FREEDOM

Also by Raymond Tallis and published by Agenda

Logos: The Mystery of How We Make Sense of the World

Of Time and Lamentation: Reflections on Transience

Seeing Ourselves: Reclaiming Humanity from God and Science

Freedom

AN IMPOSSIBLE REALITY

Raymond Tallis

Dedicated to Professor David Scott of Victoria University, not the least for an unforgettable visit to share ideas and for the friendship that it began.

First published in 2021 by Agenda Publishing

Agenda Publishing Limited
The Core
Bath Lane
Newcastle Helix
Newcastle upon Tyne
NE4 5TF
www.agendapub.com

ISBN 978-1-78821-378-3

British Library Cataloguing-in-Publication Data
A catalogue record for this book is available from the British Library

Typeset by JS Typesetting Ltd, Porthcawl, Mid Glamorgan
Printed and bound in the UK by CPI Group (UK) Ltd, Croydon, CR0 4YY

Contents

Acknowledgements   vii
Preface   ix
Prefatory Note   xiii

Overture: intention and intentionality   1

1   The impossibility of free will   11

2   Bringing the laws on side   21

3   Unpicking causation   59

4   Actions   85

5   The human agent   133

6   The limits of freedom   159

    Coda   167

Appendices   173
Notes   213
References   247
Index   255

Contents

Acknowledgements

I cannot thank Professor David Scott sufficiently for his careful reading of the manuscript. Separately acknowledging all his suggestions that I have incorporated into the text would have vastly increased the word count so I have settled for a general "thank you!". I am also grateful to Adam Rostowski for his astute comments on an earlier version of the book and for guiding me through the literature on enactivism and embodied cognition. I am also indebted to an anonymous referee whose detailed comments prompted many clarifications of key points. The trouble taken by this referee was particularly impressive given the pressures that all academics are working under in this time of plague. Publication of this book is another opportunity to express my gratitude to Steven Gerrard of Agenda for his unstinting support for my writing for over a dozen years.

Raymond Tallis

Preface

There can be few more dispiriting ideas than that our freedom is an illusion. I can testify to this when, as a teenager, I was assailed from time to time by the terrible thought that my behaviour, and indeed my whole life, might be predetermined by forces and circumstances which were not of my choosing.

The claim that we have no control over the contents of our lives requires little by way of detailed or sophisticated argument. The man in the pub or the woman on the Clapham omnibus will remind you that actions are physical events. As such, they must be the result of prior causes and subject to the laws of nature that, by definition, admit of no exception. The difference between mere happenings and human doings is therefore apparent rather than real. It must also follow that choice is an illusion since, at any given time, there is only one future. Jenann Ismael (who does not share this view) expressed it thus: "As you toss and turn in the throes of a difficult decision, there is really only one possible outcome. You are no freer to choose otherwise, than water is to flow uphill".[1]

Like many, perhaps most, determinists my teenage self did not consistently embrace the consequences of his belief. After all, he took pride in some of his achievements – sufficient to let them occasionally slip out in the conversation – and he did not hesitate to pass judgement on himself and, more often, on others. In practice, he regarded humans, for the most part, as moral agents responsible for their actions.

The theoretical impossibility of free will is, it seems, difficult to accept in practice. Arguments leading to conclusions that no-one seems to take seriously may appear to the busy world to condemn philosophy as lacking true seriousness – a fault that may seem more reprehensible in a world engulfed, as it is at the time of writing, in a pandemic. Not as irritating as, say, Zeno's paradoxes demonstrating that motion, and indeed any sort of change, is not possible, but nevertheless bad enough. Why bother to argue in defence of what, for the most time, we cannot sincerely doubt? "We know that we are free and there's an end on't", as Dr Johnson said.[2] Even so, the incompatibility between theoretical doubts about freedom and our practical belief that we are in an important sense free niggled me.

The niggles grew as, over the next half century, a more complex, and to me more interesting, case in favour of free will gathered in my mind and the gap between my practical beliefs and theoretical arguments gradually closed. Early versions of these arguments have been published over the last few years – notably in *The Mystery of Being Human: God, Free Will and the NHS* (2016), *Of Time and Lamentation: Reflections on Transience* (2017) and *Seeing Ourselves: Reclaiming Humanity from God and Science* (2020).

I was rehearsing and developing some of these arguments in a chapter of my current book *De Luce: Reflections on My Time in the Light*, when, unexpectedly, I stumbled on what seemed to me to be a more coherent account of the nature of agency and a defence of free will. The pandemic lockdown, several hundred walks in the valley behind our house on successive dawns, and the necessary cancellation of all but a few engagements, proved fruitful. The chapter-in-progress burst its boundaries and became this book.

At the heart of *Freedom: An Impossible Reality* is the conviction that not only are we humans free (within limits) but also that understanding the nature of our freedom is central to getting a clear view of what kinds of beings we are. Our mysterious freedom is on a par with the mystery of our knowledge as a marker of our distinctive nature and our unique place in the cosmos. Indeed, the mysteries are intertwined: the acquisition of knowledge is a profound expression of what it is that makes us free; and knowledge is fundamental to our capacity to act freely.

The philosophy of action, and arguments for and against free will, are some of the most fertile and interesting areas of philosophy both sides of what used to be the divide between continental and analytic philosophy.[3] Every topic touched on in this book has a literature so vast that it would require numerous incarnations to read a hundredth of the publications relevant even to the particular case presented here. The paucity of references is therefore more honest than a bibliography that would pretend to do justice to a philosophical conversation taking place in hundreds of books and thousands of journal articles.[4] If this book earns the attention that it seeks it will not be on the basis of comprehensive scholarship but on what I believe to be a new approach to the question it addresses.

Like most of my previous books, *Freedom: An Impossible Reality* is addressed to both a general and a professional readership. As a wandering scholar who has engaged with but never been part of academic philosophy, I deeply regret the merely marginal presence of the most compelling thinkers in the discipline in The Big Conversation, most notably as it touches on what kinds of beings we are. If academic philosophy matters – and I believe it does – it matters more than just to academic philosophers. A book addressed to a wider readership that does not at least acknowledge what the best and brightest in the academy are saying lets down that readership. And one that evades judgement by professional philosophers is equally deficient.

In order to reconcile the different requirements of the two audiences – or, more precisely, a spectrum of readers with different levels of engagement with academic philosophy – I have therefore located some of the more technical (but to me no less interesting) arguments in appendices that the general reader may pass over without losing the central argument. The same applies to some of the more substantial footnotes that engage with the professional philosophical literature. I hope, nevertheless, that the main text will entice non-professional readers into following the arguments to more recondite places where some of the best and brightest minds argue with each other. I very much hope that in endeavouring to please different audiences I have not ended up by pleasing none.

At a certain level, everything in philosophy connects with everything else. This, along with the fact that the book currently in your hand or on your screen grew out of a longer philosophical narrative, means that there are loose ends in what follows. While the arguments in *Freedom: An Impossible Reality* are freestanding, there will be connections with discussions – particularly about the nature of intentionality and its centrality to our human being – in my other writing to which I direct the reader.

Nevertheless, the arguments in the present book should stand on their own. If what follows does not persuade you that you are a free agent, this is an important failure. There is no more significant or profound philosophical question. Understanding the possibility of our freedom highlights our unique place in the order of things.

Prefatory note

Whether and to what extent we have free will is one of the most enduring and hotly contested topics in philosophy. For this reason, it is not surprising that the different positions have been elaborated in a wide variety of ways and the arguments have sustained a vast literature. At the risk of over-simplification, it is reasonable to classify views on free will as dividing into those that say that we have it and those that say that we don't. Views both sides of the divide respond to the claim that all events in the physical or natural world are determined. Determinism states that only one course of events is possible: the state of the world at any given time fixes its state at future times.

There are three responses to determinism. The first is that it is incompatible with free will which is consequently an illusion. We cannot shape the future or elude the past. The second – compatibilism – claims that, on the contrary, free will is compatible with determinism: in a deterministic natural world there is still room for the exercise of freedom. The third is libertarianism according to which, since agents have freedom, determinism must be false. The past does not determine a unique future.

There is a fourth view which bypasses determinism completely: "voluntarism", which has almost completed dropped out of use in contemporary philosophy. It is the doctrine that the will is a fundamental or even dominant force in the life of individuals or even the universe. It is sometimes invoked to affirm the sovereignty of the will over the intellect. (As will be seen from what follows, the intellect and the will are inseparable in the exercise of our freedom.)

The view presented in this book is a form of compatibilism. I do not deny a key aspect of determinism; namely that the natural world unfolds according to unbroken – and hence seemingly unbreakable – habits that science unpacks as laws. I shall argue, however, that this is not incompatible with true agency. At the heart of my case will be the character of human consciousness which does not fit into the world as it is portrayed by the natural sciences.

Overture: intention and intentionality

At the heart of the arguments I shall present for the reality of human freedom and, indeed, of our distinctive agency, is what is called "intentionality". Intentionality is a notion that has had a venerable history. It was there in ancient Greek and Islamic philosophy, and was important to Stoic and medieval philosophers. Since it was revived by the German philosopher Franz Brentano towards the end of the nineteenth century, intentionality has had a central presence in so-called continental philosophy and, in recent decades, in the analytical philosophy of mind. For philosophers "intentionality" may seem all-too-familiar and for non-philosophers technical and obscure. Notwithstanding the technicality of the term, it is something whose essential nature can be grasped by a moment's thought. Its apparent simplicity, however, is deceptive. Intentionality, like the concept of "the atom" in physics, has proved to be a gift that keeps on giving.

Intentionality is "the mark of the mental".[1] It is what distinguishes mental states or events such as perceptions, thoughts, beliefs, desires from other items in the world. It is "the power of minds to be about, to represent, or to stand for, things, properties, and states of affairs".[2] Importantly, these items are other than, and distinct from, those mental states. While intentionality is a fundamental and universal feature of mental states or entities, no physical entity has this feature. Physical events may be (or, as we shall see, may not be) causally related to other events but they are not *about* them.

How mental states relate to what they are about will vary according to the state in question. It will be different in perceptions, beliefs, knowledge, thoughts and desires. There is, however, something that they have in common and it is this, as we shall see, that accounts for the possibility of truly voluntary action. The relationships of "aboutness" between our mental states and the external world hold open a space between ourselves as conscious subjects and the world (or perhaps worlds) to which we relate as the theatre of our lives. Intentionality generates the virtual or non-spatial outside from which action is possible. It is the basis of the fundamentally asymmetrical relationship of presence: the material world is present to me but I am not present to the material world; the material world is "there" for me but I am not "there" for the material world.

This will be unpacked in the pages to come but a seemingly straightforward example taken from everyday vision will be useful to give a flavour of the arguments that lie ahead. Consider my seeing an object such as a cup. One explanation of how I see the cup, and favoured by many philosophers and scientists, is that it results from *a causal interaction* between the cup and my brain, mediated by light. If I truly see a cup, the cup has caused me to see it. Light bounced off the cup, enters my retina and this triggers activity in the parts of the brain associated with vision. That seems very straightforward, not the least because it makes perception similar to the processes governed by the laws and causal connections that seemingly operate elsewhere in nature.

It has been warmly embraced by materialist philosophers who want to assimilate the mind to the natural, indeed the physical, world. Daniel Dennett expressed this position with exemplary (and characteristic) clarity in his best-selling *Consciousness Explained* (1991):

> [T]here is only one sort of stuff, namely *matter* – the physical stuff of physics, chemistry and physiology – and the mind is somehow nothing but a physical phenomenon. In short, the mind is the brain ... We can (in principle!) account for every mental phenomenon using the same physical principles, laws and raw materials that suffice to explain radioactivity, continental drift, photosynthesis, reproduction, nutrition and growth.[3]

He describes this as "the prevailing wisdom" and in this respect he is correct, insofar as it is prevalent. Whether it is "wisdom" is something we shall question.

For the causal theory of perception is fatally deficient. The causal relationship I have just described accounts for how the light from the cup gets into the eye and tickles up the brain. But it does not account for the gaze looking out and seeing the item of crockery. If the gaze were entirely explained by the neural activity, then we would have a strange situation. The events in the visual pathways would seem to be required to point as it were in two directions: (1) In one direction, the events in these pathways connect with other neural activity in the brain which are their downstream causal effects, leading directly or indirectly to actions such as blinking. (2) In the other direction, they refer back up the causal chain to certain of their causal ancestors; namely, at least some of the events constituting the interaction of the light with the cup and consequently making them the basis of awareness of it.

We could express the difficulty this presents for the causal theory of perception as follows: while law-governed causation might explain how *the light gets in* – into the brain – it does not describe how *the gaze looks out*. The gaze is explicitly *about* something other than itself – in our example the cup. Causation (if it has any clear meaning – something we shall test in Chapter 3) – does not therefore explain key features of perception – namely, intentionality. Effects of cause C do not qualify as representations of C.

The very idea that material events impinging on a material the nervous system could generate, or be, a representation of those material events or of the objects that are involved in them, seems contrary to the general principle that causes and effects should be proportionate or at least commensurate, being of the same kind. This is clearly not true of light arising from a physical source – such as sunlight bouncing off a cup – supposedly causing itself to be seen and, moreover, making objects bathed in it visible. Intentionality, a universal and undeniable feature of mental phenomena such as perceptions, cannot therefore be accounted for by "using the same physical principles, laws and raw materials that suffice to explain radioactivity, continental drift, photosynthesis, reproduction, nutrition and growth". That in virtue of which a material object such as a cup interacts with another material object such as a brain does not account for the *presence* of the cup to a conscious subject.

This does not worry many philosophers or indeed neuroscientists. For them, the problem of intentionality is solved, or at rate dissolved, by assuming that, while the neural events in the visual pathways are not identical with visual experience, they nevertheless *cause* those experiences. This doesn't work – and for the same reasons as the direct causal theory of perception we have just discussed doesn't work.

First, if the events in the visual pathways were the cause of the visual experiences, those events would have two profoundly different kinds of causal descendants. One kind would be other neural events resulting from them, continuing perhaps into motor pathways if they prompt movement. The other would be the mental events, such as awareness of the object, with the various mental consequences they have. Such a fork in the causal pathway – one branch into the realm of physical events and the other into the realm of mental events – is (to put it politely) anomalous (to put to a different use a term borrowed from the American philosopher Donald Davidson) and would thwart the ambition that materialist philosophers have of gathering perception into the physical world. Secondly, it would require the events in the brain to be about events outside the brain, in order to deliver the intentionality of perception and other elements of consciousness.

Consider a paradigm case of a causal interaction between two material objects: the collision between billiard balls. When moving Ball 1 collides with static Ball 2, the first ball imparts some of its momentum to the second ball. Nothing happening in Ball 2 is *about* what is happening in Ball 1. Ball 1 is not revealed whole or in part to Ball 2; or the effect in Ball 2 is not "about" the cause in Ball 1, except insofar as a conscious human subject makes the connection. And the same would be true of any interaction between material objects.

Admittedly, one of the protagonists in the causal theory of perception is a rather special material object – namely the brain of a living organism, which is rather more sophisticated than a billiard ball. And admittedly, the neural consequences of the impact of light energy on a photosensitive retina are a long way from the collision between billiard balls. Nevertheless, the stuffs and the physical principles, laws and raw materials in play in these interactions are, as Dennett reminds us, essentially the same. What's more, the vast majority of events taking place in the brain, even in the "highest" reaches such as the cerebral cortex, do not have this capability of being about that which triggered them. The spinal cord, the cerebellum, and most of the cerebral hemispheres are not associated with consciousness and appear to be innocent of being in an outside world. And those nerve impulses that are said to be associated with consciousness are not fundamentally different from other neural events.

At this point, we need to anticipate, in order to pre-empt, the claim that intentionality can be explained as an *emergent* property of matter, a property that emerges when matter takes the form of brains. After all, it has been argued, the liquidity of water is not a property of the molecules of which it is made. And trees, that are made of matter, do things – such as shed their leaves on a seasonal basis and use the fruits of photosynthesis to sustain their growth – that the matter of which rocks are made does not do. Nevertheless, it is possible to give an account, or the beginning of an account, of how these properties may emerge, using "the same physical principles, laws and raw materials" (to use Dennett's phrase) that are evident throughout nature.

The appeal to "emergent properties" does not, however, explain how matter might acquire awareness of itself in becoming the intentional object of a conscious subject. Emergence – which could certainly be appealed to in an endeavour to understand how photosynthesis in leaves or the photochemical sensitivity of multi-cellular organisms comes about – seems to have little to offer in explaining the origin or basis of seeing the sun and locating it "out there". However often emergence is invoked as an explanation of intentionality, it still looks like something between a statement of faith and a promissory note.

There is another problem with the causal account of intentional consciousness. What is it that accounts for the backward-reaching intentionality alighting at an object of interest such as a cup rather than somewhere else; for example, falling short of the cup at what is going on in the retina; or bypassing it and stopping at some predecessor event somewhere in the journey of the light before it reaches the cup?[4]

The example of vision illustrates with a particular clarity how intentional consciousness enables the perceiving subject to be in contact with the world (the cup is revealed to me) while at the same time be at a distance from it (the cup is "over there" while I am "over here"). In virtue of perception, we are related to the material world but are not *wired into it* by law-governed causes. Acknowledging the reality and real nature of intentionality enables us to meet the challenge of identifying a basis for freedom without appealing to magic. We are required only to acknowledge the undeniable sense in which intentionality – and conscious subjects – lie outside the natural world as seen through the lens of natural science.

Importantly, this does not imply that the portrait of the world seen through the natural sciences is false, rather that it is incomplete. There is a gap between perceiving subject and perceived object that is not captured by physics, chemistry, and the rest. As I shall discuss, this gap creates the space for genuine agency – including the extraordinary expression of agency that permits the uncovering of the habits of nature as the laws of science. How we, as conscious subjects, interact with the world is consequently quite different from how material objects interact with other material objects – even material objects such as my body or my brain. This is the clue to our ability to act upon the material world as if from outside of it. The sense in which the object of perception is outside the perceiving subject is fundamentally different from that in which material objects are outside other material objects, including the material object that is our body. It also addresses the seeming paradox that conscious experiences are not mere effects of the perceived world and yet are not causally impotent – merely epiphenomenal, having no traction on what happens.

The causal theory of perception, that construes experiences as events comparable to those that are seen more widely in the physical world, therefore overlooks (or denies) the distinctive nature of perception and more broadly of other contents of consciousness.[5] A standard causal interaction between the cup and a nervous system mediated by light would put the perceiver's body in indirect contact with the cup. It would not, however, open up, and hold open, the distance from which the perceiver sees the cup as being "over there", as something that exists in itself, and as other than me who is "over here". The spatial separation between the body (more particularly the visual apparatus) of the perceiver and the perceived object (such as the cup) is transformed into something in virtue of which the object is outside of the perceiving subject. While spatial relations belong to the natural world, the property of being "outside" in this sense does not. More broadly, the presence of a material object to a conscious subject and the way it may be connected with other material objects also present as part of a world is quite different from the way it is connected with other material objects in a purely physical nature.

Why is this relevant to the question of free will, of agency? Perception provides the ground floor of a virtual outside from which the perceiving subject *faces* the material world. As I shall argue, this outside is the basis of the capacity of the perceiving subject to engage with that world on terms that are not solely dictated by natural forces though she exploits those forces. The outside maintained by such conscious experiences is fundamentally different from the spatial relationship between two material objects, such as the cup and the saucer or the cup and the brain of the subject conscious of it.

The arguments against the causal theory of perceptions and other mental items may seem rather obvious but the position these arguments sustain is radically at odds with the view of many, perhaps the majority of, contemporary philosophers in the anglophone tradition. The most popular view is that the human subject is neurally wired into her surroundings, making agency impossible to understand.

Besides, we may have cut the causal theory of perception too much slack. For, as we shall discuss in Chapter 3, there are problems with the very idea of a cause. That is for a later time. For the present, I want to highlight two other aspects of intentionality which enable conscious subjects to build on the virtual outside, made available courtesy of vision and other modalities of perception, to open up more complex modes of non-physical outsideness.

First, when I see an object, I see that there is more to it than what I am currently perceiving. I am conscious of the perspectival nature of my perceptions: I am seeing the object from a particular viewpoint. Evidently, it has other possible visible appearances – how it would look from the back, from further away or closer up, and so on – which I might anticipate. I also know from other experiences that a cup has tensile strength, weight, temperature, and so on. It is this that underpins my confidence that, when I reach out for it, I will be able to grasp something solid – which accounts for my surprise when my expectations are not fulfilled and what I think is a cup turns out to be a hologram. This "full-blown" intentional relationship between a perceiving subject and a perceived object opens up the sense of possibility – of what *might* be the case – that supplements anything that is the case.[6] The sense of possibility focused on perceived objects is further augmented by the sense that there are other things "out there" that I cannot presently experience. The visual field, for example, is populated with items that are visibly hidden – because they are concealed behind intervening items, or round a corner, or beyond an horizon.

The sense of the *possible* is another, fundamental problem for the causal theory of perception: perception may (and in fact very often does) propose objects or states of affairs that do not exist. By this I do not mean exotica such as unicorns but common-or-garden coinages of mistaken expectations. While non-existent objects clearly lack causal power, we can see or be afraid of things that are not there. Admittedly, illusions and such like are parasitic on perceptions of things that really exist; but that does not alter what illusions tell us about the nature of mental states. There are no illusions – non-existent objects – in the material world except those generated by conscious subjects. Even where anticipations are justified, the intentional object of anticipation is not precisely congruent with what actually happens. After all nothing directly imagined or anticipated through the mediation of a description would capture the details of any actual event or state of affairs. The intuition of possibility built into perception lies at the heart of agency, as we shall discuss in Section 4.2.

Secondly, the intentional relationship is also elaborated by the joining of intentionality between subjects.[7] You and I share experiences of a public realm that is present to us and, we assume, to others. We believe that the landscape we are both looking at is visible to each other and, indeed, to anyone else who happened to be in our vicinity – now or at some other unspecified time. Shared, joined or collective intentionality – mediated through non-verbal modes of communication such as gestures (notably pointing) and facial expression and, of course, hugely elaborated through language – ultimately leads to a body of knowledge that is not directly dependent on sense experience, though it may be tested against such experience. The experience does not have to be my own. None of my knowledge of the Amazon rainforest or the Pleistocene era – or even of the lives of the people three streets away – has been directly exposed to the tribunal of my own sensory experience.

Brentano's pupil Edmund Husserl, the giant of phenomenological philosophy, highlighted how shared experience, or more broadly intersubjectivity, is central to our intuition of objects having an existence in themselves. I am aware that others who encounter what I experience do so from a different standpoint. That different standpoint is made explicit at a very basic level, in for example when someone draws my attention to what I am not presently seeing.[8] What they see of an object or a landscape that I am not currently seeing is a revelation of the fact that the object or landscape has aspects presently hidden from me. This develops my sense that what is out there exceeds my experience of it. As Husserl argued,[9] objects of perception are "transcendental" in that, at any given time, they will have a quantity of unperceived features, that may be revealed, but not exhausted, in the course of further perceptions. Those unperceived features may be indirectly revealed by others who refer to them: they become objects of (my or anyone's) knowledge.

The virtual outside opened up by knowledge is vastly greater than that which is made available by individual experiences. Factual knowledge – knowing that and know-how – has, as we shall discuss, a central role in the pooling of agency, and the invention, manufacture, and employment of ever more complex skills, tools, facilities, and institutions through which we act directly and indirectly in and on the world, exerting, and magnifying, our power. Knowledge also enables us to reach from the present into a future fashioned individually or collectively from an acknowledged past and a shared present.[10] These are dimensions of "outsideness" that we shall examine in more detail in the chapters to come.

The central point is that the interaction between a perceived object and a perceiving subject is a kind of interruption in the otherwise uninterrupted flow of events in the material world. The subject intercepts the seamless flow of events by turning to face it. As we have noted, the light from the cup stimulates the visual pathways and there is a further flow of events through other parts of the nervous system, as in the case of automatic reactions, onwards to motor pathways. But the intentionality of perception points in the opposite direction such that the perceiving subject looking at a world is a place in which the objectively uninterrupted flow of material events is marked by "here" and "now". Courtesy of intentionality, we face the material world from a standpoint instead of merely being part of it. That is why the distance between the subject and the cup she is looking at or reaching out for is not a purely physical, spatial distance identical to that between the object and her body.

And we face the world collectively as well as individually, especially when we engage with it as an object of knowledge. It is here that we find a starting point for building an individual or collective outside, a human world, which is the platform for agency in which individual subjects are a genuine source of events that are actions. While subjects – "I am" and "we are" – are made possible by the human organism that is itself a product of a universe of material things, energies, and forces, the lives of subjects are starting points for unique

journeys, composed of a multitude of overlapping ends, towards chosen destinations, significantly defined by agency.

Behind the arguments in this Overture – which are absolutely central to
my case for the possibility of free will – is something that is at once obvious
and yet elusive. Intentionality is that in virtue of which the natural world is
made explicit.[11] Such explicitness – culminating in the scientific account of
the natural world[12] – is undeniable. It is, however, inexplicable in the context
of a world picture that (*pace* Dennett) confines itself "to the same physical
principles, laws and raw materials that suffice to explain radioactivity, continental drift, photosynthesis, reproduction, nutrition and growth". We may
capture explicitness in the notion of "thatter" in virtue of which what-is, or
Being in the absence of consciousness, becomes "that it is the case"; or, if that
seems too sweeping, there emerges a realm of factual truths such that matter,
or fragments of it, acquire names, even inverted commas. Or, to stay with
Dennett, the physical stuff of physics becomes "the physical stuff of physics".

It is easy to overlook the gap between Being or what-is and "that it is" or
between x and "that x is the case" – particularly when, as we shall discuss in
Chapter 3, the word "information" is employed so widely. Nevertheless, it is in
that gap that we shall find the roots of human agency and of the fact that we
are not simply wired into the natural world such that our lives would be mere
local manifestations of the unfolding of the universe. As I know from bitter
experience, reminders of that gap prompt many philosophers of a naturalist
persuasion to reach for the smelling salts. And yet it is absolutely central to
understanding our distinctive nature and it is the key to the possibility of
freedom and to the arguments of this book.

It is important, of course, not to imagine that this gap which permits us
humans a significant margin of agency, entirely liberates us from the laws of
nature. As a doctor who spent nearly 40 years treating patients rendered more
or less helpless by the habits of nature operating in their own bodies, and as
a senior citizen anticipating similar events that will extinguish my agency, I
am not deluded as to the scope of our freedom. Freedom is limited, as I shall
discuss in the final chapter. The outside made available to us by intentionality
does not place us beyond the reach of the laws of physics but enables us to
discover and exploit those laws in order to pursue ends that we truly own.

One final point. Franz Brentano, who introduced "intentionality" into
modern philosophical discourse, sometimes regretted reviving this term. He
was concerned that it had been misunderstood: "[S]ome people thought that it
had something to do with intention and the pursuit of goals. In view of this, I
might have done better to avoid it altogether".[13] Actually, it has a lot to do with
those things. Intentionality, I shall argue, is the necessary condition not only of

forming but also of fulfilling intentions. Intentionality – to reiterate the argument central to this book – opens up the distance, the outside, from which we are able to act upon the material world. It lies at the heart of our agency. Indeed, I could have called this book "Intention and Intentionality" and, by making it sound like a lost Jane Austen novel, promoted a misunderstanding that might have increased its readership.[14]

CHAPTER 1

The impossibility of free will

"If determinism is true, then our acts are the consequences of the laws of nature and events in the remote past. But it is not up to us what went on before we were born, and neither is it up to us what the laws of nature are. Therefore, the consequences of those things (including our present acts) are not up to us"

Peter van Inwagen[1]

1.1 ARGUMENTS AGAINST FREE WILL: LAWS AND CAUSES

Before we look at the case against free will, it is a good idea to settle on a definition of what is being attacked and, indeed, what is being defended in this book. The definition by Robert Kane in his excellent *The Significance of Free Will* captures what matters: "the power of agents to be the ultimate creators (or originators) and sustainers of their own ends and purposes".[2]

Perhaps "*ultimate* creators (or originators)" is to make a claim that is difficult to sustain. So let us drop "ultimate" and unpack what is important in a less ambitious idea of free will. It implies:

1. That we can truly say of at least some of our behaviour that "I am responsible for this".
2. That our actions have deflected the course of events: we make a difference and that difference is not merely an inflection by our bodies of the predetermined course of events passing through us.

3. That our actions express something within us that we can truly own and justifiably own up to.
4. That as agents we have explicit ends and purposes that truly belong to us.
5. And that what we have done is one of several possibilities genuinely open to us such that we could have done or chosen otherwise.[3]

Since I do not claim that we exercise our freedom by breaking or entirely bypassing the so-called laws of nature, my position is *compatibilist*: I will argue that determinism in the natural world is compatible with human freedom.

My position is a modest one, in that I do not believe that everything that human agents do is driven by something called the will. Nor does the claim that we are the originators of our actions imply that, unassisted, we magic ourselves and our actions into being. As we shall discuss in Chapter 6 and elsewhere, asserting that we have freedom of the will does *not* require us to believe that (1) *everything* an agent does is free; (2) agents are the sole source of what they are capable of doing; (3) every part of a free action is explicitly done and freely executed; or (4) that an agent is free to do anything.

Even freedom limited in this way seems to some philosophers incompatible with our actions being (among other things) bodily movements: they are material events arising out of a material body interacting with a material world. The material element may be a minute part of an action – as in the case of a wink that may be hugely consequential. Nevertheless, it is indispensable: an individual totally paralysed with curare could not express agency.

However strongly we feel that we are the origin of our actions, that we are a place where the buck starts, an objective view seems to tell us otherwise. Or so the argument goes. As Thomas Nagel expresses it: "Something peculiar happens when we view action from an objective or external standpoint. Some of its most important features seem to vanish under the objective gaze. Actions seem no longer amenable to individual agents as sources, but become instead components of the flux of events in the world of which the agent is a part".[4]

That flux of events is, so we are told, shaped by causes and laws.

Causes

Let us focus first on causes. According to the widely accepted principle of causal closure, every physical event – which must include what we classify as our own actions insofar as they have, and are intended to have, physical effects

– has a sufficient immediate physical cause. Since the cause is sufficient, it does not require any distinct assistance from a human agent. And since the cause is immediate, there is no space for the agent to intervene.

This principle of causal closure therefore seems to undermine the claim that our actions originate with us. Everything that has a physical effect must itself always have prior causes which in turn have prior causes and so on – until we reach events which took place before we appeared on the scene. The future we imagine we are shaping is therefore itself shaped by the past that shaped us. No being, not even a human being, has a privileged, even a separate, role in determining its own future. Consequently, we only *seem* to perform our actions; in reality, we are merely the site of them. We are not the source of any of the events that take place in our lives but, being causally wired into the material world, we are conduits through which events pass, like an Aeolian harp played by the wind.

This dismal claim seems unassailable when we stand back from individual moments in our lives and look at our entire life history and recall that we had no role in assembling ourselves *in utero*. The development of the foetus involves as little agency as the growth of a tree or even the precipitation of a crystal out of a solution. We begin, it seems, as a given we have not chosen. Why should we not continue in this way? After all, our passage to a sufficient maturity where we seem to have agency is in crucial respects preprogrammed. In addition, development is dependent on many other internal and external circumstances we do not and cannot choose. My acquisition of the capacity to make moral choices for which I am responsible seems to be the ultimate expression of moral luck. I cannot, it seems, freely choose to be the kind of being that is capable of free choice.

Thus summarized, the case against freedom starts to look merely platitudinous. We have to *be* something we have not chosen to be in order to exercise freedom – on behalf of that something: free will is always someone's free will and that someone cannot choose her coming into being. How can this unchosen creature we are given to be grow into something that is sufficiently self-chosen to exercise free choice? Can we freely build on what is given to acquire an increasing margin of freedom? If the answer is "No", is there any respect in which we can take credit (or be justly blamed) for what we are and what we do? The answer again seems to be "No".

So much for causes: whatever we do has a causal ancestry that precedes our actions, and indeed our very existence. We cannot, it seems, shake off the past in order to be the ultimate source of our actions. There is no way that we can *intervene* between causes and their effects, to make this event happen and stop that other event from happening.

Laws

As we shall discuss in Chapter 3, the status, and hence the power, of causes is contested. But would-be agents seem to be subject to double jeopardy. If causes don't imprison us, the laws of nature that govern the way the universe unfolds will. Actions and agents are products of the laws of nature that must, by definition, be unbreakable. If causal ancestry makes the agent the prisoner of her past, law-governed nature predestines her future. The agent's destination is preordained and apparent choice is rather like that offered by Henry Ford to his customers: "You can have any colour you like so long as it is black".

What is more, it seems that we *rely on* those laws to be, or to dictate, exceptionless[5] regularities if we are to be able to act and our actions are going to bring about their desired effects. Any loosening of the law-governed connectedness of the material world, and of our interactions with it, would be incompatible with our achieving our ends or indeed with our continuing survival. Walking to the shops, throwing a ball, talking to someone and being heard, all require the material world to be impeccably law-abiding. The years of training that go into the making of world-beating snooker players would be pointless if they could not rely on the conservation of linear momentum.

If the laws of nature were suspended for our convenience, we would be chaotic pockets in the order of the universe. Worse still, given that there is no limit to the consequences of any event (though they will eventually be lost in the noise of other events), the law-breaking behaviour of an indefinite number of agents would result in an incoherent universe. And our dependency on the reliability of the laws of nature is even more intimate. While the biological mechanisms instantiated in our bodies are not sufficient to account for agency, they are necessary for it, as becomes all too obvious when they fail.

It appears, therefore, that agency *requires* precisely what seems to frustrate it: a deterministic universe, regulated by laws and glued together by causation. In short, so it would appear, it depends on having our cake and eating it: relying on the stable order of things while rejecting the implacability of that stable order.[6]

Thus, the traditional case for determinism, according to which only one course of events is possible and we have no independent role in bringing it about. This is clearly incompatible with free will.

1.2 NEURODETERMINISM

Philosophers, scientists, and, increasingly, the general public subscribe to the belief that human persons and their conscious experiences are identical with their brains or what is going on in parts of that organ.

This view, as I have argued extensively elsewhere, is ill-founded.[7] Even so, the temptation to investigate the metaphysical question of our freedom using brain science has proved overwhelming. The laboratory, after all, seems to some to be a more respectable (and better funded) place for inquiry into the nature of things than the philosopher's study. Consequently, the traditional arguments against free will have been supplemented by arguments originating from neuroscience-besotted philosophy. Given that brains are material objects, subject to the laws of physics, chemistry, and biology, and that we are our brains, we must be likewise subject to those laws. The prison of the universe is personalized in the prison of the brain.

In truth, neuroscience has little to contribute to the argument against free will and I was half-minded to assign this section to an appendix. There are, however, several reasons for giving neurodeterminism a place in the main text. First, it is widely believed that it has reinforced the traditional determinist views we have just discussed.[8] Secondly, the deficiencies of the experiments designed to demonstrate that we have no free will perform the inadvertent service of reminding us of the nature of real actions, an essential preliminary to understanding freedom. In addition, I have a personal reason. As one who spent most of his career in clinical neuroscience, I dislike seeing one of humanity's greatest intellectual monuments sullied by being associated with bad philosophy. Nevertheless, readers who are already persuaded of the vacuity of the claims that neuroscience has shown us that our brains are calling the shots may skip this section.

The experiments

A typical neuroscience experiment, supposedly demonstrating that we are not free, requires subjects to perform some very simple action, such as moving a hand or pressing a button at a time of their choosing. The action is voluntary because it is not in response to an external stimulus, subjects act without pre-planning, and the required movement is not at a predetermined moment. Brain activity is monitored either using electroencephalography (EEG) or functional magnetic resonance imagining (fMRI) and the experimenters record the activity that has been associated with the brain being prepared to make a move. The subjects are also required to note the time when they feel the urge or intention to make the movement required of them.

In the famous experiments of Benjamin Libet,[9] subjects were requested to move the fingers of one hand when they wished to do so. In order to assign a time to the urge to move, they were also required to note the position of a moving spot on a screen when they were aware of the urge to move. Experimenters also recorded certain EEG activity in the brain – the so-called Readiness Potential – which was considered to mark the brain's preparedness to make a move.

In the much later experiments of John-Dylan Haynes[10] and his team, brain activity was recorded with a more sophisticated technology: functional magnetic resonance imaging (fMRI). In this case, the subjects not only had discretion over the *when* of the movement (as they did in Libet's experiments) but also the *what*: they could freely choose between pressing one button with the right hand or a different button with the left hand. They timed their decision as to the button to press by noting which of a succession of letters on a screen was visible when they made their decision.

What has caused considerable interest among neuroscientists and some philosophers is that evidence of the brain's preparedness to make a voluntary movement is seen *before* the time at which the subject is aware of having made a decision to move. In Libet's experiments, the Readiness Potential was a consistent third of a second ahead of the subject's timing of her decision to move. In Haynes' experiment, the neural correlate of the decision to press the right button or the left button was evident in brain activity of prefrontal and frontal cortex up to 10 seconds before it entered the subject's own awareness. Even more alarmingly (to some) Haynes was able to predict (admittedly with only 60 per cent accuracy) which hand was going to be moved and hence which button was to be pressed, on the basis of brain activity preceding the timed decision. In short, it seemed to the experimenters as if the brain was preparing to move either the left or the right hand before the subject had decided which hand to move.

Interpretations of these experiments have been, to put it mildly, over-excited. For some they prove that our brains are calling the shots: even when we are choosing to make a voluntary movement in our own time, we are at our brain's bidding. The organ, or its cortex, seems to have decided what we are going to do and when we are going to do it. At the very least, it appears that our actions are initiated by unconscious processes before we have determined what we are going to do and when we are going to do it, although we may have the power of veto. Free will, it is concluded, has no role in generation of our actions. Our sense of being in control of our actions is, as one experimenter has put it, like that of a child moving the plastic toy steering wheel next to the real thing held by its parent, unaware that its voluntary actions are causally inert or merely epiphenomenal.[11]

Critique: methodology

Fortunately, we need not take these studies too seriously. They have two sorts of problems: methodological and philosophical. The latter are more important for our argument and we shall come to them presently. But the former also deserve a look.[12]

Subsequent research using Libet's experimental design has shown that individuals who are timing their own intentions rely on external cues rather than directly introspecting them. In short, we *infer* that we have had the urge to make a movement. At the very least this could account for a delay in the timing we ascribe to our urges so that they seem to occur after the brain has already prepared to make the apparently voluntary move. Secondly, the Readiness Potential, supposedly the marker of the brain's preparing itself to move, does not seem reliably to be connected with making the movement; it appears rather to be broadly connected with awareness of participating in the experiment. It is most closely connected with paying attention to the clock in order to time the urge to move.[13]

It might be argued that the problem with determining the temporal order of the decision to move and the activity in the brain associated with preparation to move is less pressing in the case of Haynes' experiments because there is a larger interval – 10 seconds – between them. Even so, there are serious methodological issues with Haynes' experiments.

One relates to the apparently disturbing observation that scientists seemed to be able to predict, on the basis of observed brain activity, which button is to be pressed, before the subject was aware of having made a decision. However, the choice of left or right button may not be truly random and the predictions are based on statistical techniques that inadvertently pick up patterns of responses. Moreover, the frequency of correct predictions as to which hand the subject was going to move was only just above chance. Indeed, it is worse than this: the reason the actions were able to be predicted several seconds before the decision was made to move the left or the right hand probably lay in the statistical techniques used to predict the actions.[14]

Critique: looking in the wrong place

But the methodological flaws of these experiments are less important than something they show us by default. That is to say, their value is not to be found in anything they do, or do not, say about the extent to which we are, or are not, the prisoners of our nervous systems. Rather they (entirely unintentionally) remind us by default of the nature of free action and where we should expect to find expression of our free will. And this is not in the place where Libet and Haynes and other experimental neuroscientists are looking.

It is, I think, worth spelling this out in some detail.

1. The subject's involvement in the experiment goes far beyond the trivial movement that is the focus of the neuroscientist's attention. Let us remind ourselves what participation requires. There is the task of getting to the laboratory on time, after a complicated journey by transport ("Don't forget the bus pass!") and on foot ("Follow the written instructions!") to the relevant room. It might involve setting the alarm the night before to make sure that the appointment is not missed, and possibly other complex arrangements so that the appointment is honoured.[15]

2. Subjects are required to understand the general purpose of the experiment and the part they are to play in it, to follow the instructions, and accept reassurances that participation is entirely safe, notwithstanding the intimidating equipment and all the folk in lab coats. None of this is reflected in a simple movement of the finger or hand and any urge that is supposed to drive it.

3. The trivial movement, the product of a reasonless choice, therefore counts as an expression of agency only inasmuch as it is a small part of a much greater whole, as an element of the action of voluntarily participating in the experiment. The crucial expression of agency is not the decision to move the hand but a large-scale commitment to taking part in the experiment, something that has to be sustained over a long period of time. That commitment – and the reasons for it, such as wanting to help those clever scientists understand the brain as it might help develop treatments for brain injury – is where free will is to be found. As such, it is hardly something captured by studying an urge or a succession of urges. Reducing the subject's action in participating in the experiment to hand movement is analogous to seeing a much-trailed handshake between two national leaders as just an arm movement.

4. This reminds us that our agency is not expressed through a series of discrete decisions as to movements propelled by a series of urges. As we shall discuss in Section 4.3, we advance on a broad, temporally deep front.

5. The choice in Libet's experiment between moving the hand now and moving the hand in, say, 10 seconds' time is trivial. Likewise, the choice

in Haynes' experiment between moving the left hand or moving the right hand. In neither case is there anything significant at stake or indeed connected with anything else in the experimental subject's life. True agency, however, is about choices that have significance and are justified by what we value.[16]

6. In the experiments, subjects are required to time their own urge to move their limb. This is itself a highly sophisticated action, involving introspection and connecting introspected experiences with a highly conventionalized display of time – the position of a spot on a clock-face (Libet) or the identification of letters on a screen (Haynes). It hardly needs saying that conscious intention must have had a role in this act of timing the urge to move one's finger. We are therefore entitled to ask how the intention to time the intention or urge to move fits into neural activity and the ordering of events around, say, the Readiness Potential. It is odd to think of the urge as being anchored to a particular moment in physical time in the way that nerve impulses are, given that the urge is directed towards a future state – something that will be a major consideration when we think about the tensed nature of action in Chapter 4.

This brings into view the wider question of the nature of the urge to move. Is this also something that can be detected by EEGs or scans? Those who identify the mind, the subject, or the agent with neural activity would say yes. But how would it be generated? In view of what we have said of the subject's participation, the urge must be rooted in the entire circumstance of the experiment. As such, it could hardly be innocent of what else is going on, given that it makes no sense out of its somewhat egregious context. How would localized brain activity capture or reflect that?

Firstly, it has been suggested that the Readiness Potential is not so much the brain girding itself up for action before the subject is aware of making a decision but a spontaneous event that the subject is aware of and sees as a wave to catch. In short, that the urge does not follow in the wake of the Readiness Potential but utilizes it. Second, we need to consider the role of the other protagonists in the experiment. I am talking about the experimental team – led by Professor Libet or Professor Haynes – who have been working in neuroscience for many years, have acquired the necessary skills to design the experiment, and have secured the funding and collaborative expertise to carry it out, write it up, and publish in the relevant professional journals. None of this looks like something cooked up in an isolated brain calling the shots or even localized clusters of causally interacting brains. Finally, widening our attention beyond the subject to the experimental team highlights even more clearly how the experiment – like most normal, cooperative human activity – is not the product of a succession of discrete urges strung together but something that grows out of immensely complex networks of agreements based on shared knowledge and aims. At any rate, it appears to be necessary within the experimental design to ignore how much of what looks like free will conventionally understood that is required to set up the experiments designed to demonstrate that we do not have free will.

I hope that you will by now be persuaded that neuroscience adds nothing to the traditional arguments against free will. As something that cannot be discovered by brain research, free will is in good company. Nothing in the brain, after all, can explain or reveal the consciousness of brain scientists consciously looking for free will and coming into the laboratory each morning to resume their quest. This said, we should perhaps be grateful to neurodeterminists for the inadvertent service they have done in reminding us, by default, of the real character of true, meaningful actions.[17]

We shall return to this in the next chapter, where we shall see how scientific research is itself a particularly striking expression of human freedom. This is part of our critical examination of the supposed obstacles to free will: the laws of nature and the causal connections that together, so we are told, fix the course of events.[18]

CHAPTER 2

Bringing the laws on side

For many determinists their vision of the world and of their place in it is what we might call Laplacian, after the great physicist Pierre Laplace. In his *Essai philosophique sur les probabilities*, Laplace argued as follows:

> We may regard the present state of the universe as the effect of its past and the cause of its future. An intellect which at a certain moment would know all the forces that set nature in motion, and all positions of all items of which nature is composed, if this intellect were also vast enough to submit these data to analysis, it would embrace in a single formula the movements of the greatest bodies of the universe and those of the tiniest atom; for such an intellect nothing would be uncertain and the future just like the past would be present before its eyes.[1]

The future state of the universe, including of those entities in it who fancy themselves as free agents, is entirely predictable because it is fixed once initial conditions are established. Everything unfolds in accordance with the laws of nature. An omniscient being – Laplace's oddly named (but not by Laplace) Demon – could predict what would happen to me and how I would behave long before I had any idea of either of these things. As Peter van Inwagen has put it, "there is, at any instant exactly one physical possible future".[2] The idea of my exercising choice – and hence choosing between one future and another – is fantasy.

As we shall see, the "intelligence" to which Laplace referred, the demon, has no place in the Laplacian universe. Nor would Laplace himself, the discoverer of his eponymous law, be accommodated in the law-bound world picture he offers in the passage we have quoted. But we are getting ahead of ourselves.

And then there is causal necessity. Is it not true that my actions – material events arising in a material body – are the effects of prior causes whose ancestry precedes my being born, stretching back, perhaps, to the Big Bang?

Thus, a double whammy for any claim to true agency, to my being a genuine source of my actions, shaping my own future and that of at least a small part of the universe. Every event – in nature and consequently in my life – is necessitated by prior events and conditions that follow one another according to the seemingly unbreakable laws of nature. My post-natal life is therefore as much the product of natural processes, and as little under my control, as my life *in utero* or the world before I was born. The law-governed causation that brought me into being has predetermined the course of my life.

The barriers to free will erected by the laws of nature seem insuperable if human beings are after all parts of nature; if, for example, persons are (their)[3] brains. It is difficult to know why we go to the trouble of intending events if what we intend was going to happen anyway; or, if intendings are simply part of the law-governed causal chain connecting the world before our birth with the world after our death. Moreover, if intentions are material events in our brains on a par with the falling of stones in a gravitational field, it is puzzling how they come to seem to be so different – most importantly if they present themselves as points of origin of actions we claim as our own. Are we not deluded?

This argument about intentions will seem less decisive when, as we shall do in Chapter 4, we look at how they relate to real actions. In respect of what prompts them and how their elements are put together, they do indeed seem fundamentally different from the kinds of events that populate the Laplacian universe.

First, however, we must confront Laplace's argument directly and question the very ideas of laws and causes and their dictatorial powers which have been nodded through. The key to their overthrow will be found in the procedures by which the laws of science are discovered (and exploited) and causes identified (among other things as potential handles by which we might manipulate what happens). This will give us an insight into our capacity to mobilize law-governed causes in the service of our freedom. We shall cast light on the truth behind the seemingly dubious claim put forward in this arresting passage from a posthumously published essay by John Stuart Mill: "Though we cannot emancipate ourselves from the laws of nature as a whole, we can escape from any particular law of nature if we are able to withdraw ourselves from the circumstances in which it acts. Though we can do nothing except through laws of nature, we can use one law to counteract another".[4]

Our first step is to look critically at the very idea of a law of nature (Section 2.1) and then reflect on the implications of the fact that, through scientific inquiry, we have made progress in understanding what makes nature tick (Sections 2.2 and 2.3). Next, we shall inspect the very idea of a cause and find that what remains of it after a critical examination is not as inimical to agency as it might at first seem (Chapter 3). When we do this, we shall see that genuine agency is compatible with what science has discovered about the natural world.

Incidentally, that compatibility won't be found in, or be confined to, places round the edges of the classic laws, either in quantum indeterminacy or, alternatively, in so-called chaotic indeterminacy. A few pre-emptive observations on this score are justified.

Quantum indeterminacy, according to which there is a necessary indeterminacy in the behaviour of elementary particles, is not available to creatures such as you and me – since it does not scale up to the macroscopic level and would, anyway, not be under our control. For these reasons, we are not in a position to manipulate or exploit quantum indeterminacy, except in certain highly specialized circumstances, as in random number generators which amplify quantum effects into usable signals. Even if we were able to exploit quantum indeterminacy more widely, this would offer no escape because the *probabilities* of underdetermined quantum physical events are fixed by sufficient immediate physical circumstances. The evolution of the universal state vector is entirely deterministic. Quantum indeterminacy would not seem to open a space for us freely to decide to carry out a criminal act or refrain from doing so. Besides, the play of chance at the level of elementary particles would, even if it could be scaled up to levels relevant to our behaviour would give us less, rather than more, control. We are not the players of the play of chance; and unpredictability is hardly an ally of agency, not the least because we want to be able to predict and indeed control the outcome of our actions.

Some of those who invoke indeterminism often seem to confuse two things: events not being predetermined and events not being predictable. Take the flipping of a coin, where the outcome is not certain, only probable. The fact that I cannot predict whether my sixpence will fall heads or tails is not the consequence of coin tossing being outside of the scope of the laws of classical physics. Rather it is that the relevant laws and the initial conditions that are fed into them are unknown to me. The profoundly chaotic nature of coin-tossing – with so many uncontrolled and indeed unknown variables – is concealed from us because we focus on only one aspect of the trajectory of the coin – whether it settles heads up or heads down. The uniqueness of each coin-tossing event leading to one of two classes of outcome is hidden.

The search for freedom in chaotic indeterminacy, therefore, confuses the unpredictability of chaotic systems sensitive to minute changes in initial condition with genuine indeterminacy.[5] Laplace connected the predetermined nature of the future with the capacity of a suitably equipped demon to predict it. Predictability is a function of cognitive competence, not of the presence or absence of deterministic laws.

In this chapter, I focus on "laws". I have not tried to encompass, or tease out the relations between, laws, forces, entities, models, theories, theorems, equations, as different explanatory aspects of the science of nature. It is a task that is beyond my paygrade. I do not however think the argument that follows depends on a radical clean-up of the conceptual geography of the field of the philosophy of science, an ongoing project that seems to be defeating the best and brightest practitioners.[6] Nevertheless, it will be necessary to show that it is consistent to hold a sceptical (or at least more nuanced) understanding of these items while embracing a realist account of human agency. To this we shall return in Section 5.2.

Some of the present chapter may seem like a mighty digression from our central concern: whether or not we have free will and whether we must conclude that free will is impossible in a universe whose unfolding is most accurately described by the laws of science. It is no such thing and for this reason: that the very procedures by which science advances are manifestations of the extent to which we can stand outside of nature and any putative laws it may have. That capacity "to stand outside" is a particularly sophisticated development of the features of consciousness that we discussed in the Overture. And it will also be employed in agency that exploits our understanding – encompassing the most basic common sense and the most advanced science – as to how what is around us "works".

I hope the reader will trust this claim sufficiently to have the patience to follow the arguments of this chapter.

2.1 DO LAWS HAVE LEGISLATIVE POWER?

Let's begin with the common notion that the laws of nature have regulative powers, such that, among the other things they decree, they force us to do what we imagine we are doing of our own accord. If they are or have powers and we are made of stuff subject to those powers, we are helpless. We are places where things happen, not agents who genuinely *do* things.

Are the laws, to borrow a term from Tim Maudlin, "pushy explainers" in this way? And, if pushy, are they pushy in the sense of being the engine of change, in a universe that would otherwise be inert? Or do they merely have directive powers, acting as rails along which what happens is channeled? This latter view presupposes that dynamism is already built into the universe: it is running as soon as it is up. The laws merely narrow the range of possible ways of unfolding, ensuring that one path is taken rather than another. The laws, that is to say, are not horses but only horse-riders; not making things happen but making them happen this way rather than that.[7] As Helen Beebee has wittily expressed it, it is as if the laws were "somehow 'out there', prior to and watching over matters of fact to make sure they don't step out of line";[8] as if they were additional to nature, supervening "on the overall distribution of matters of fact".[9]

This idea of the legislative power of laws presupposes that something additional is necessary to ensure the continuation of the natural order such that the world goes round rather than all over the place; there would be no regularity without regulation; that disorder is more spontaneous than order so that things have to be ordered about; and nature, left to itself, would be chaotic.[10] (If this were the case, then it is difficult to see how the laws to tame the chaos would arise out of intrinsically chaotic nature.) Thus understood, laws are a quasi-agency – something that is perhaps a distant echo of the idea of an extra-natural, omnipotent God.[11]

The difference between horse and horse-rider may not be clear cut. While the laws may "dictate" one trajectory rather than another – and not that there is a trajectory at all – some pushiness is still required to ensure that path A is taken rather than path B. Rails that deflect or contain the unfolding still do some work: while horse-riders may do less work than the horse, they still have some work to do.

The contrast between pushiness ensuring change and mere constraint directing the traffic rests on certain other assumptions. Pushiness seems to imply that the natural state of the universe is stasis and that it requires assistance to keep it unfolding. Contrariwise, the idea of laws as constraints seems to presuppose that dynamism is already built into the order of things: it doesn't require anything to maintain a state of change.[12] It is possible for example that the idea that the natural state of the universe is stasis, so that things have to be *made* to happen, may be connected with the freezing of the flow of process when we chop the world into discrete facts capturing a succession of states. (We shall return to this suggestion when we discuss causation.)

Both alternatives – horse or rider – require us to engage with the difficult notion of the laws of nature as either having or being powers – as if they were acting upon nature, determining what happens, from outside, with the latter being a kind of substrate. It makes the laws a higher-level force, even extra-natural, a secular *deus* acting on the *machina*. The idea that "lawfulness" is an over-arching force chivvying the universe either into movement or to move in one direction rather than another is therefore problematic. It is, perhaps, the result of mistaking a description of how things are for a force shaping how they must be.

We have entered the scene of an argument that goes back to David Hume and has generated a large philosophical literature in subsequent centuries. Beebee contrasts two views of the laws of nature – as being on the one hand "relations of necessity" of how things must be or on the other as "mere generalisations of the broadest and most accurate kinds" expressing how things just happen to be. One sees law-like behaviour as something mandated from without that behaviour; and the other sees laws merely as summarizing the way things pan out. The latter sees the laws as the regularity of patterns of events and way they are connected and the former explains how that regularity is secured.

The wish to find an explanation of nature's regularity is the result of extrapolating to the whole of things the idea that everything happens for a reason. Nothing "just happens". The idea of "pushy" or "coercive" or "constraining" laws may be a projection into the material world of the idea of agency – something to which we shall return in Chapter 3, when we think about causation. It is, after all, as obstacles to the fulfilment of our intentions that we experience universal laws as (local) constraints – though they are also enablers.

If we downgrade the laws of nature to mere regularities that can be relied upon, they look less like explanations than authoritative, accurate, most general descriptions of what just happens to happen; or if connecting particular events with descriptive laws counts as explanation, it is an explanation that eventually hits the buffers of "This is how things are". Or as the articulation of principles of coherence in the natural world. They do not shape what happens but are simply the shape of what happens.

If laws-as-mere-regularities rather than as regulators look or taste like explanations, it is when they are invoked to account for particular events covered by them – as when we invoke the laws of motion to explain the particular trajectory taken by a flying object. Or when a lower-order law is seen as a local manifestation of a higher-order law – as when Boyle's law connecting the pressure and volume of a gas is seen to be a manifestation of the kinetic theory of gases. The arrow of what feels like explanation goes from particular events to general laws and from less general laws to more general laws: "this is how this thing goes this way because this is how all things of this class go". This "because" is, however, rather attenuated as a bearer of explanatory force.[13]

The least burdened account of laws, then, would set aside the idea of them as principles of material necessity built into the universe driving or otherwise regulating change in favour of their being the most general and reliable accounts of nature's regularities – regularities that do not require to be maintained by an independent regulator. The natural world is not the obedient servant of a legislative master. The laws do not, however, have a kind of (mindless) agency built into them. The only obligation is that things should continue to be as they have always been and that, as they unfold on a particular occasion, they should unfold on all similar occasions. Even "obligation" is too strong a term. It is better perhaps to settle for "things continuing as they are". Necessity is verbal, logical, or theological; as such, it has no place in grown up natural science.

Let us speak, therefore, of the mere habits of nature. While the term "habits" is unburdened with dubious notions of legislative authority, it is not entirely satisfactory. It is rather homely and low-key and hardly does justice to the unfolding magnificence of nature. What's more a habit is something that we typically think of as being acquired and, equally, as being set aside or overcome. Clearly, this does not apply to habits used in the present context: its regularities are not something the universe can kick or grow out of. This said, I cannot at present find a term that better captures the uniform unfolding of nature that is not mandated from without and which are reflected to differing degrees in the laws of science. If there were a better term, I would happily embrace it. Meanwhile "habit" will have to punch above its weight.

How will this address the seeming conflict between lawful nature and the possibility of true agency? Denying laws intrinsic powers does not seem to offer much comfort to those who seek to defend the possibility of genuine freedom. The natural world seems no more biddable if its laws are recast as "habits". Habits that science tells us have been in place for billions of years are not going to be kicked for *parvenus* such as human beings. As things were, so they will be: the universal principles of precedence and of the uniformity of nature are upheld. Even if the flow of nature were not driven by commands *ex machina* we would still have to go with the flow.

The advance of science and the discovery of laws that encompass more of the natural world and permit ever more precise predictions seem only to tighten the noose. And when, in addition, we appreciate that everything that takes place at the level of the cell and the organism within our own bodies – the proximate source and ground of any agency we may have – is equally subject to the habits that are apparent elsewhere in nature, that sense of helplessness seems like an acknowledgement of reality. Physiology, biochemistry, molecular biology, etc. are reminders of the unchosen biological conditions of our seeming to be able to make choices.

There is an apparently less daunting interpretation of the intransigence of the laws of nature. Laws seem to be "unbreakable" because they would cease to qualify as laws if they were broken. Any robust, significant observation at odds with predictions based on existing laws prompts a search for a better law. And the new law – which typically has a wider reach than the one it supersedes – will be tested against other observations that do not fit with the old law. An example would be the constancy of the speed of light in a vacuum that prompted the replacement of Newton's laws of motion by special and then general relativity. Laws, in other words, must be unbroken to qualify as laws; otherwise, they will be replaced by another law that can accommodate the data that do not fit. In short, the jury seems to be rigged because a law that proves not to be exceptionless will lose its standing as a law.

There is not much comfort to be had here either. The replacement of one set of laws by another set of laws that have a wider scope and greater predictive power – range and precision – will not retrospectively confer a margin of freedom on those who lived, or thought they lived, under the rule of the earlier set of laws. Firstly, the principle of apparent unbreakability itself remains unbroken. Secondly, the regime of the discarded law is no more forgiving than that of its successor. A Newtonian natural world is not noticeably less constraining than an Einsteinian one.

The history of science in which one law is superseded by another, however, gives us a clue as to how the very idea of laws of nature and the processes by which they are discovered and refined may reveal the truth of our freedom. We shall come back to this presently.

The point for the moment is that denying quasi-legislative powers to the habits of nature does not disarm their apparent antagonism to the freedom of an agent to choose her own life or at least a significant part of it. And although the way the habits of nature[14] are reflected in the laws of science evolves dramatically as science advances and corrects itself, this does not mean that they do not reveal something fundamental about the material world including my body. Besides, you cannot acknowledge the extraordinary power of science-based technologies to transform our lives and still doubt that what is captured in the laws of science is an ever-closer approximation to the nature of the material world and certainly closer than what is revealed in the casual impressions of daily life.

As American philosopher Hilary Putnam argued half a century ago, a so-called "anti-realist" view of science that suggests its laws are social or institutional constructs, would make its spectacular successes inexplicable: "The positive argument for realism is that it is the only philosophy that doesn't make the success of science a miracle".[15] The explanatory and predictive successes and technological efficacy of the laws seem to argue for their truth. Even anti-realism would not prove that what laws we have – however approximate – prove that the habits of nature are any less limiting to our freedom. Discovering that, after all, the gravitational field is curvature of space-time does not make it retrospectively any easier to bend the Newtonian physical world to our will.

There is, however, a point hereabouts that goes to the heart of our concern about the compatibility of law-governed nature with genuine agency. As science evolves over time and one law is replaced by another (ditto forces, entities, models, theories, etc.) it is assumed that science is converging ever closer on nature. Irrespective of whether this optimistic story – to some degree anti-realist about the past of science and realist about its trajectory and its ultimate future – is true, it reminds us of something of crucial importance: at any given moment in the history of science there is a separation between the habits of nature and the laws of science. It is reflected in what seems to be a permanent feature of science: the replacement of one law by another presumed to be more accurate and of wider scope.

This highlights something central to the argument that follows. The laws of science, not being identical with the inherent habits of nature – which we must assume have not changed, or not at least in the short time since human beings first became scientists – must belong to a virtual space outside of nature, occupied by humanity. It is from this space that the habits of nature are partially or incompletely uncovered as the laws of science. That position outside of nature, I will argue, is also that from which its habits may be exploited in the service of our agency. The compatibility between determinism in the natural world and genuine agency illustrates something that it is easy to overlook when we look at the world through the lens of science: the experimental procedures by which we discover the laws of science. The habits of nature – necessary for our actions to have their desired consequences – may therefore be more friendly to the idea of free action than might appear.[16]

There are, however, a few more steps to be taken before we reach that cheering conclusion.

2.2 THE UNNATURAL NATURE OF THE SCIENCE OF NATURE[17]

> "Nature has not made it a priority for us to discover its secrets".
> Albert Einstein[18]

We have taken the laws of nature down a peg, by stripping them of a role in "governing" (to use Helen Beebee's term) the universe, in necessitating or dictating the unfolding of events. Instead, we have reabsorbed them into nature itself as its habits. "Habits" – a term C. S. Peirce used for laws of nature – are intrinsic to natural processes; they are not imposed. They are how things generally go, underpin reliable expectations, and implant a sense of necessity in the way things follow one another.

Re-badging natural laws as habits does not, however, make nature less implacable. We must look elsewhere for that in virtue of which we may exercise freedom. We can find it in something neither realists or anti-realists about science will deny: the divergence between on the one hand the putative habits of nature, and on the other the particular laws that scientists have promulgated – and relied upon – in their various disciplines at various times in their history. The term "laws of nature" is misleading: it bridges, or even conflates, the ideas of the intrinsic, permanent habits of the universe and the laws of science into which they are incompletely translated.

To appreciate this is to acknowledge the unnatural nature of the laws of science. Equally unnatural are the processes that have led to their discovery (or, for anti-realists, their invention or construction). I will invoke the distance from nature that the discovery and articulation of the laws of science represent to support the claim that, far from being entirely helpless participants in the habits of nature, we are able to exploit those habits – most faithfully represented in the laws of science – to exercise and extend the scope of our free will. For that distance is a particularly striking expression of our unique relationship to the natural world and of the outside that was flagged up in the Overture when we discussed intentionality.

The curriculum of science

We have distinguished between (a) the habits of nature, (b) the so-called laws of nature, and (c) the laws of science. It is the latter that are our central concern. By the laws of science, we mean the kinds of things we see in science textbooks and that are exploited in science-based technology. Examples would include Boyle's law connecting the pressure and volume of gases, Newton's laws of motion that had seemed for several centuries to summarize the movements of large and small items in the universe, the Henderson-Hasselbalch rule making it possible to estimate the acidity of a buffered solution, and the field equations of general relativity that gather up gravitational and inertial manifestations of mass. They are products of quality-controlled research, and are exploited in the advanced technologies that vastly enhance our capacity to transform the world around us according to our perceived needs. These technologies are also mobilized to further our ability to develop and enhance and refine our image of the natural world. There is an iterative loop whereby science-based technology is utilized to create instruments used to advance science.

Irrespective of how much we know of the many habits – or kinds of habits – or even kinds of stuff – nature has, it seems unlikely there is a one-to-one correspondence between the multiplicity of the laws of science and what there is "out there". Nature no more reflects the accidents of the history of science than it falls of its own accord into curricula assigning events to different disciplines or to different aspects of the same discipline and allocating its inquiries to the professional responsibilities of different individuals. No processes are intrinsically biochemical – that is to say adding up their chemical elements or being added up to biological ones; and "of concern to a biochemist" does not designate a natural kind. The multiplicity of laws is a reflection of the particular direction of the curiosity and interest of scientists – and sometimes their paymasters. In times of war, the science of mechanics branches off into a separate discipline of ballistics. The textbook laws are the children of the internal history of science and the accidents by which it is differentiated into special sciences.

Let us dig a little deeper into the distinction between the habits of nature and the laws of science. The distinction is particularly obvious when two or more laws are identified as operating at the same level and applying to the same stuff. Consider, for example, Boyle's law and Charles's law. According to Boyle's law, the volume occupied by a certain quantity of gas is inversely proportional to its pressure, so long as the temperature is kept constant. As the applied pressure goes up, the volume goes down. According to Charles's law, the volume occupied by a gas is proportional to the temperature, assuming the applied pressure is kept constant. It hardly needs saying that, in nature, there is no separation within gases between pressure, volume and temperature: gases have to have all three. They are not separately in thrall to laws connecting volume with pressure and volume with temperature.

That there are two distinct laws (and, of course, many more) is to this extent an artefact of observations driven by accidents of the history of an emerging discipline. As we have noted, the habits of the nature do not map on to the multiplicity of laws that the history of science has thrown up. The latter will be shaped, among other things, by the scale and direction of attention of the scientist, and the transmission of influence between successive practitioners of a discipline, who inherit interests, techniques, and ways of structuring observations, and a version of "the story so far" from predecessors and contemporaries.

Of course, the structure of science is not permanently fixed by the curriculum and technologies of a particular epoch of inquiry. One of the regulative ideas driving scientific advance is the belief that seemingly disconnected and disparate phenomena will fall under, or be connected through, a decreasing number of laws: that the sciences of this, that, and the other will eventually be unified; and, consequently, the multiplicity of laws of nature at any stage in the history of science is a temporary state of affairs. The aspiration to unification is connected with the notion of a hierarchy within science, with physics being the prince of sciences as it is closest to nature, according to certain criteria; namely that it is most general in its application; and it engages with the fundamental stuff of which all of nature – rocks, clouds, trees, animal bodies, human brains – is composed. While the entities that are described by biologists or biochemists have to conform to physical laws, the compliment is not returned: physical entities such as rocks do not have biological or biochemical properties. Even within physics, seemingly the most fundamental of the sciences, there are distinct laws – optics, heat, electromagnetism, mechanics, the physics of sub-atomic particles – applying separately to aspects or items that are not separate in the physical world. If the laws of science were a direct account of the intrinsic nature of the physical world, the scope of individual laws would not be confined to aspects of that world, which are not in themselves separated.

The history of physics offers striking examples of progressive unification of laws, evident long before we reach what subsequent generations of scientists will regard as fundamental. Take our two relatively homely examples, Charles's law and Boyle's law. They are subsumed under the kinetic theory of gases that predict both the relationships between volume and pressure, and between volume and temperature. The laws of electricity and magnetism merge into those of electromagnetism. The latter will be gathered up in the laws of motion and gravity in relativity theory. And so on.

This has raised the expectation that, eventually, we will find one law covering the entirety of the natural world rather than an anomalous collection of laws applicable to aspects of nature. The universe will prove to be one kind of stuff with a master-habit of unfolding in a certain way. This vision of a (single) Theory of Everything is based on the faith that the laws found, say, in chemistry or biology or even economics or sociology will not be in conflict, or even belong to a fundamentally different reality, but will prove to be different manifestations of a single Order of Nature; of a law or laws that apply at all places and at all times.[19] The laws that are discovered en route will still retain their relatively local validity – and implacability – but they are now seen to be underwritten by the higher-order laws of which they are approximate and local expressions.

There is, however, a rather awkward consequence of this optimistic idea of the progressive convergence between the discovered laws of natural science and nature herself. It is this: as we progress to ever more fundamental and basic laws, the last drop of the particular is squeezed out and we have a featureless universe. A world entirely described or explained by or reduced to (for example) $E=mc^2$ would not be a very enticing tourist destination. The brochure could not even include something as ordinary as a jacket on the back of a chair. And Schrodinger's universe would seem to be able to accommodate simultaneously two incompatible states of a cat – dead or alive – but not the cat itself. The Theory of Everything, as The Theory of Nothing-in-Particular, comes to look a bit like The Theory of Nothing.

If the account of the universe seen through the lens of fundamental (mathematical) physics were the only true (or most nearly true) account of how things really are, then it would leave the rich variety of the experienced world unexplained. It would perhaps be unreal; or have a second-order or derivative reality whose origin remains unexplained. If this is not challenged, it is because it is assumed that the universe is fundamentally simple and that complexity is unreal.

The important point – crucial to the argument about the relationship between habit-following nature and free will – is that natural science is not ventriloquising or mirroring nature. Even less is it an undistorted expression of the habits of nature. An obvious justification for saying this is something we have touched on already: the evolution of science; the historical fact that some laws have a limited shelf life, even though they may be practically useful or bridges to other laws. In some cases, they prove to be simply wrong or turn out to have a more limited application than was at first thought. In more interesting cases they are superseded because they are discovered to be expressions of a more fundamental law that has wider scope and subsumes more than one law. Meanwhile, the habits of nature, we may assume, remain unchanged.

The divergence between nature and the curriculum of inquiry and discovery into which science is divided and the separate laws that belong to different disciplines at different times in their history has a significance that cuts deeper than the argument between realist and anti-realist philosophers of science. To carve nature at joints that do not belong to her and yet thereby to produce accounts that apparently amplify our power to manipulate the natural world is a striking marker of our capacity for action that is not subordinate to putative universal habits of nature's unfolding.

To get things wrong or only approximately right and nevertheless seem to enhance our capacity as individual or collective agents through science-based technology says something very profound about the source of our agency.

Newton's laws of motion and the billiard ball atom served humanity very well before they were superseded by general relativity and the strange inhabitants of the standard model of the atom. The instrumental power of science may not demonstrate the 100 per cent or even 50 per cent truth of the laws and the reality of the hidden entities and invisible forces that they invoke. What they do demonstrate is that we can enhance our power to achieve our ends by exploiting scientific laws that are to some degree false, inasmuch as they do not precisely map on to the habits of nature. This is an indirect revelation of something fundamental about the relationship humans have to the habits of nature: the relationship is not entirely one-sided, with nature in the driving seat.

More work needs to be done to clarify the basis of this claim. We need to turn our attention to something that is overlooked: the *experiments* by which the habits of nature are uncovered as, or are transformed into, the laws of science. It is here that we can see more clearly the compatibility between free will and seemingly universally applicable laws of nature.

It is time to examine the methodology of science.

Putting nature on the rack[20]

Let us return to our earlier example of two laws applying to the volume occupied by a quantity of gas: Boyle's law according to which the volume of a gas is inversely proportional to the pressure; and Charles's law according to which the volume of a gas is directly proportional to the temperature.

We have already pointed out that nothing intrinsic in gases as found in nature corresponds to the separation between a stand-alone Boyle element and a stand-alone Charles element. A gas cannot have a volume without also having both a pressure *and* a temperature – and indeed other properties. It is we, not the gases, who effect that separation for investigative purposes. So, for example, I may keep the temperature constant while I change the volume in a controlled way and examine the resulting pressure, as when I am discovering, testing or exploiting Boyle's law. Or I might keep the pressure constant and vary the temperature to discover, test or exploit Charles's law.

This elementary example casts light on the fundamental distinction between the habits regulating the unfolding of nature and the scientific laws we extract from the natural world and highlights the work that has gone into transforming its habits into the laws of science. This distinction lies not only at the heart of the activity that is experimental science but is also present in a primitive form in the informal experiments we carry out in daily life when we are trying to work out why something happens or how we might better manipulate the world to our advantage. "Try changing this and see what happens", we might suggest to ourselves, as we are endeavouring to see how things "work". In the case of science, we are seeking generalizable observations and it involves something rather abstract: the isolation and manipulation of parameters or variables. In a typical law-seeking or law-testing (or, later, law-exploiting) scientific experiment there is a distinction between those parameters whose relationship is being investigated (for example the relationship between pressure and volume) and other parameters that are kept constant (for example temperature) because they might conceal the relationship being sought.

This extraordinary human behaviour – and it is extraordinary – tends to be taken for granted. Let us return to Boyle's law. There are three characters in this story. We have temperature which is controlled; and pressure and volume which are the variables whose relationship is being investigated. Either of these latter variables can be selected as the independent variable (the one that is deliberately altered) or as the dependent variable (the one that changes as a consequence). If we are interested in seeing how increased pressure impacts on volume, then pressure will fill the role of independent variable and the volume that of dependent variable. If on the other hand we are interested in seeing how reducing available volume increases pressure, volume will be the independent variable and pressure the dependent variable. All three characters are measured separately: the temperature to make sure it remains unchanged; the pressure in order that it can be applied in a controlled way, to a certain measured value; and the volume to see the effect of changes in pressure.

No such separations are evident in nature: the "controlled", the "independent", and the "dependent" variables are not roles assumed by aspects of the material world. A gas is obliged to have a pressure, a volume, and a temperature all at once. And yet this teasing out of what is out there into discrete variables goes to the heart of science. Events as served up raw by nature are not the values of variables or, indeed, instantiations of collections of teased-out variables. The state of an entity is not simply "a certain volume" or "a certain temperature".

We are so accustomed to seeing, and using, equations relating pressure and volume or mass and gravitational attraction that we do not see them for what they are: views on the habits of nature from an outside that is required for their transformation into the laws of science. The extra-natural view, the outside, is not itself captured in those laws. To put it another way: the laws of nature are not uncovered by natural processes. To this extent a laboratory – and our world insofar as it is the theatre of inquiry and a place where we exploit the results of inquiry – is outside of nature.

It is a conclusion that holds irrespective of the outcome of any argument between realists and anti-realists about whether the laws of science are realistic accounts of the world or merely instruments that help us to grasp the world cognitively and hence manipulate it. While it is obvious that anti-realism places the laws of science outside of nature, it is, I hope now clear that the manipulation of nature necessary to reveal its most general habits must take place in a space that is outside of those habits, even if the laws of science were a realistic portrait of the habits.

We are en route to the conclusion that the laws of science that seem to determinists to prove that we have no free will could not be discovered except through the exercise of free will. It will, at least, be clear that the experimentation that gives rise to the laws of science is built on a human capacity for an unnatural manipulation of nature: the controlled alteration of the values of isolated variables. As already mentioned, experimentation in the lab is a development of behaviour seen in daily life – as when I manipulate things to "see what is going on"; for example, when I squash or blow up a ball to test it for leaks. In the experimental situation pressure and volume, however, are more decisively separated than they are in the single act of squashing or inflating. And the difference is connected with the search, in the laboratory, for observations that are explicitly generalizable; that stand for a class of observations with an unlimited number of members.

The capacity to separate variables in controlled experimental conditions is a startling example of a kind of behaviour that one might expect the unbiddable habits of nature to preclude. The progressive widening of that separation, evident in equations such as "P/V = k" (Pressure divided by Volume is a Constant), written down, transmitted, and consulted as potential recipes for manipulating the material world, is the key to the enhancement of human agency made possible by science. But it is also a testament to the undeniable operation of human agency in the performance of science.

We are perhaps getting ahead of ourselves. To take the argument further, it will help to focus on something central to scientific inquiry, to the process of discovering laws, and to making practical use of what has been discovered. It is all that goes into ensuring that "other things are equal".

Ceteris paribus: laws as powerful idealizations

At the risk of being a bit boring but for the sake of clarity, I want to stick with the homely example of Boyle's law.[21] As with all other laws, it applies – or rather it can be seen to apply – *only so long as certain conditions in which the experiment takes place are controlled.* The most important conditions are, firstly, that the quantity of gas is unchanged and, secondly, that the temperature is kept constant. (There are other variables that are not relevant and do not have to be kept constant. For example, it does not matter whether the experiment takes place in Boyle's house, in the meeting room of the Royal Society, in England or in France, in the seventeenth century or the present, in a secondary school classroom.) That is why most laws carry Terms and Conditions which can be summarized in the phrase *ceteris paribus*: "other things (relevant to the effects under investigation) being equal".

This may seem an innocent, common-sense requirement – nothing to get excited about. But it has profound significance. The key to good experimental science is actively *keeping* those other things equal; taking certain precautions to secure this. Failing to do so will result in a flawed study with results which will prove to be misleading. So-called "confounding factors" – uncontrolled sources of variation – will be noise that may obscure the sought-after signal: the lawful relationship between parameters.[22]

Most of the most fundamental or general habits of nature are, and remain, hidden from the casual gaze. Likewise, what emerge as the laws of science. This is because the natural world or its unfolding over time does not of itself break down into variables, even less into controlled and uncontrolled ones. In the wild, there is no protocol or experimental design that keeps the *ceteris* sufficiently *paribus* for changes not to count. Gases in the natural world are not, for example, insulated from changes in their temperature, volume, or pressure. The inter-relations between variables are maintained: they do not, however, have to be shielded from interference in order to be upheld. They have managed without humanity thank you very much. The inverse relationship between pressure and volume of a gas was in force before it was discovered. It is only where it is a question of teasing out and exploiting separate laws that the protected circumstance of the laboratory is needed. The uncaged air outside of the apparatus is still subject to Boyle's and Charles's laws and indeed to other laws of science active at the macroscopic and microscopic level. The individual laws, however, are not visible because nothing is controlled and all laws are in play at once; or rather the tendencies that can be teased out of the habits of nature have not been disaggregated into discrete laws of science.

The variables uncontrolled outside of the laboratory that are stigmatized as confounding factors within it are no less law-abiding than the dependent and independent variables scientists are interested in investigating; it is just that they are manifestations of habits different from the ones that are being investigated or exploited. And the laws that are discovered in the protected environment of the laboratory are, if they are valid, equally present in the world at large, only not visible. Nature does not recognize the boundaries between that which belongs to and that which does not belong to an experiment; nor does it uphold a separation between the laboratory and the outside world or even the space inside the apparatus from the space outside of it. Boyle's law applies with equal precision in Robert Boyle's body – breathing with increasing rapidity as it dawns on him that he may be on to something – as in his apparatus. As he increases the volume of his chest cavity, so the pressure in his lungs falls and air consequently rushes in through his airways. This bewigged individual gives us a striking example of how the scientist manipulating the habits of nature may poke them into revealing themselves as scientific laws while themselves not being in breach of those laws.

Nature, in short, is not snobbish, unlike scientists who focus, and hence restrict, their interests at any given time. They seek "signals" freed of "noise", and dismiss the latter as uninvited manifestations of uncontrolled conditions that must be excluded if inquiry is to meet the standards of good, that is to-be-relied-on, science. Nature is not prejudiced against any of its own modes of unfolding, downgrading them to mere confounds or contaminants that may prevent the discovery even of laws of vast scope. All events are equally expressive of its fundamental habits. There are no signals and no noise. So-called noise is as habit-abiding as are so-called signals. A badly run laboratory conforms to nature's habits as a well-run one. There are no "ideal gases" that obey Charles's and Boyle's law and delinquent ones that do not.

Take another seventeenth-century discovery: the law of falling bodies. Feathers fall more slowly than pebbles and this deceived folk scientists for thousands of years as to the habits underlying the behaviour of falling objects, making them believe that heavy objects necessarily fall faster than lighter ones. The leisurely descent of feathers compared with that of pebbles does not, however, disprove the law of gravitational attraction; rather it conceals that law because of the differential effect of the viscosity of the air on objects of different density, and different – more or less streamlined – shape. As science advances, so the efforts to shield the experimental situation from outside noise become ever more complex. Of the thousands of scientists and supporting personnel seeking evidence of the presence, that is to say the influence, of the Higgs boson at CERN most were employed directly or indirectly excluding confounding factors that would conceal real sightings or create false ones. In some cases, where noise cannot be excluded, experiments are repeated again and again and statistical techniques such as averaging are used to pick out signals from noise. What is filtered out by these techniques is as true to the habits of nature as what is retained and published as "data".

Because the idea of controlled conditions is universal in science and we are introduced to it at the very beginning of our science education, it is difficult to see how strange, and not to say unnatural, it is. While the glory of science seems to lie in the vast scope of its most fundamental laws such as $E=mc^2$, the mystery of scientific enquiry is equally present in more local laws hedged about with *ceteris paribus* clauses demarcating boundaries of their application – boundaries that are not, of course, laid down by nature. The sense that there are constant, if invisible, principles underlying change in the universe motivates Boyle's homely enquiries that resulted in his law just as much as it informs the investigations carried out using the Large Hadron Collider.

There is a sense, therefore, in which scientific laws are idealizations, for all that our knowledge of them has enhanced our power to manipulate the real, stubborn, material world. Feathers and iron are equally obedient to gravitational forces but this is evident only in the ideal situation of an absolute vacuum where descent is not impeded by the viscosity of the medium in which it is taking place. "Ideal" is not, of course, a natural category – not the least because it is a normative term. Again, nature does not discriminate between her own manifestations.

The purified inquiry taking place in controlled conditions necessary to generate robust, usable, laws of science that are sufficiently faithful to the habits of nature, indicates the extent to which individual laws are not part of nature, in the sense that the parameters they tease out and connect do not unfold independently of one another. While it is difficult to discern the operation of laws in the real, uncontrolled mess of the ordinary world, neither the laws being investigated nor other laws are broken in the messy place outside of the laboratory: they are merely concealed by each other; or rather they may be simultaneous manifestations of more than one law – in the case of bodies falling through the air, first, the law of gravity and second, the laws relevant to the viscosity of gases.

The separation of controlled, dependent, and independent variables and other ways of shielding signals from noise, are evidence that the interaction between scientists and their apparatus is unlike anything else in nature, even though it, too, must conform to the habits of nature. There could be no more striking expression of our capacity to manipulate nature, rather than being manipulated by it, than the ability "to keep things equal" exercised in the lab. The egregious nature of experimentation is especially evident in contemporary Big Science. But it is a feature of all science, from the discovery and testing of Archimedes' principle, to the search for the Higgs boson. It is not necessary to travel to Geneva to see the distance between the habits of nature and the processes by which they are discovered and for the very idea of experimental design (not to speak of apparatus) to be seen for what it is: something that fits awkwardly into our idea of the natural world.

For this reason, it is worth dwelling a little more on Boyle's experiments "touching the spring of air" in a closed space (a J-shaped tube) that revealed his eponymous law. The actions involved in compressing the air and measuring its pressure (frustrated by repeated "casual breaking of the tube" that Boyle complained of) did not break the habits of nature; but neither were they natural product of those, and other, habits. The manufacture of the apparatus and the solutions he found to the problem of its infuriating habit of its falling apart was a series of events that would not have come together without the orchestration of Boyle's inspired intuition-driven curiosity that occasioned the transformation of perception into active experimentation. The "casual breaking of the tube" was as respectful of the laws of nature as the transmission of the ink from Boyle's quill pen to the paper on which the results were transcribed, or the increased rate of the passage of air into and out of Boyle's lungs as he grew more irritated with the frailties of his apparatus.[23] Experiments that go wrong are as natural as those that go right. They are not, however, as respectful of scientists' intentions.

Preparing the experiment, carrying it out, repeating it on numerous occasions, and collating the results of endless repetitions, demonstrating it to fellow scientists to persuade them of its truth, do not look like an expression of nature's habits on a par with the effect of pressure on the volume of the gas. They look even less like it when we appreciate the vast cognitive and cultural hinterland behind Boyle's iconic experiments, encompassing technological developments underlying the manufacture of his kit and the intellectual climate building in the wake of Francis Bacon's foundational works on "experimental philosophy".[24] The apparatus with its infuriating conformity to the habits of nature resulting in "casual breakage" is not a mere reagent. Nor is the increasingly annoyed bewigged gentleman immortalized in his eponymous law just a piece of the nature he is putting "on the rack".[25] In short, he is clearly an agent, rather than a reagent.

Transforming solicited physical events into observations, and these in turn into numerical results, gathering up those results into a dataset (as in a graph or a table) and elevating that sequence into evidence of a law, are steps that take us far from the realm occupied by the material objects that are employed in the experiment.

These are reminders, if reminder were needed, that the habits of nature do not proclaim themselves. They have to be revealed by processes that are not prescribed by, or flow spontaneously out of, though they do not transgress, those habits. The very flaws, inadequacy, inaccuracy, approximations, or incompleteness of the laws of evolving science throughout its history are markers of their distance from the (unchanging) habits of nature. As seems obvious, nature does not have the wherewithal to generate a complete account of itself; but even less does it tease itself apart to generate the kind of partial, incomplete, localized account of the totality offered by elementary laws such as those laws discovered by Boyle.

The distance between the habits of nature and the actions by which they have been discovered as scientific laws in highly regulated settings is made concrete in the strange, cognitively privileged space that is a laboratory. There is no limit to that distance. Consider again the massive cognitive and technological edifice of CERN. CERN is not a natural product like a crystal, a hive or a nest. This extraordinary child of intentionality joined across intellectual communities, nations, and centuries is a monument to the extra-legal – but not law-breaking – processes by which the habits of nature, in the form of scientific laws, are revealed, tested and connected with other laws. It is a spectacular development of the exploitation of those same laws in daily life and in the development of advanced technology. CERN, what is more, is a particularly striking example of the process by which we use sophisticated science to carry out science yet more sophisticated still.

In the Overture, we discussed a virtual outside, rooted in intentionality, evident in the spectatorial stance in accordance with which we are turned to face the world in a manner that, except in the case of other conscious beings, the world does not face us. As an experimenter committed to obtaining reliable, valid, repeatable results, Boyle was grasping nature and its habits not merely from the outside opened up by his own perceptual apparatus but from a refined, objective (or at least intersubjective) standpoint. Even more than ordinary experience, naïve perception, and casual observation, this standpoint is from further outside of nature – as we shall see presently, when we discuss measurement – notwithstanding the aspiration to set aside distortions arising out of the individual subjective viewpoint and to, as it were, "take the side of nature". Hypothesis generation and speculation about possible laws and their connection with other laws lies further still outside of nature. It is deeply ironical, therefore, that the success of objective science has concealed its origins in the primordial outside of the human subject.

There are many other ways in which natural science is unnatural. For example, an experiment may investigate the change in a dependent variable from a starting value, from *initial conditions*, when another variable is altered. Just as there are no dependent, independent and controlled variables in nature, there are also no starting points, no initial conditions or indeed terminal conditions – states of affairs that count as *outcomes*. There are no reference points in the natural world from which one state of affairs is a start and another an ending. As will become evident when we discuss causation, there is seamless unfolding, rather than a stopping that makes a place for starting.[26]

Measurement

Scientists extract observations from the flow of events. The seamless unfolding of things seems to be arrested in a series of snapshots, which are then preserved.[27] Less controversially, we may agree that the most important and universal aspect of scientific inquiry is also the most unnatural. I am referring to measurement. The more clearly we see measurement, the more astonishing it appears.

Empiricists often describe measurements that underpin and test theories as "experiences" or, more respectfully, "observations". While this is true, they are nonetheless fundamentally different from the kind of unsolicited experiences that fill our waking hours and our casual noticings as we go about our daily business. Most of what is strange about measurement is evident long before scientists start using sophisticated kit such as voltmeters and Geiger counters or the less sophisticated kit employed by gentlemen scientists such as Mr Boyle. It is already there in the use of the ruler.

In order to make a measurement, it is necessary to dismount from the spontaneous flow of events and associated experiences. It is a deliberate act performed in pursuit of a special kind of perception designed to ensure as far as possible that, by criteria that have been established collectively, what it reveals should not be distorted; that in some sense the object being observed should be allowed to speak for itself. At the heart of the action of measurement is a self-effacement of the subject – of her angle of vision or "take" on what is before her. Her personal reason for making the measurement, what she is feeling when she makes it, are also swept aside as irrelevant background. While measurement is a highly sophisticated experience solicited by a self-conscious actor, at the same time, as it is turned into a result, it is necessarily impoverished.

Even in the case of something as simple as my determining the length of a table, scarcely anything of what I experience during the course of the measurement is preserved in the result that is obtained and recorded. Walking across the room to pick up the ruler and subsequently putting it back in its box does not count as part of the measurement. As for the table itself, much of it is pushed to the margins – indeed is effectively out of sight. When its length is being measured, its colour, illumination, texture, weight, position, ownership, etc. are erased. Likewise, the colour, weight, and ownership of (say) the ruler, the fall of light on it as it is placed along the table, whether it is made of plastic or wood, and to whom it belongs. As for the record of the measurement, it doesn't matter whether it is written down at once or later, where it is inscribed, and whether the inscription is in black or blue ink or pencil or a number or a dot on a screen.

The mismatch between the quantity of experience needed to secure the measurement and the result obtained is even more striking in advanced science. Think of the experiences lying behind the data-points gathered up in CERN. All those plane and train journeys (and connected arguments over reimbursement of travel expenses), those plans, those grant applications, the writing and publication of the references upon which the application depends, that training, those conversations … my point, I hope, is made.

A measurement is thus trebly distanced from, and elevated above, the unsolicited flow of experience that is served up by the natural world: it is elective; it is quality-controlled; and it is purified to the point of exsanguination as it becomes a result, a quantity, a data-point, extracted from a complex qualitative experience associated with the action. In science, the measurement is increasingly guided by theory, as is the manufacture of the instruments used to make measurements. It is remote from ordinary noticing, being sheathed in rules, knowledge and theory. We use science-based technologies to help us in our aim of getting nature to perform in such a way as to enable us to extend the degree to which the habits of nature are encompassed by the laws of science.

The most cursory glance at measurement exposes the inaccuracy of the claim made by (brilliant) nineteenth-century philosopher and physicist Ernst Mach that "there is no break in continuity between science … and modes of behaviour characteristic of the entire animal world".[28] Dismounting, stepping back, from the flow of experience to seek out a particular purified experience-by-appointment, remote from appetites or immediate needs, is hardly the way of the beast, or indeed of the natural world.

In summary, a measurement extracts something of supreme simplicity, even poverty, from the interaction between the elements in a complex situation (person, measuring tool, measured object, the conventions and skills of measurement): a number attached to a unit. Everything else has been stripped off. Neither the number nor the unit tells us anything about the object. If I say of an item that it is 24 inches long, you would not be able to attach any significance to this assertion. It would not tell you anything about it – not even whether it was long or short, unless you already knew what I was talking about – a caterpillar or a tree. The idea of a data *point* – something vanishingly small and featureless – reflects the exsanguination of the experience of measurement as we pass to a result. This is particularly clear when data-points are located in an entirely extra-natural or non-natural space defined by axes as when they are added to a graph.[29]

Units are a striking marker of the special space in which measurement is located and its distance from ordinary experience of the natural world. As Max Born expressed it:

> The foundation of every space and time measurement is laid by fixing the unit. The phrase "a length of so and so many meters" denotes the ratio of the length to be measured to the length of the meter. The phrase "a time of so many seconds" denotes the ratio of the time to be measured to the duration of the second. Thus we are always dealing with ratios, relative data concerning units which are themselves to a high degree arbitrary, and are chosen for reasons of their being easily reproduced, easily transported, durable, and so forth.[30]

Inches and pounds do not exist in nature: they have to be imported from without – from the further reaches of sophisticated discourse made possible by the joined intentionality of many hundreds or thousands of individuals the overwhelming majority of whom are unknown to the individuals making the measurement.

The extraordinary nature of unitization is evident even in primitive units based on the human body. To "pace out" a distance is to repurpose an action, usually aimed at getting somewhere, to serve an entirely different aim: that of quantifying the size of a space. Equally extraordinary is our capacity to take an objective stance on parts of our own bodies as the basis for agreed units of size. The idea of a standardized "cubit" (forearm), foot, or "inch" (finger) reveals an ability to stand outside of our own bodies not only to the degree that is required to reduce them to their own lengths but also to regard them as mere instances of a general body parts.

It is important, therefore, not to lose sight of the unnatural nature of even the homeliest measurement. While objects with straight edges and successions of events with equal time intervals between them may be naturally occurring, there is no natural process that transforms these items into rulers and clocks. Einstein was acutely aware of this, as evidenced in an arresting remark that he made towards the end of his life. He was struck how the theory of relativity: "[I]introduces two kinds of physical things, i.e. (1) measuring rods and clocks, and (2) all other things, e.g., the electromagnetic field, the material point, etc. This, in a certain sense, is inconsistent…; strictly speaking, measuring rods and clocks would have to be represented as solutions of the basic equations (objects consisting of moving atomic configurations) not, as it were, theoretically self-sufficient entities".[31] It is the observer – who belongs to a complex community of minds – who transforms straight rods into rulers and periodic events into clocks. And here, as elsewhere in physics, the conscious observer is both necessary and an embarrassment.[32]

How far we have to travel from the habits of nature in order to transform them into the laws of science! It is this distance between the habits of nature and the laws of science that may explain our tendency to see the laws unveiled by science as being natural laws that have *regulative* role – as being something imposed on nature from without rather than the most general description of the way things most generally go. In other words, construing laws of nature as items that act upon nature from without may be a projection of the outside-of-nature from which the laws are revealed to us.

One determinant of the path taken in the journey from the habits of nature to the laws of science is our mode of attention to the world. The reader who is already persuaded of the distance between the habits of nature and the laws of science and of the unnatural nature of the scientific enterprise is rewarded with permission to skip the next sub-section.

Scales and direction of attention

We have already registered the multiplicity of robust scientific laws, some but not all of which are superseded by laws of greater scope or wider or more accurate predictive power. What lies behind this multiplicity and what may break down special laws into something rather less elevated – typical patterns, and so on – is the grain and direction of attention of interested humanity. We may focus on something close to ordinary observation as in ornithology whose laws have a limited range. Or we may or at least imagine, as an asymptote of scientific enquiry, a single law covering every event in the universe. The nature of that universal law – and whether it would be a theory, an equation, or a model – is not clear, particularly as it would homogenize everything and thus leave the variousness of the experienced world unaccounted for.

There is also the question of the size of the entities to which the law applies. Some take for granted the privileging of micro-physics among the sciences: because everything is made of atoms, the behaviour of atoms ultimately explains the behaviour of everything: everything that happens really happens at the smallest scale. This is apparently justified because the laws of micro-physics have the greatest generality and its entities the widest distribution. Chaffinches are made of atoms, but atoms are not made of chaffinches.

While the privileging of the micro-physical scale may seem justified to many, it brings numerous problems. An obvious one is that quantum mechanics questions the very idea that the ultimate constituents of what we call matter are elementary particles localized in space and time whizzing around and banging into each other. Indeed, if as quantum theory seems to imply, there are no discrete elements, it is difficult to see what meaning remains of the idea of scale. If, for example, the universe were a single wave function, what happens to the granularity which permits the scientific gaze to scale up or down the acuity of its gaze? The second is that it is difficult to see how macroscopic entities, most notably organisms with their distinctive properties and causal interactions, and *a fortiori* conscious organisms, could emerge from the colourless, etc. realm of atoms.

This seems to justify the view expressed by Mariam Thalos (to whom these arguments about scale are indebted): "Our universe is scale free. By this I mean it is active at multiple scales, potentially at every scale. It's not true that all the 'real' action happens at the smallest size scales; it's false that the large-scale features are simply inert, and that all of us – large and slow-moving beasts that we are – are banished from the true dance of the universe. The one-scale model of activity in the universe is a dogma too old for new tricks".[33]

It is, to put it mildly, a bold assumption that the habits of the universe operate on a particular scale and that that scale is the one illuminated by elementary particle physics; that that scale is justified in having the status of being fundamental – not only in the sense of being most general in application but also in the sense of being closest to the habits.

As already noted, that there are laws of physics *and* of chemistry *and* of biology does not reflect inherent distinctions in the material world. Indeed, the fact that some of the most fundamental laws of chemistry have been discovered to be a manifestation of yet more fundamental laws of physics – quantum mechanics as it happens – is a powerful reminder that the variety of the laws is a reflection of the variety of disciplines rather than the variety of nature.[34] Nature, as we have already noted, is not inherently a chemist or, come to that, a physicist: even the most fundamental laws of physics, testable to 1 part in 10^n, are provisional, as the unresolved conflict between its most powerful theories – relativity and quantum mechanics[35] – demonstrates.

It is obvious that nature is not, and cannot be understood as being at odds with itself, unable to decide whether it is chemistry or physics: it is what it is. Obvious or not, it is nonetheless significant for our understanding of the status of the laws of science and of the activity of the scientists who reveal them. The multiplicity of laws reflects the discretion available to humanity in determining its own scale and direction of attention – an extension of the primordial privilege of the spectator distanced from what-is by intentionality.[36]

Those for whom the truth about the universe is, or will be, captured in physics also believe that the so-called "special" sciences – that fall short of fundamental physics in respect of having a narrower scope – are in some sense constrained by physics because everything in the universe that exists is physically constituted.[37] Notwithstanding the current head-on collision between relativity and quantum theory it is generally assumed that it is within physics that we shall find any unification of the sciences, the point of convergence of our knowledge of nature in a Final Theory or a Theory of Everything.[38]

This view seems to survive the discovery that at the most fundamental level, scientific laws lack particular content of any kind: what we have are mathematical structures. The other side of the fact that particle physics applies equally to rocks, chaffinches and human beings is that there is nothing in it that captures the very real differences between them. In its progression to mathematical purity and utter generality it loses those differences.[39] The mathematical picture of the world becomes more empty as it widens its scope.

This is a matter for another time. Our point, for the present, is that the distinctive aspects of the universe that are captured in the more parochial laws of the special sciences may not be separated in nature or even inherent in it, any more than the back view and the front view of a mountain, its being remote or near, or its being a collection of smaller items, a single item in itself, or a part of a mountainous terrain, are inherent in the mountain. The multiplicity of such laws corresponds not to the different habits of nature but to different modes – directions, scales – of attention. The circumstances bring the less-than-fundamental laws to the fore are also those that pick out individual materials or events from the continuum of nature – something that we shall discuss when we examine the very idea of causes.

The key point is that what is picked out by the laws of science or the sciences is *not* inherent in nature as its intrinsic habits or master-habit. This is not just a temporary state of affairs, that will obtain until we arrive at a 100 per cent accurate complete account of underlying principles or a single principle governing change when the laws of science will be identical with the habits of nature. The fact, however, that we are able to use those laws – which reflect different scales of attention and inquiry not reflecting anything intrinsic in nature – to enhance our powers is a reminder of how as agents we act upon nature from a virtual outside.

A quick look back at neurodeterminism

The question as to whether the processes that result in the discovery of the laws of science are themselves unmediated expressions of the habits of nature has particular salience when science turns its attention to consciousness – the very ground on which the multi-storied edifice of science stands.

The scientific account of consciousness typically identifies it with neural discharges in particular parts of the brain – something that we saw in the Overture as deeply problematic. It becomes more problematic when this claim is extended to all cognitive activity, including that which underpins scientific inquiry.

It is difficult to see how, if human consciousness were entirely constructed out of neural activity, it could stand outside of nature sufficiently to discover that this capacity to stand outside of nature is located in neural activity entirely subordinate to the laws of nature. By what means could the physical events that are neural discharges reveal that they are sufficiently correlated with consciousness to justify the conclusion that they are identical with consciousness? How could they stand outside of themselves this way (a) to make the necessary observations and (b) to extrapolate from those observations to general conclusions about their basis? By what means can a brain ascend to a view on itself from which it could draw conclusions about all brains and all consciousness? If neural activity entirely accounted for that outsideness, how could it stand outside of it to see its origin in neural activity? Specifically, what neural activity could correspond to the thought that all thoughts, including itself, are neural activity?[40]

The neuroscientific experiments we discussed in Section 1.2 designed to test whether we have free will or whether the brain is calling the shots are direct attempts to gather back into nature that in virtue of which we are able actively to investigate nature. We need only ask whose brain was calling the shots when the question about free will was posed, when the experiment was designed, and when the wherewithal (including equipment, experimenters and participants, and the money to pay for them) was assembled, to highlight how misconceived the experiments were. If it were not triumphalist to do so, it would be tempting to declare that there could be no more impressive demonstration of our free will than the experiments that Libet and Haynes carried out and which for some prove that we have no free will.

Conclusion

The methods by which *Homo scientificus* seems to close in on the habits of nature are not themselves explicable in terms of those habits. What goes on in the special space of the laboratory where the habits are revealed as the laws of science reveals a capacity to stand outside of, or at least take a carefully constructed external stance on, the habits of nature in a way that suggests the exercise of a freedom not subordinated to or explained by those habits. Scientific inquiry requires a vast amplification of the distance from nature that is opened up by the intentionality of perception. We cannot credit the habits of nature, as formulated by physics, chemistry, with initiating and maintaining the complex, arduous 2,500-year cognitive journey by which the habits themselves have been revealed to human beings – who are, after all, a minute part of the natural world and very recent arrivals in it.

The ingenuity, struggles, and the carefully structured methods that make possible the observations, experimentation, apparatus, measurements, arguments, and confirmations behind the discovery of the simplest law, are remote from "V/P = constant" or "$E=mc^2$". Human beings, if they were entirely subject to the habits of nature, would seem an unlikely bridge between the habits of nature partly reflected in $E=mc^2$ and the law of science expressed in the formula "$E=mc^2$". It seems to be an egregious expression of the habits of nature to put other habits into inverted commas as the laws of science. This distance between the habits of nature and the laws of science is easy to overlook when we look at nature through the lens of natural science, just as we do not see the spectacles through which we see the world. Indeed, they become less visible the more effective they are.

Enough has been said, I trust, to support the conclusion that the processes by which what we regard as the laws of nature are discovered and tested are highly unnatural. This is the profound mystery behind the seemingly innocent, indeed sensible notion, that laws apply only where "other things are equal". In the rough and tumble of nature, other things are not equal, nor do they have to be. More precisely there is no distinction between "things" and "other things". Nor is there anything to account for the difference between the chaotic surface image of the world as presented to the casual gaze and the hidden apparent order portrayed in science and how we get from one to the other.

Scientific inquiry at a level of sophistication sufficient to reveal the natural laws is located at the end of a long journey away from any putative material, law-governed substrate of nature and natural causes. The journey begins with perception; proceeds to active observation; and then, via experimentation and measurement and hypothesis-driven generalization, eventually arrives at scientific laws.[41] None of these vast steps looks like something that physics, chemistry, or even biology can accommodate, even if (as they are not) those disciplines were a straightforward portrait of the habits of the universe. The shared, and often contested, and rapidly changing, story about the world we live in, is a long way from the processes of nature. Even common sense is already remote from the kind of cognitive stance we associate with beasts.[42]

This is why I believe we should reject the views of Quine who wanted to naturalize all knowledge, including scientific knowledge: "But, like the animal's simple deduction over innate similarities, [science] is still a biological device for anticipating experience".[43] Hardly. Science-mediated anticipations are explicitly rooted in principles, are based on specially generated experiences, and are quantitative and unit-based. Measurements do not happen: they are made. Scientific data are given only to those who have positioned themselves to receive them. What is more, the principles are established separately from any particular person's observations made at any particular time or place. Boyle's law is not anchored to the experiences of the particular genius who gave it his name. Boyle's life is confined to Boyle whereas Boyle's law belongs to the whole world mediated through human consciousness.

The procedures by which the habits of nature are formulated as the laws of science are an extra-natural expression of the very freedom that the laws are supposed by incompatibilist determinists to demonstrate to be impossible. It seems reasonable to conclude that, if we can step outside of the habits of nature sufficiently to uncover them as the laws of science, we can also exercise genuine free will outside as well as inside the laboratory in exploiting those laws to serve our freely chosen ends. *The means by which we discover the laws of science are also those by which we can exploit them in freely chosen actions to serve our purposes.* The complex consciousness that informs scientific and indeed pre-scientific inquiry into the ways of the natural world is a marker of our distance from the habits of nature. Nature does not declare its own most general properties, let alone gather itself up and name itself "nature". What-is does not of itself generate the "that" and the "how" that declares *that* it is and *how* it is.

There is an echo of this sentiment in an arresting passage from Karl Popper: "Nature has no theories about itself. Our intellect does not draw its laws from nature, but tries – with varying degrees of success – to impose upon nature laws which it freely invents".[44] This is somewhat of an exaggeration: speculation is free but nature calls the shots when it is a matter of separating true from false, useful or useless, fertile or sterile, conjectures.

If the central argument of this section is not as obvious as one might expect it to be, it is because the distance between *what-is* and *that-it-is* is concealed when the communal, written, artefactual nature of science hides the role of the subject and her intentionality in making it possible. That we can advance our understanding of the habits of nature and transform them into the laws of science which we can exploit proves that we are not entirely subject to the former. The so-called laws of nature could not account for the revelation of the habits of nature as the laws of science. If we were soluble fish we would not be oceanographers.

2.3 EXPLOITING THE HABITS OF NATURE VIA LAWS OF SCIENCE

From discovery to exploitation

The case against free will appears unanswerable if we acknowledge that we seem to *depend on* the 100 per cent reliable habits of nature for our actions to be possible and for them to have their desired consequences. If for example action and reaction were not equal and opposite, we could not walk to the shops or, indeed, get out of bed and the outcome of our actions would be unpredictable and beyond our control. The impossibility of free will could be summarized thus: agency requires the wall-to-wall adherence of nature to its habits, the very determinism, that is seemingly incompatible with it. This is the challenge faced by those such as the present author who claim that free will is compatible with a deterministic natural world.

The case, it appears, is closed. Until, that is, we reflect on the procedures by which we have discovered what we believe to be the laws of nature to which we are in lifelong fealty. If we can unpack the habits of nature as laws of science by manipulating the natural world *inside* the laboratory, we surely must be able to manipulate the natural world *outside* of the laboratory. What is more, our capacity to manipulate the natural world is enhanced by our knowledge of the laws we have discovered. None of this would be possible if we were indistinguishable from a nature regulated by those laws.

The key to the defence of the compatibilism to which this book is committed is that *the laws of science are a product of a mode of engagement with nature that cannot be explained by those laws, a mode of engagement, from a virtual outside, that is compatible with, indeed presupposes, distance from them.*[45] I say "virtual" outside because the outside in question is not the literal outside of spatial separation – in the way that objects and events are outside of each other. Rather it lies in the distance between intentional consciousness and its objects, between subjects and that which they experience, or knowledge and that which is known. The manner in which, say, a cup and my hand reaching towards it are outside of one another is mutual and symmetrical: the cup is outside of the hand and the hand is outside of the cup. The same is not true of the way the cup is outside of me: the cup is "over there" for me but I am not "over there" for the cup.

If there is such a thing as science uncovering usable truths – and we may assume that this is not an illusion, given its universal, practical consequences in our lives – then there is something like free will; for the experiments upon which science depends are not just a succession of pilotless law-governed events passing through the physical spaces occupied by the scientific community.

And if there is such a thing as progress in science (and it is difficult to deny that there is), then it seems reasonable to think of scientific discourse closing in on the habits of nature; and any idea of "closing in" must be predicated on the notion of beginning from a (virtual) outside whose most homely manifestation is in the relationship between the cup and the hand.

The exercise of free will does not, of course, depend on the application of sophisticated science – not the least because it would not be possible to see how science could get off the ground. Science-enhanced agency is just the highest, and a comparatively recent, expression of the immemorial poking and prodding that has enabled us to arrive at a general sense of how things go and thus more effectively to manipulate them in pursuit of our ends. Science takes its rise from the habits of unstructured investigation – some of which are seen in non-human animals – though it has soared far beyond them in the ways described in the previous section.[46]

We are now in a position to return to the passage quoted earlier from J. S. Mill, armed with a better understanding of how his claim about the possibility of free action in an apparently law-governed universe might stand up: "Though we cannot emancipate ourselves from the laws of nature as a whole we can escape from any particular law of nature if we are able to withdraw ourselves from the circumstances in which it acts. Though we can do nothing except through laws of nature, we can use one law to counteract another".[47]

"Withdrawing ourselves from the circumstances in which [one particular law] acts" is precisely what we see happening in a laboratory, where some variables are controlled and others are unconstrained. The multiplicity of laws teased out by science acting at one place – that makes it possible to withdraw from particular laws and to exploit one law to manipulate a situation governed by another – enables us to be law-abiding (or habit-abiding) while not being helpless substrates upon which laws (or nature's habits) operate. That multiplicity is evident throughout natural science.[48]

So much for the multiplicity of laws. But how, when every event conforms to the habits of nature, can we "escape from any particular law [or habit] of nature" by "withdraw[ing] ourselves from the circumstances in which it acts"? By what means can we position ourselves in this way? Sticking for a moment to Mill's terminology, how can we "use one law to counteract another", given that "we can do nothing except through laws of nature"? This "divide and conquer" approach seems to require us to stand outside of nature and its laws. Surely, it will be protested, this is impossible, given that any such withdrawal must require what Mill said was not possible; namely that we "emancipate ourselves from the laws of nature as a whole". And yet, as we have seen, this is close to what we actually do when we are engaged in using some habits of nature to uncover other habits as the laws of science. The strategic manipulations, in the laboratory, of our encounter with the material world that have enabled us to discover the laws of science are refinements of those we use in everyday life, though our manipulative powers are greatly enhanced by our discovery of the most general habits of nature as portrayed in the laws of science.

Mill therefore is right in this sense: while you can't buck the laws of nature you can set one local law against another. You can exploit the conformity of a gas to Charles's law by increasing its temperature while, by allowing it to expand freely, avoiding any alteration in its pressure. In short, we can fore-ground what we may call Charles's or Boyle's effects depending on how we manipulate the gas and the circumstances in which the manipulation takes place. Likewise, we can give Boyle's law uncontaminated expression if we so order things that the gas we are observing is shielded from changes that would conceal the proportionality between volume and pressure.

If we can do this inside of the laboratory – which is as subject to the habits of nature as anywhere else in the universe – then we can do it outside the laboratory. Laboratories are privileged spaces but they are not metaphysically privileged.[49] If we can truly manipulate the material or natural world inside them, we can manipulate the world outside of them. The establishment and maintenance of controlled conditions, or more broadly setting up an exper-imental situation, in a shielded system, is a striking example of the ability, evident throughout daily life, to regulate the circumstances in which we act.[50]

It is in this sense that experiments are *done*: they do not merely *happen* as a result of the habits of nature somehow discovering themselves as the laws of science. And this island of doing is opened by human beings importing a viewpoint – endlessly elaborated through various modes of shared intention-ality into structured standpoints – into what-is. It is by these means that the habits of nature are made visible as the laws of science.

In experimental science, therefore, we see a particularly clear example of Mill's principle of using "one law to counteract another" – something that is evident more broadly in human agency. The multiplicity of laws to which Mill refers arises from a multiplicity of aspects of any event or unfolding state of affairs that reveals one law in operation rather than another.[51] Separating out aspects that are not separated in nature – after all, gases are obliged to have both pressures and volumes and temperatures all at the same time – is evident in the experimentation that reveals the laws that connect picked-out variables. It is we who introduce "aspects of nature" into nature. And this is reflected not only in foregrounding certain laws but in the distinction between a foreground governed by certain laws and a background of conditions that are not governed by those particular laws. Our embodied subjectivity opens up a particular "outside" which transforms "what there is" into "what is there" and "what is there" into conditions from which one set of habits may be exploited to serve our ends; "we can use one law to counteract another". Counteract or exploit.

That we do in fact exploit the laws of nature – or the laws of science that pick out aspects of the habitual modes of the unfolding of what-is – is beyond doubt. It is a matter of empirical fact. We are able to utilize those laws to make predictions and directly or indirectly bring about states of affairs that conform more closely to our wishes. To deny this would be to deny the most obvious fact about our human history – namely that our ability to achieve our goals, and indeed our lives, has been transformed by the application of science building on pre-scientific technology using common-sense levels of understanding of how the world hangs together.

We have shaped the world to an extent not matched by any other creature. It is not for nothing that the present epoch of the earth is labelled the Anthropocene. And while the scale of our impact on the planet does not compare with the scale of the processes that gave rise to the solar system, unlike the latter it has been driven by explicit purposes. At any rate, we cannot be deluded as to our ability to exploit habits of nature in the form of the laws of science, given that we are able to fly to the moon or speak to our friends tens of thousands of miles away by means of signals bounced off distant satellites, without even raising our voices.

Granted, other creatures have shaped the world dramatically but there is a fundamental difference between ourselves and beasts that is not just one of scale. It is to be found in the central role of *explicit purpose* guiding our impact on our surroundings – notwithstanding that the overall consequences of our activity, such as climate change, may be unintended and hugely unwelcome. Human purposes are not simply observable from without. Unlike the "purposes" seen by human observers in the natural world – as for example in mechanisms such as a heliotropic organism turning to the sun – human purposes are to a considerable degree known from within. They are (to use a term that will be important in our discussion in the next chapter) "entertained" – awoken and energized – by a sense of a future.

More generally, by seeing how things "work" we can make them work for us. We use the near 100 per cent reliability of many scientific laws to our advantage to control the outcomes of our actions, as we manipulate nature using those laws as guides to our choice of levers. Again, there is nothing in natural processes that would generate this capacity to see "how things work"; or not at any rate its being acquired through the lens of general theories rather than a process of trial and error which merely aligns the habits of our behaviour to the habits of the universe.[52]

Intentionality and shared intentionality in the lab and beyond

Our double status as parts of nature and as beings who act on nature from a virtual outside is already evident in perception where we are connected with nature and at the same time distanced from it by intentionality which confers the spectatorial privilege of beings who *face* nature as their world and endeavours to make practical sense of it. The observations that are made are intended to be exemplary: to exemplify a limitless class of possible experiences.

Boyle's investigations were in another important respect freed from his current material circumstances. They were curiosity-driven and, from the point of view of his immediate needs, that curiosity was idle. (Not as idle, of course, as the celestial mechanics that lay at the beginning of the scientific revolution in Europe and ultimately delivered our modern artefactscape, though it could not have anticipated this outcome.) What was sought was not a particular answer to a particular question but an underlying principle that would apply to situations that are neither individual nor present, to general, largely absent, situations.

The blue-skies nature of science has ultimately delivered more than inquiry hard-headedly rooted in immediate practical need. While the interval between fundamental discoveries and practical application has narrowed in the last century, the history of science has been one of discovering general principles that do not necessarily have even a future application.

I dwell on this to underline the many distances from the natural world opened up by the cognitive enterprise of seeking "the laws of nature". It remains important to keep in the forefront of one's mind the original source of that distance in the spectatorial privilege of a subject facing the material world – an asymmetrical relationship between an "I" and an "it". The nature of the distance is illustrated by the intentionality of visual perception which permits access to what is "out there" without direct contact with it. In the case of full-blown perception, the "out there" is populated by objects that are assumed to exist in themselves, independently of being experienced – either by myself or by anyone else. This is the element of truth in Quine's otherwise misleading claim that "the positing of bodies is already rudimentary physical science"[53] The positing of bodies is the precondition of science rather than the lower slopes of this extraordinary ascent to a viewpoint on the universe.

While it is possible that other conscious animals undertake searches, the scents that they follow are not prompted in the way that scientific research is prompted – by odourless intuitions susceptible of being formalized and generalized, and the sense of an underlying principle or of invariable connections between changes understood as the changing values of parameters. Those intuitions – vastly more sophisticated than experiences and expectations trig-gered by bumping into things – are in part shaped by a legacy of knowledge, methods, and existing areas of inquiry. It is this that permits the spectatorial distance afforded by perception – which can be imported into the agency of practical applications – to be greatly expanded, permitting ever more distantly mediated interaction with the material world.

The cognitive monument that is science and the advantage that it brings to agents is the most developed consequence of the joining of intentionality, creating the community of minds, that is human society. What is the most striking aspect of science is its progress, as measured by its practical applica-tions. We manipulate nature – even place it "on the rack" – to disclose its most general and enduring habits in the form of the laws of science. We then use our knowledge of those laws to develop apparatus to refine experimentation and further our knowledge of those habits. There is a process of cognitive upwards ratcheting.

This is a huge topic. Suffice for the present to note the vast and expanding distance opened up between the realm of "what-is" and the realm of knowl-edge or "*that-it-is*" marked by the capturing of the habits of nature in the laws of science, which presupposes our having a capacity as agents, has also hugely extended our agency. Our capacity to capture nature's habits by creating the conditions in which they are partially visible is the same capacity as that which enables us to use one habit to manipulate other habits. The *ceteris paribus* condition we maintain in research and in the exploitation of laws is a par-ticularly sophisticated expression of our wider, pre-scientific capacity to hold things steady to create a platform from which we may exercise our agency.

Such platforms are many and various and we shall discuss them in Chapter 4. For the present, we may note that the journey to the positioning and fixing of conditions in which we exercise our agency is the lifelong project of indi-vidual and connected human agents. It is ultimately built on our ability to be outside of the present moment, courtesy of intentionality. And it is from this standpoint that we can privilege some aspects of nature and downgrade others, differentiating the object of interest and our aims with respect to it and the background that permits it; the ground – literal and metaphorically – on which we proceed to our goals. Nature itself recognizes no such privileges or differentiations.

All of this highlights the irony of the fact that the natural science that has extended our agency – and resulted in longer life, health, and fun expectancy for at least some of the human race and (politics permitting) may yet bring these gifts to the remainder – has been cited by some to demonstrate our lack of freedom. The failure of physical science to accommodate the human subject and free will – neither of these is visible to brain scientists – has been taken as proof that the very idea of human agents as the source of their actions is flawed. Our bodies, as material objects comprehensible through the eyes of physics, chemistry, biochemistry and biology, are, so we are told, simply parts of nature and entirely subject to its laws, the inmost keep of our determinist prison.

In short, we overlook our capacity to *see* the laws to which we are supposedly subject and to know of, and chafe against, the natural constraints on human possibility. Why is this the case? It is perhaps because when we learn about, or utilize, the laws of science, the knowing, experimenting agent is off-stage. There are no signs of Robert Boyle in the law-like behaviour of gases or of Albert Einstein in the field equations of general relativity or of the scientific community and its endeavours in the laws of science.

Jennan Ismael has commented penetratingly on the "weirdness" that follows when we reify the laws of nature: "We invert the order of determination … so that it looks like the laws are not simply descriptions of patterns that are partly constituted by our actions but are instead iron rails built into the spatial and temporal landscape that won't let us act in any way not in accord with them".[54]

It is indeed "weird" that the product of our unique capacity to see how the universe works, which has greatly enhanced our potency – namely the laws of science – has then been turned against us to support the conclusion that we are powerless. While humans enjoyed freedom before there was physics – otherwise there would be no physics – it is true that it has extended the scope of what freedom we had before physics gave birth to the powerful tools that surround us in our daily life. The weirdness is compounded when, as science becomes more powerful, the conviction grows that we are disempowered by the very laws we have discovered. As the laws of science seem to give us ever more precise predictive power regarding every aspect of the universe including our own body, to some the noose of determinism seems to tighten. The science that is supposed to show that we are not free has as a matter of undeniable fact vastly extended our agency.

Which is not to say that there isn't a mystery. It is difficult to grasp how, as very late arrivals in the scheme of things, we could start ordering the world around. Nevertheless, this will seem to be an argument against the reality of freedom only so long as we forget the intentionality that enables us to engage with the world at a distance from which, armed by possibilities (of which more presently), we can inquire into its nature and, imagining how it might work, get it to work for us. Which is not to say that how we do – and where we do not – fit into the unfolding history of the material universe is easy to understand.[55]

Home scientificus is a particularly egregious expression of the wider mystery of human consciousness and where it fits into an overwhelmingly insentient universe – a mystery that is exacerbated when we form a picture of that universe as being defined by the laws of natural science. Mystery it may be but without consciousness and the free will that it underpins there would be no basis for any world picture, not the least one arrived at by painstaking experimentation. And we cannot deny that we do have world pictures transformed by such experimentation.

One final point, to head off a misunderstanding. Asserting that we are outside of nature inasmuch as we transform the habits of nature into the laws of science may seem to some a mere truism irrelevant to the question of whether we can exercise genuine freedom. That the laws of science are outside of nature, it will be argued, says nothing more than that a description of nature is outside of that which is described. This is to miss the fundamental significance of the fact that there are such descriptions and of the means by which they are generated and, indeed, quality-controlled and revised. While knowing a law does not entail any exemption from the habits of nature, the complex, deliberate processes by which we come to know the law indicates a relationship to nature that is remote from the subservience that would flow from total engulfment in the natural world.[56]

And so, we come to the other apparent enemy of free will: the causal necessity built into the connectedness of the world.

CHAPTER 3

Unpicking causation

"The human intellect cannot grasp the full range of causes behind any phenomenon. But the need to discover causes is deeply ingrained in the spirit of man. And so the human intellect ignores the infinite permutations and sheer complexity of all the circumstances surrounding a phenomenon, any one of which could be individually construed as the thing that causes it, latches on to the first and easiest approximation, and says 'This is the cause!'"

Leo Tolstoy, *War and Peace*

Some determinists argue that all physical events are not only law-governed but also the inescapable effects of prior events – their causes. Since behaviour must take place in, and make a difference to, the physical world, the idea of actions as a metaphysically privileged category of happenings expressing an agency free from the bondage of causation is therefore fantasy. Even when actions are motivated by "internal events" such as explicit intentions, beliefs, hopes, or the idea of an immediate or distant goal, so the argument continues, they are no less determined from without. Internal events are the effects (and subsequently causes) of external events.

Intentions, reasons, wishes and such-like are simply intermediate (presumably physical) causes located between physical inputs understood as stimuli and physical outputs understood as responses. These intermediaries have either been implanted as biological instincts or "drives"; or they are the consequences of cultural conditioning, the latter being rooted in biology and hence ultimately in the physical world. Even when we do exactly as we want we are not acting freely because we have not chosen the wants that cause our actions. Those wants have a causal ancestry that ultimately lies outside of us.

In short, actions are part of the natural order and are themselves natural phenomena. This is necessary if they are to interact on level terms with the rest of the natural world. The movement of the arm of a person who picks up a stone to throw it is, and must be, as subject to Newton's laws as is the flight of the stone and what happens when the stone falls to the ground.

"Laws *and* causes" may seem an unnecessary doubling of the jeopardy of agents.[1] It is sufficient, surely, that actions should be law-bound or even law-generated to damn them as mere happenings. Causation seems to turn the key in a door that has already been slammed tight shut by the laws. Should we not think of laws and causes less as a double whammy than as a single whammy with two sides? Perhaps.

Or perhaps not. Treating laws and causes separately, with the latter being the events that realize the general laws in particular places, exposes certain assumptions built into the case for determinism that tend to be passed by on the nod. We shall in due course look critically at the assumption that the natural world breaks up into discrete events that are first effects of prior causes and then assume the role of causes of subsequent effects. And we shall examine much-contested ideas of what it is that connects these discrete events: of causation as "oomph", as material necessity, as "productive quality" that David Hume (*vide infra*) dismissed as a meaningless metaphysical term, as an occult force hidden from perception; or as a kind of glue or cement – securing the coherence or at least continuity of the unfolding order of things.

Dismantling the idea of causation – as a source of material necessity, supplementary to the habits of nature captured in the laws of science, built into the sequence of events – will arm us against seeing voluntary actions as mere stretches of causal chains that pass through the agents to which they are ascribed. Seeing actions in this way would scupper the idea of true agency by stitching what agents do into the physical world and removing any grounds for seeing actions as fundamentally different from other events.

3.1 HUME-ILIATING CAUSES

The obvious place to start is with the Scottish Enlightenment philosopher David Hume. He examined causation in his *Treatise on Human Nature* (1737–8) and his subsequent *Enquiry Concerning Human Understanding* (1748) and laid down the terms of the debate in anglophone philosophy for the next quarter of a millennium. Famously, he defined causation as follows: "We may define a cause to be an object followed by another, and where all the objects, similar to the first, are followed by objects similar to the second. Or, in other words, where, if the first object had not been, the second had never existed".[2] We may read "object" to include "event".

As has often been pointed out, Hume offers two distinct characterizations of causation in this short passage. In the second sentence, we are offered what contemporary philosophers call a "counterfactual" account of a cause – something to which we shall return. In respect of the first characterization of causation, Hume identifies those aspects of the relationship between successive events that we really can perceive: the constant contiguity of the types of events; and a temporal order which places the cause before the effect. What we *cannot* perceive is a *necessary connection* between cause and effect. That seemingly necessary connection is "no more than a determination to carry our thoughts from one object to another".[3] It is the strength of our expectations that make us seem that certain events necessitate their successors.

Since we cannot perceive causation, we have no adequate grounds for believing there is such a principle of necessity inherent in the natural world. There is nothing corresponding to what the German Enlightenment philosopher Georg Christoph Lichtenberg mocked as "an occult force":[4] a *power* inherent in causes to bring about effects. It is a mistake, Hume argues, to infer from the uniformity of nature and the fact that some sequences of events are highly predictable, and their course is actively controlled, that how things typically follow one another is a necessary, irresistible order of things. We are not entitled to conclude, from the fact that, given the right circumstances, events of type A are always followed by events of type B, that events of type A *must* always be followed by events of type B. All there is to causation is regularity; and the habits of nature partly reflected in the laws of science will take care of the regularities.

Causal necessity, therefore, is something we project into nature from our own confident, and (seemingly) overwhelmingly justified, expectations. When in our experience an event of type A is always followed by an event of type B (other things being equal), we conclude that the type A events *make* the type B events happen: "Upon the whole, necessity is something that exists in the mind, not in objects ... Either we have no idea of necessity, or necessity is nothing but that determination of the thought to pass from the causes to the effects, and from effects to causes, according to their experienced union".[5] Hume saw this sense of necessity as a manifestation of a general tendency of the mind "to spread itself on external objects".[6]

Whether the observation of "constant conjunction" between types of events is the only, or even the main, source of our causal intuitions, is a matter of dispute and perhaps open to correction by empirical psychologists. After all, outside of the lab, in everyday life, we trace the causes of singular events – "What's making that funny noise?" – to other singular events "It's the door swinging in the wind" – without explicitly locating them under general types of events or referring to regular, repeated experiences of constant conjunction.[7] The descent from general conceptions of causal connections to particular causal links is contested. Any general principles of causal linkage are submerged in a background of expectation based on experience that may not be in sharp focus. The fact remains, however, that, as Lichtenberg put it, "Man is a cause-seeking animal; in the spiritual order he could be called the cause-seeker. Other minds perhaps think of things in other – to us inconceivable – categories."[8]

Kant was persuaded by his reading of Hume also to locate causal connectedness in the mind. He went further and his hyper-radical response could be seen as a case of throwing the bathroom as well as the baby out with the bathwater: causation was, he asserted, but one of several categories of the understanding that transform the blizzard of sensations into experience of a structured world "out there" – a world ordered *a priori*, by the forms of sensible intuition, in space and in time.[9] The notion that every event has a cause is one of "the conditions of possibility" of organizing experience into a world.

Whether or not one accepts Kant's radical transformation of causation as a response to Humean scepticism, the awkwardness of the idea of "material necessity", of necessity baked into the succession of events, cannot be denied. For some philosophers, the very idea of causation imports into nature – or the idea of it – something whose home base is propositions. Ordinarily, so the argument goes, necessity seems to be a logical relation: there is *de dicto* (in words) but not *de re* (in things) necessity.[10] Implacability or inevitability in the progression of material events hardly looks like a relationship analogous to that which connects a premise with a valid conclusion. The effect of a cause and the conclusion of a syllogism may share the property of inescapability but their modes of inescapability are fundamentally different. There is no "must" in nature any more than there is an "ought". Nature is what it is – not what it must be, even less what it ought to be. "If lightning, then thunder" is not analogous to "If p, then not not-p". (As we shall see, there is also no "might be" in the material world – something that will be central to our understanding of the relationship between possibility and action.)

The outcome of this argument over material necessity does not bear on the position to be developed in this section; namely that connections between events are invoked in order to overcome *dis*connection. My concern in what follows will be with the nature and origin of this disconnection as it is reflected in the discreteness of events.

Among the problems with Hume's psychologizing of causation is one that he was aware of: it provides an insecure basis for a distinction that is important in practical life. Mere correlation between the occurrence of A and the immediately subsequent occurrence of B does not, however regular, guarantee that B will always follow A. We cannot draw safe general conclusions about how things will go, even to the extent of being confident that day will follow night just because it always has done. Indeed, if causes really are separate from effects and the relationship between them is contingent, there is no obligation on nature to continue behaving in the future as it has in the past. Hence the problem of induction: the challenge of discovering something more robust than a psychological basis for our confidence in a future sequence of events that will be like that of the past; of finding an unshakable ground for expectation of what is going to happen next.

One thing that seems to distinguish genuine causation from mere association or correlation, between lawful and accidental regularities of association, is an identified *mechanism* connecting observed causes and effects. Even the tobacco companies gave up denying a causal relationship between smoking and lung cancer when it was experimentally demonstrated that cigarette smoke was able to induce cancerous changes in lung tissue. In short, the identification of a biological mechanism linking smoking and cancer seemed to bind the two together more tightly. The inhalation of much smoke and subsequent coughing blood ceased to be two types of distinct events but earlier and later stages of the same process. However, there remains a problem. The mechanism is a protracted, if continuous, process. Breaking it down into discrete events opens the possibility that the earlier stages may not guarantee the later stages.[11]

The discovery of an intermediate mechanism – or intermediate mechanisms – uncovers an underlying continuity. We can see this in the well-worn example of lightning causing thunder. (Now is not the time for distracting originality.) Although there may be a clear interval between the flash and the bang – so that we think of them as separate events – a deeper grasp of what is going on sees them as parts of the same processes, with the interval filled with the rapid expansion of the air around the bolt of lightning for a few thousandths of a second that compresses air that cannot at first expand. It then expands outwards explosively and thunder results.

The viewpoint and/or description-dependency of the separation and unification of events is universally evident. I can speak of a banging causing a noise or of "a banging noise"; of "a singing bird" or a bird producing a song. We are more prone to tease a cause-and-effect pair out of a process or an event when there is a delay between our perceiving part of the process and seeing it entire. Then (for example) we translate the banging noise into the effect caused by a swinging door; or the singing bird into a song having its source in, being caused by, the actions of a bird.

Agency, or the idea of getting a handle on things, is an important driver to picking out discrete events from a continuous process. We shall discuss this presently but there is one aspect of this that is worth touching on at present. The difference between mere correlation – constant conjunction – and what we are prepared to count as causation is highlighted by amenability to manipulation. To use a well-worn example, the prior fall of the needle on a barometer correlates with the occurrence of rain but one cannot cause rainfall by moving the needle. This is because the needle's position under normal circumstances and rainfall are both effects of reduced atmospheric pressure: they have a common ancestor rather than being in a relationship of cause to effect.

This example illustrates what is meant by manipulability as a mark of a genuine causal relationship. To anticipate a later discussion, there is an alternative "interventionist" account of causation: that X counts as a cause of Y if I can reliably change the value of Y by altering the value of X. Such interventionist accounts are ways of making causation more friendly to the idea of voluntary action, as we shall see presently.

Meanwhile, let us look at a couple of other problems with the Humean psychologization of causation. First, by what means does the transformation of the observation of constant contiguity into the sense of a causal relationship come about? It is difficult not to suspect that there is, just below the surface, a sense of a kind of real causal necessity in the process by which the questionable sense of causal necessity is implanted in our minds. Hume seems to offer a causal explanation of our causal beliefs, by this means simultaneously deconstructing and partly restoring causation. (Indeed, there is a later section in this part of his *Treatise* entitled "Of the Causes of Belief"!).[12]

Secondly, if causation were a mental sewing together, by a bond of quasi-necessity, of events that are not in fact separate but contiguous, it is difficult to understand how they come also to be experienced as apart in the sense of being distinct and only contingently related.[13]

Restoring the continuum: causes as glue (or cement) or oomph

Which brings us to a more fundamental point. It concerns the extent to which the natural world is or is not seamless, an unfolding continuum, or whether it is intrinsically broken up into discrete successive events or dis-crete successive states. Hume himself seems to argue for this seamlessness: "Though distant objects may sometimes seem productive of each other, they are commonly found upon examination to be linked by a chain of causes which are contiguous among themselves, and to the distant objects; and when in particular we cannot discover this connection, we still presume it to exist. We may therefore consider the relation of *contiguity* as essential to that of causation".[14]

This passage reflects an ambivalence that haunts the very idea of causa-tion – and not only in Hume's mind.[15] Insofar as causation is thought of as a connection – between items that are intrinsically separated, and have a purely contingent relationship – as a kind of glue ("the cement of the universe"[16]), it is supposed to act as a principle that brings them together through a bond of necessity. Insofar as cause and effect are *not* separated but are contiguous there would seem to be no need for any kind of additional connection. It is not clear what the objective difference is between two contiguous events and a single process. Nature, it appears, unfolds seamlessly rather than breaking up into, or being, a succession of discrete events.[17] The need to be united by a causal bond is created by an act of separation that (for example) breaks up a continuous process into a succession of events. Only then do events have successors that they have to force to happen.

We can see this splinter-and-reconnect process of understanding at work when we think of an example we touched on earlier: the relationship between smoking (cause) and lung cancer (effect). The smoking which takes place over 20 years and the cancer that emerges long after smoking started – even after a period of abstinence from smoking – may seem discrete events or processes. Once the nature of connection between them is fully understood, however, they are found to be phases of the same process. The smoking that delivers car-cinogens to lung tissue brings about biochemical changes that in turn cause mutations in cells as a result of which they have uncontrolled replication. It is only the coarse grain of attention, and intermittent observation of the process, that gathers up the partners – "smoking" and "lung cancer" – into unified elements that are separated and have then to be reconnected.

The causal link, it seems, has to be invoked only to unite that which has been separated in our gaze. While the separation may be evident at the mac-roscopic level, or at the level of everyday observation the underlying processes are continuous. This invites us to go further than Hume. We might speculate that the causal bond of material necessity is constructed to re-unite *that which the mind had separated* – picked out, divided, pulled apart – in virtue of its directed and scaled attention. Causation is posited in order to restore the continuity of an intrinsically continuous universe fragmented by the scale of our attention.

Behind any realist approach to causation is the intuition that *whatever happens must have to be made to happen* – and what makes it happen is something that precedes it which was in turn made to happen. This makes sense only in the context of two presuppositions: firstly, that the unfolding of the universe is made of discrete, bounded events; and secondly, that the dynamism of the universe is maintained only through something that secures its transmission to its successive states or events that are supposed to comprise those states. The second presupposition is connected with the belief, discussed in Section 2.1, that the laws of nature are required to nudge the universe into activity and keep it active. In the case of causation, the idea is that something is required to act locally either to keep the show going or to keep the show on the right road; that some kind of necessitation is required to mandate successive states of affairs, such that each one controls the character of its successors. Causes are the powers invested in particular events that represent the law-governed unfolding of nature operating at localities.

The idea that some kind of local intervention – local necessity, an occult force – is required seems to result from a gaze, that (a) fragments what is presented to it into discrete, separate elements and (b) by this means presents it in a succession of freeze frames. The former reflects the manner in which the subject splinters the universe into items caught in the beam of her attention. The latter reflects the manner in which that attention arrests the dynamism of its unfolding, breaking it up into a succession of states or events. There is stasis built into the very idea of a *state* or even of an event that is seen as completed. This completeness is most evident when we think of events as members of a class, most obviously when that class is designated by a noun or noun phrase ("a rumble of thunder") or as a fact ("There was a rumble of thunder"). When they are referred to or in some other way gathered under a class, happenings are seen from without as completed events rather than from within as (ongoing) processes. The causal connection – oomph transmitted from one event to the next or glue linking successive events – restores the dynamism of unfolding processes that is lost when they are broken up into completed fragments. When the flux is paused, what happens next – individual events – has to be made to happen. If causes are seen to be required to supplement laws, it may be because particular events have to be reconnected with the natural world from which they have been isolated by the circumscribed attention paid to them.

The impression of arrest is reinforced when one state or event is seen as the start of a process or sequence of events. Causation as oomph is a resume-and-continue secured by the postulated efficacy of a state or event bringing about a successor state or event that counts as its effect.[18] Conscious subjects are not, of course, in a position to decree the way in which things are connected in the flow of events. Their contribution is to break the flow into discrete elements that have then to be reconnected. By ascribing to the mind not only the causal necessity connecting events but also that which picked them apart in the first place, and created the need for the causal link, we are out-Humeing Hume.

Of course, we do not always intuit a causal relationship between types of events that are contiguous and always follow one another. For example, day always follows night but we do not believe that night causes day. There are two reasons for this. First the temporal succession between day and night is reversible: day follows night and night follows day. But secondly, we can see the continuity between them and we cannot overlook that they are aspects of a single process and are consequently not deceived by the nouns that divide the 24-hour cycle into two parts into overlooking their continuity. Night passes into day via dawning and day to night via dusking. There is continuous cycling rather than the flicking of an "on" and "off" switch.

Downgrading causal necessity to something we project into mere constant conjunction of events or type of events that left to themselves would anyway be parts of a continuous unfolding does not, however, make the behaviour of the universe more biddable, particularly as constant conjunction seen in particular types of events broadens seamlessly into a universal uniformity of all sequences as attention zooms outwards and its scale become more encompassing. The habits of a continuously unfolding universe give no more breathing space for agency than does a universe composed of events wired by the putative glue or the oomph of an intrinsic causal necessity. There is still no room for the power to deflect the course of things originating within an agent acting independently of the unfolding of nature. The double whammy of laws *and* causes as barriers to agency may boil down to a single whammy with two aspects: habit-governed behaviour whose local expression looks like causal connection. But it is a whammy, nonetheless.

Nevertheless, there is reassurance in the suggestion – made by many philosophers – that the very idea of causation cannot be entirely extricated from human interests. Picking out, from the flow of unfolding nature, one event as a cause and another as its effect, reflects parochial concerns. It is another aspect of what we uncovered in the process by which the habits of nature come to be portrayed in the laws of science. So it is worth developing this a bit more.

Causal relations as viewpoint-dependent

The interest-dependent nature of what is identified as a cause is well under-stood among philosophers but its full implications for the possibility or other-wise of free will have not been as widely appreciated as they should be.

Let us return to the example of thunder and lightning. Does the lightning "bring about" the thunder? Yes – in the minimal counterfactual sense (some-thing we shall discuss presently) that there would be no thunder without light-ning. Even so, lightning is not intrinsically a point of origin. We could say, with equal validity, that the causal ancestors of the lightning also caused the thunder. So, there is no starting "cause", no beginning except (perhaps) the Big Bang. Likewise, the consequences of the lightning will include other effects than the thunder itself – a flickering of light on the farmyard pond – and the effects of the thunder – such as the alarm felt in the breast of a robin. There is a boundless rippling out of effects from both thunder and lightning. So there is no terminal "effect". The lightning is not a beginning and the thunder is not an end. There are neither initial nor terminal conditions, settings out or arrivals.

The example underlines something that is clear enough: no event is intrin-sically a cause or an effect. Its status as either one or the other has to be conferred. It might be objected that there is a difference between causally con-nected and causally disconnected events. And yes, indeed, there are pairs of events that seem to be causally disconnected; for example, contemporaneous events such as the sound of my typing and the flight of a bird outside of my study's window; or temporally separated events such as The Battle of Hastings and a pupil making an error over its date. Nevertheless, we may assume that, if the universe is seamlessly connected, all events will have a common ultimate ancestor. This will certainly be true if we accept the standard story of the origin of the universe in a single moment of creation – The Big Bang understood as an event. The correlations between types of events will, of course, be weaker as their common ancestor is more distant; and their causal kinship will be con-cealed in the greater separation of the cousinage. Nevertheless, there is ulti-mately no intrinsic difference between events that are and events that are not causally connected. And, apart from the Big Bang, every event that is given the status of a cause is equally entitled to the status of an effect; more accurately, without the assistance of an external viewpoint of a conscious observer, it is entitled to neither. If an event is to seem to qualify as a cause, rather than an effect, it does so only in relation to a successor event that has been picked out. If it is to seem to qualify as an effect, it does so only in relation to prior event that has been picked out. In both cases, the relationship exists only insofar as it is made explicit and it is made explicit by a conscious subject.

The reason for labouring this perhaps obvious point is to emphasize the extent to which the roles of cause and effect are imported by the conscious subject who, having "smithereened" unfolding nature into discrete elements – or, more accurately, having inherited or bought into the smithereened natural world shared with her fellow humans – wishes to find a link between spatio-temporally contiguous events that goes beyond their mere contiguity.

The "cause-to-effect" story is a proto-narrative fragment, with causation being invoked as a bridge, connecting events that are picked out by our individual or collective attention – particularly our verbally structured attention – from one another as bounded entities. What regulates or at least guides that attention in the business of illuminating and dividing up the world are the basic needs and more sophisticated interests of the conscious subject. And so we return to the conclusion that if causation is a glue that puts together what is not in itself apart, or an oomph that brings about the succession of one event by another, it stitches together a world atomized by our interests, repairing an unfolding strand which has been blown apart by the irruption of conscious subjects into a world that is otherwise continuous. In summary, the human subject is the original source of both discontinuity and restored unity in a universe, connecting that which has been disconnected. Whether or not what is seen as a causal chain or conversely as part of an unfolding continuum will be perspective-, or description-dependent on how objects and events are or are not dissected by individuals or communities.[19]

We can see this viewpoint-dependent privileging at work even at the most basic level when, to reach shamelessly for another hackneyed example, we think about one billiard ball A striking another B. Ball A is seen as the striker because we begin a sequence with the ball struck by the cue (and hence closer to the human agent who is seen as a kind of beginning); and ball B is seen as the struck because it is further from the action of the player. If, however, we begin with the trajectory of ball B that strikes a third ball C, then the movement of B is the cause and the movement of C the effect. As for the balls, they are, all three of them, both strikers and (as when C hits the side of the table) and struck.[20]

To argue as I have just now may suggest to some readers that I am ascribing extraordinary powers to the conscious subject to divide the continuum any way she wants. This would be clearly untrue. While the very idea of Nature as the Given which is passively received by or imposed on subjects is problematic, there is much that we have to take account of – if we are to live our lives – that does not fall within our individual or collective ability to shape, even less to dictate. Indeed, we live in largely unchosen circumstances. What

I am suggesting is something much less radical: namely that the world as we divide it up – and then connect up – is not simply as it exists in itself in the absence of consciousness. How deep goes this ability to shape, through our interest-directed attention that which we encounter as the Given, is not something that I am qualified to say. Nor, so far as I can tell, is anyone else. It is, however, sufficient to justify allocating a significant role to the mind of conscious subjects and their implicit or explicit viewpoints in conferring upon an event the status of a cause, of an effect, or of a mere bystander. It would follow from this that a viewpointless account of the universe as a whole would not contain any causal connections. This has been expressed by Judea Pearl: "If you wish to include the whole universe in the model, causality disappears because interventions disappear – the manipulator and the manipulated lose their distinction".[21]

The central argument of this section is that Hume's claim that causation is the glueing together in the human mind of items in the world that are in themselves "loose and separate" is the other side of the fact that it is the mind – or the conscious subject – that splinters the world into loose and separate items. In short, the Humean mind tidies up the mess it has itself created by intuiting necessary connections between things it has itself disconnected.[22] As a result of this disconnection, laws expressing the unfolding of the universe seem to lose their grip. They have to be reattached and a universal dynamic continuity has to be restored or resumed through the operation of powerful particulars – namely causes that necessitate effects and so keep the show on the road.

Tensed time, minds and causation

As has often been pointed out, picking out one event as the cause of another is to elevate it to the status of a quasi-agent, albeit a mindless, innocent one. This is the consequence of seeing things (events, processes, states of affairs) as happening only because they are *made to happen* by other things – by other events, processes, or states of affairs. Indeed, several philosophers, notably the eighteenth-century Scottish philosopher Thomas Reid, have argued that our seeing causes in the natural world is a projection of our experience of ourselves as agents. The fear that agency is reduced to a stretch in a causally closed world – a causal reduction of agency – is replaced by an agent-theory of causation. "Cause" and "effect" can be translated into "means" and "end". Suddenly, causation is no longer looking like an obstacle to free action but the child of it or, if that is too strong, its necessary partner.

It does not follow from this that we can exercise complete discretion in allocating the roles of cause and effect to pairs of events. Once we have placed a boundary around a thunderstorm and divided the thunder from the lightning, we cannot decide that the thunder is the cause of the lightning or deny that the lightning is the cause of the thunder. The most obvious and universal constraints come from the temporal asymmetry between causes and effects: effects cannot precede their causes nor causes succeed their effects. This "asymmetry of influence" is a viewpoint-*in*dependent element of causation. It has been addressed by many philosophers,[23] but Huw Price's treatment is especially illiminating.[24]

Price begins by acknowledging the point made earlier that causes as discrete entities are viewpoint dependent. But he develops a more radical version of our claim that the allocation of causal roles is also viewpoint dependent. According to Price, "causal asymmetry isn't really in the world at all. *The appearance that it is* is a product of our own standpoint".[25] This is in turn the child of our own asymmetry in time, rooted in our experience as agents "using one thing to achieve another".[26] More strikingly, so he argues, we should "put causation in its proper metaphysical perspective as something like a secondary quality"[27] – comparable to colours and the feeling of warmth, which are not intrinsic features of the material world. The asymmetry between cause and effect is in us not in the physical world.[28]

If we were to accept Price's position, would this finally disarm causation as a contribution to our imprisonment separate from that of the implacable habits of the universe as expressed in the laws of science? It might seem so: the suspicion that the time asymmetry of causation is connected with the time asymmetry of our lives as agents is well-founded. At the very least, we have to acknowledge that agency points forward to a future that we can alter and does not point backwards to a past that is done and dusted.

We have arrived at something central to agency: tensed time. This is not a feature of the material world as presented through its most authoritative portrait – namely, physics. The division of time into past and future must always be with respect to a reference point – which is supplied by conscious subjects. The most general term for this reference point is "Now". The absence of tensed time in the universe as seen through the eye of physics is expressed rather poignantly by Einstein in a not terribly consoling letter of condolence when he wrote to the recently bereaved wife of his oldest friend, Michele Besso. In a slightly misguided effort to cheer her up, he reflected that while Besso "has departed from this strange world a little ahead of me. That means nothing. For us believing physicists, the distinction between past, present, and future is only a stubborn illusion".[29] The present, as Now, transforms the time either side of it, dividing it into the unalterable, closed past and the alterable, open future. It is the present which requires action of us, though it is guided by the past and serves the future.

The asymmetry of influence, then, is both undeniable and at the same time inexplicable in terms of the laws of science according to which there is no tensed time.[30] The most general account of the laws of macroscopic Nature – the general theory of relativity – delivers a block universe, frozen in four-dimensional geometry, that lacks time-asymmetry. It is a Parmenidean universe in which nothing happens. If this truth is not apparent – and the universe is a rather jollier place than this portrait would suggest – it is because, as Huw Price argues, we project on to the physical world the temporal asymmetry we have as agents.[31]

Tensed time and the asymmetry of influence, evident in the idea of the relationship between a cause and an effect, is even more obviously present in the idea of the transformation of events into items to be exploited by agents to produces effects. That exploitation reaches beyond the present. While the past is not under our control – what is done is done – we can dip into it through memory and make it present at will and so that in various ways it will shape how we populate the future and thereby serve the future-pointing present.[32] This is closely connected with something we shall discuss in Section 4.2: the way agency grows out of the envisaging of possibility and, linked with this, the emergence of tensed time.

Whether or not you are persuaded that these arguments tame causation, the contrast between time-reversible laws and the time-irreversible passage from cause to effect should discourage us from bundling together laws and causes as co-conspirators in the frustration of agency and indeed undermining its very possibility. More particularly, it is a further reminder, if any were still needed, that not only the laws, but also the relationship between causes and effects, and common sense and scientific ways of envisaging nature, cannot be parts of nature themselves, otherwise nature would be contradicting itself. Singling out (prior) causes and (posterior) effects is not a natural process, an effect of physical causes. Being a cause or an effect is not an intrinsic property of any material event, any more than division of the unfolding of nature into discrete events is an intrinsic property of any part of nature. Depending on the viewpoint that is assumed, any given event can be a cause – a quasi-active deliverer of "oomph" – or an effect – a quasi-passive recipient of oomph.[33] That is why events-as-causes cannot be seen as difference-making, as doing independent work, because they receive as much as they give. They are ultimately part of the overall process that is the unfolding universe.[34] "Causation-as-material necessity" is not an independent source of the intransigence of nature.

Knowledge as neither an effect nor a cause: an anticipatory aside[35]

We first encountered causation in this book in the Overture when it failed to account for the intentionality of consciousness. Indeed, it seemed to run counter to it. Any explanatory value causation might have in, for example, the case of vision, would cover the light getting into and tickling up the brain but it would not account for the gaze looking out. That failure extends to higher-order aspects of consciousness – such as intentions, wishes, desires, and above all, knowledge – which will be central to our understanding of the nature of voluntary action. To be informed, and to use information to guide an action, does not sit within any putative material causal chain in which oomph is transmitted from link to link.

My being apprised of a factual state of affairs is not reducible to the transfer of energy from your mouth to my ears and auditory system. All attempts to reduce the semantic contents of communications to the physics of their vehicles (speech, writing) are doomed. Equally, my making use of what you have told me – at a time of my choosing – is not a mere material effect of a material cause. The ultimate justification for saying this is to be found in the shared intentionality that is the basis of knowledge; the way knowledge is about, or points to, a general possibility both as something of which someone is apprised and as something that is acted upon. Possibilities, as we shall discuss in the next chapter, do not inhere in the material world – which is composed solely of actualities. "Nature at time t_1" is "Nature at time t_1" and not "Nature at time t_1 plus what it might become at time t_2". The possibilities of "Nature at time t_1" have actuality only insofar as they are envisaged – or seen in retrospect – by a conscious subject.

This obvious truth has been obscured by many habits of thought. Prominent among them in recent philosophical discussion has been the pandemic spread of the word "information" to apply to all sorts of states and happenings that have nothing to do with the sharing or acquisition of knowledge by conscious subjects. "Information" – which is ubiquitous in all sciences, ranging from quantum mechanics via molecular biology to cognitive science – pops up in many discussions of causation. When Ladyman *et al.* assert that "all that is generally important in the idea of causation is information flow along asymmetric gradients"[36] they are reflecting a widespread understanding of information exchange as being present throughout the universe. This usage squeezes out the distance between conscious subjects – informants and informees – and the material world. There is no basis for the distinctive roles of the one who is informed and of the one who is doing the informing. Any emission or reception of information in the material world must be in the eyes of an observer to whom the succession of events is a resolution of expectations of future events generated by present or past events. It may seem surprising that to make this seemingly obvious point is in fact to swim against a mighty current of opinion but it is. This is no place to mount a critique of "paninformationalism" but the reader may want to pursue this further.[37]

There is much more to be said about knowledge and its role in agency and we shall return to it in the next chapter.

3.2 FURTHER HUME-ILIATION OF CAUSES

Many contemporary philosophers prefer to see causes not as oomph-bearing events with causation being the process of delivery of that oomph ensuring that other events occur but in *counterfactual* terms: a cause is an event without which another event would not have happened, or would not have happened when it did, or would not have happened in the manner or to the degree that it did. Thunder does not happen without prior lightning: this clap of thunder would not have occurred without that flash of lightning.

According to this view, causes are necessary, but not sufficient, for the effects that are ascribed to them.[38] To put this another way, any counterfactual role that causes may have is conditional. While Event of type B may not occur without Event of type A, this dependency will itself depend on what else is going on – on the circumstances. "Circumstances" will be a mixture of standing conditions and other occurrent events. The tile that falls from a roof will fracture my skull if the tile is made of hard stuff, if it falls from a sufficient height and is not obstructed in its descent, if my head is positioned so as to harvest a sufficient share of its linear momentum, and my skull has a certain fragility and has not been reinforced by titanium.

The counterfactual theory of causation more closely merges the notions of causes and conditions, of protagonists and supportive bystanders. This is one of the reasons why it seems to capture less of our ordinary intuitions of what a cause is supposed to be. It is, however, worth exploring because it is very much aligned with the viewpoint-dependency of what counts as a cause; how the focus, direction, and scale of attention provide the relevant criteria. Most importantly – and in my view (but not that of all philosophers) damningly – it places things that do *not* happen as being causally on a par with things that do. This is "absence causation".

Supposing (to take a favourite example among philosophers) you agree to water my garden while I am on holiday. You forget. When I return all my flowers have wilted. Intuitively, the heat of the sun seems more like a cause of the wilting than your absent-mindedness, though they are both in equally good standing as counterfactuals. If the sun had not been so hot or if you had not not-watered the flowers, they would not have wilted.

By widening the criteria for what counts as a cause, even to encompass things that don't happen, counterfactual accounts seem to take the oomph out of causation: the absence of counterfactuals – "factuals" we might suppose – would not of themselves make anything else happen. It would also seem to take away any role causation might play in glueing together the universe through one event bringing about its successors. If the non-event of your failing to water the flowers seems to have causal consequences, it is ascribed this status only as a result of my following an audit trail that connects you with the wilting of the flowers and lays responsibility at your door. The connection is not with a discrete event – such as your failing to water the flowers specifically at 4 pm on Tuesday – but with any potentially capable agent. And the flowers would not have wilted if the president of the United States had watered them or William the Conqueror had come back from the dead armed with a watering can. Your failure to water flowers is clearly not a discrete event or action. It is not something that took place in my garden or indeed anywhere else. Nor did it take place at a particular time, for example over the entire week – the 168 hours of my wakefulness and sleep – that I was away or at a particular period in that week. What you failed to do is a whole *class* of actions that would fall under the category of your watering the flowers between such and such a time and another time. It doesn't look like the kind of thing we think of as a cause which at the very least is an occurrent event that has no missing details, even though most of its details – say occurring at 4 pm vs at 4:30 pm – are irrelevant.

The counterfactual theory of causation highlights something unwelcome to those who want to embrace a realist theory of causation as an intrinsic and universal property of the natural world, as a necessary connectedness driving the unfolding of things, and to invoke it in the case against free will. It embraces the extent to which something qualifying as a cause is interest-dependent. Your failure to water the flowers – a non-event – is identified as a cause because it is relevant to something that matters to me, namely the health of my flowers, and its dependence on a contractual relationship between human beings. It is picked out as a necessary condition of the wilting of the flowers because you could have prevented this horticultural tragedy. The weather is, of course, equally to blame – if it had rained your omission would not have had the unwelcome consequence I am complaining about – but it is of less interest as a causal factor since it is innocent. The sun shines alike on flowers that could do with less of it and bricks that are indifferent to it. Its influence is not localized. Likewise, the wilting of the flowers in the garden of some people living in another city – which could likewise have been prevented by your watering them – is also not linked with your behaviour because you had no contract with these strangers.

Counterfactual theories not only make more explicit the extent to which the identification of causes is interest-relevant. They also bring imputations of causation closer to allocation of blame. When, just now, I said that the hot weather was equally – indeed more – to blame for the wilting of the flowers than anyone's failure to water them, I was, of course, joking, not the least because the sun was not in a position to behave differently. Material objects are not moral entities. So, we focus on something that is an appropriate subject of moral judgement: the failure to keep a promise. That is how your failure to water the flowers earns its status – out of millions of other candidate non-events – as the counterfactual cause of the wilting.

It will be evident from this example that counterfactual theories offer no basis for differentiating the causes and conditions of an event. This may be seen as a plus. As J. S. Mill famously pointed out, "Nothing better can show the absence of any scientific ground for the distinction between the cause of a phenomenon and its conditions than the capricious manner in which we select from amongst the conditions that which we choose to denominate the cause".[39] The difficulty of disentangling causes and conditions is all the greater for the fact that causes will produce their effects only so long as certain conditions are met. Lightning will not produce thunder in a world where everyone has gone deaf. (Nor will it dazzle in the country of the blind.) It will start bush fires in hot dry conditions but not when it is raining. Causes and conditions (and indeed mere circumstances or contexts and, in between, modulating factors) are picked out with respect to an event, indeed an outcome, of *interest*. There is nothing in the wilting of flowers that makes it a discrete effect – separable from that the wilting of the weeds. It is just an event, or part of a process that is the life-cycle of the plants – though it is not clear that the life-cycle of a plant, as opposed to that of an ecosystem, is discrete, either.

What will be clear is that counterfactual theory, far from rescuing causation, making it respectable by removing the taint of "occult forces" and "material necessity" in fact furthers its Hume-iliation. This is perhaps unsurprising as it picks up an aspect of Hume's deconstruction of causes that we cited earlier: "We may define a cause to be an object followed by another, and where all the objects, similar to the first, are followed by objects similar to the second. *Or, in other words, where, if the first object had not been, the second had never existed*" (italics mine). In short it offers little by way of explanation why things happen in order to satisfy those who believe what happens has to be made to happen by prior happenings. The promotion of non-events to the status of causes highlights how causes are individuated by the interests of conscious subjects.[40]

To say that the counterfactual account of causation highlights its interest-dependency is an understatement. It places it front and centre. Of equal importance is that it connects causation with *possibility*: the possibility of how things might have turned out if an event had or had not taken place. This lies at the heart of another alternative account of causation:[41] the statistical account according to which a cause is not an event that brings about another event – its effect – by obliging it to happen. Rather it merely raises the statistical chances of that second event taking place. It is as it were advisory rather than mandatory. Its half-hearted oomph or loose glue brings more to the table than counterfactual causation but less than traditional causal obligation.

According to the statistical theory, causal power is measured by the strength of the statistical correlation or the closeness of the covariance between types of events categorized as, respectively, causes and effects.[42] As with the counterfactual theory, it does not provide a robust basis for a difference between causes and conditions and conditions and mere background circumstances. The latter will, of course, influence the chances of an event happening. For example, my walking in the same city as you are walking will – even if we are moving independently but are not actively trying to avoid each other – increase the chances of an encounter.

The statistical account of causation, what is more, does not capture the distinction between events that are supposedly causally connected and those that are merely associated through having a common causal ancestry. Consider for example the rotation of two horses on a merry-go-round. The movement of one will increase the chances of the other moving from near zero to near 100 per cent. In short, two events that are picked out as separate parts of the same process would meet the statistical criteria for causal association: 100 per cent.

As for the relationship between events separated in time, it is clear that successive phases of the same process will also be statistically highly correlated. Consider a ball thrown through the air. The trajectory goes from Point 1 (P1) to Point 2 (P2) to Point 3 (P3). If we consider P1-to-P2 and P2-to-P3 as separate events, the former increases the chances of the passage from P2 to P3 but we would hardly think of the former as being the cause of the latter.[43] Rather, we would think of them as phases of the same process initiated by the person throwing the ball.

The probabilistic account of causation therefore does not differentiate causation from correlation and mere continuation; and the notion of universal, widespread correlation of events ultimately dissolves causation into the regularity of the habits of the universe, into dimensions of its coherence captured in part by the laws of science. In short it is the theory that most completely assimilates causation to law-like unfolding. Our two examples – the horses on the roundabout and the successive phases of the trajectory of the thrown ball – remind us by default that causation is traditionally regarded as being between two events whose relationship is contingent – events that are "loose and separate".

Any appeal to causal bonds to glue or otherwise connect the universe presupposes a discontinuity in the unfolding of things – fragmentation into discrete events – that causation is supposed somehow to heal so that an orderly, continuous unfolding of the universe is maintained. Counterfactuals or statistical probabilities do not deliver this. They merely describe how it is with events in the plural and how they co-occur with other events. These accounts of causation do not suggest that causation brings anything separate to the party.

The probabilistic account of causation has another problem that touches closely on something we shall address in the next chapter: the very idea of probability or (more generally) possibility. If we think of a cause as an event that raises the possibility of another, subsequent, event, we have to ask in what sense it is appropriate to think of the material world as having, at any moment, more than one possible future, so that an event might or might not occur. This is at odds with the Laplacian notion of the universe unfolding according to a fixed, unswerving and "unswervable" path. If the cause and effect occurred under the aegis of these laws, the cause could contribute nothing distinct or independent to the unfolding of things: it could not of itself raise the probability of a subsequent event. There would be no additional power that particulars would deliver.

The conviction that particulars-as-causes do so arises out of two mistakes. The first we have already dealt with: that of imagining that the event identified as the cause is somehow self-defining, thus bringing its own packet of influence to the party. The second is conflating our (human) sense of the probabilities of events with something inherent in nature. If lightning occurs, it is reasonable to expect that thunder will follow; so, we shall have an increased sense of the possibility of thunder that is usually justified in practice. This is not, however, due to the intrinsic efficacy of lightning, something additional that it brings of itself; for, as already pointed out, it is itself an effect of causes that are themselves effects, etc. It gives no more than it receives. What's more, seeing lightning as a discrete cause rather than as part of an unfolding material universe is to elevate it to the status of a beginning when there are no beginnings in nature except (perhaps) the Big Bang. There is no reference point from which probabilities are to be estimated. Without such reference points, probability estimates have no target, however objective we may feel the statistics are.

We shall return to possibilities and probabilities in the next chapter (Section 4.2). For the present, we note that the belief that causation directs the unfolding of the universe and this provides an independent obstacle to free will is in ruins. What Hume started has ended in complete Hume-iliation.

Concluding comments: the slipperiness of causation: oomph and glue

It is certainly true that there was a fairly long period in the twentieth century when large numbers of philosophers sought not to appeal, ever, to the concept of causation. Thus, for example, van Inwagen says of "cause" that it is "a horrible little word", and adds: "causation is a morass in which I for one refuse to set foot. Or not unless I am pushed".[44] A sentiment echoed by J. J. Smart, "Causation? Pah! It's all right for plumbers and brain surgeons".[45]

If causation were an intrinsic property of nature, a material necessity binding all the events in the material world, we might be justified in viewing our actions as mere links in a causal network that weaves itself unbroken from the Big Bang to the Big Crunch. The contrary view advanced by Huw Price and many others that the status of being a cause is conferred may seem too anthropocentric to some. Nevertheless, we can I hope at least agree that, given that causes are identified as points of origin, and given that the world has no local points of origin, even less local destinations, we should accept that the roles of causes and effects are not intrinsic characters of events. The lightning is no more a beginning than the thunder is an end.

There is an important sense therefore that the status of events as causes is conferred from outside. That "outside" is the same as the outside we discussed in Sections 2.2 and 2.3 as that from which the habits of nature are revealed as the laws of science – the laws which we discover through manipulating and tweaking the world in a purposeful, systematic way. While our search for causes in everyday life often demands less of us than the search for laws – they are closer to the surface and are more evident to informal observation – the principle still applies.

We typically seek local, individual causes when we are surprised or intrigued by an event or when we wish to prevent something from happening or make it happen. And we can of course seek causes directly without seeking or seeing any underlying law. For example, I can look out of the window to identify the source of a noise and see that it is due to someone chopping wood. I don't have to be aware of any underlying laws – for example of mechanics or acoustics – in order to establish what I count as the cause of the noise. On the other hand, there are events – for example the development of lung cancer or the anomalous perihelion of Mercury – that will require much research to determine laws connecting them with what will be agreed to be their causes. Under such circumstances, the causes will be local instantiation of general processes that are in turn an expression of certain high-level laws. In either case, events do not qualify as "causes" entirely on the basis of their intrinsic properties. If we determine that smoking is the cause of lung cancer, it is in part because we see the behaviour of the smoker as a point of origin, perhaps susceptible to manipulation, something to which we shall return. We could look further upstream to the cultural factors that explain why anyone should do anything as strange as smoking a cigarette and smoke should be imported into the lungs.

Two further points need to be made before we complete our exorcism of causal ancestry as a barrier to the possibility of free action additional to that posed by the implacable habits of nature.

The first is that if causation were universal and the universe were causally closed, it is difficult to see how we could adopt a position from which causes could be discovered and manipulated to bring about desired effects. This is analogous to the argument we have made in relation to the discovery and exploitation of laws.

The second is that the notion of a cause is irredeemably untidy. The wide variety of ways of interpreting causation justifies suspicions as to whether anything definite corresponds to it. Nancy Cartwright has characterized causation as "a concept with rough, shifting, porous boundaries, a congestion of different ideas and implications that can in various combinations be brought into focus for different purposes and in different contexts".[46]

It is not clear, for example, to what extent causes can be replaced by "powers", "capacities", "properties" and "dispositions" or "dispositional properties".[47] One might treat these terms with even more suspicion, given that they seem to rest on something not evident in the physical world: a connection between an actual present state and a possible future one. The brittleness of glass, for example, connects its current state with a state it might have if something was dropped on it. Even if this connection is drained of tense and we replace "present" state and "future" state with state at t_1 and state at t_2 there would still be the idea of a reaching out of one moment to another, something that is not seen in the material world as construed by physics. In short, "powers", "properties", "capacities" and "dispositions" seem to presuppose a world in which there are possibilities. But (as we shall discuss in Section 4.2) there is only actuality in the natural world.

Perhaps the most profound ambivalence in the very idea of a cause is reflected in its two faces as "glue" or "cement" on the one hand and "oomph" and "biff" on the other. They offer different kinds of healing to a universe, splintered at least in part by the irruption of the subject and our discourse about the world, breaking it into "loose and separate" fragments. Glue/cement focuses on the restoration of spatio-temporal continuity; and oomph focuses on the transmission of dynamism across spatio-temporal intervals. In the case of cement, healing the spatio-temporal discontinuity restores connectedness. Oomph makes things happen by restoring the dynamism of the totality that is lost to a fragment that is isolated: the flux is paused, as facts that are alighted upon, picked out, so that what happens next then has to be made to happen. In either case – the discontinuity or the pause in the flux – a point of reference makes one moment, one state, one event a starting point.[48]

I have several times used the interactions between billiard balls as an example of causes and this may cause uneasiness. There are many other supposed causal connections that are remote from mechanical collisions on the baize. The irreparable untidiness of the idea of the "cause" is evident when we think of how it is employed when we use it to refer to the interactions between atoms or their macroscopic representatives such as billiard balls; the relationship between lightning and thunder; the attraction of an micro-organism towards the light; what a tactless comment does to someone's mood; the impact of Russian interference on the outcome of the 2016 US presidential election; the influence of upbringing on political views or the capacity to be able to reflect on those views; or the reasons for the breakdown of the relationship between nations. Nevertheless, the explanatory force of the idea of cause in these quite different, higher-level contexts owes much to the very basic examples and to what is on display when in the interaction between billiard balls, where the oomph transfer is visible to the most casual gaze – rather than in something of the character of the relations between nations, where oomph is nowhere to be seen.

The point is that much of the explanatory work performed by the word "cause" is carried by the lower-level uses – physical interactions in the natural world. The higher-level ones seem derivative or even merely metaphorical – at the very least parasitic on the intuitive sense causal connection seems to make when we think about physical events – especially where it is a case of one item colliding with another. To put this another way, widening the meaning of causation beyond its canonical setting of billiard balls and more broadly the physical world weakens its explanatory power. While "cause" may have well-established but widely different uses in different contexts – fundamental science, biology, social sciences, the law, everyday life – there is no guarantee that as the notion spreads out what for some is its home base (or bases) in for example billiard-ball mechanics or even in clinical science, it will retain any of its original meaning or explanatory force. And there are problems even there.[49]

At the billiard ball level, moreover, causes lack something fundamental to human action: normative criteria – the difference between doing the right and the wrong, or between the necessary and the pointless, thing – that lie at the very heart of the logic of the "becausation" of actions. That is why in the next chapter we shall be so hard on the idea that the reasons for actions count as their causes; or reasons count as causes. So, while the appeal to the idea of cause may satisfy the desire for explanation of the physical stuff of human actions, what it delivers bypasses their essential nature. This will be important when we come to consider the tenacity with which causation has on the minds of many philosophers of action, even unto talking about something called "agent causation".

The notion of causation does not seem robust enough to survive unchanged, or indeed to survive at all, when it is applied outside of some putative home territory – for example in the context of mechanics. The double whammy to free will of laws *and* causes is a single whammy, if whammy it is. As Wittgenstein expressed it: "If there were a law of causality, it might be put in the following way: There are laws of nature".[50]

It does prompt this question, however: why are causes invoked in addition to laws to explain or merely describe the regularities of the experienced world? Is it perhaps that they seem to be required in order that the oomph of unfolding according to the habits of nature or the laws of science – which have no particular target, being by definition general in their application – should be directed to particular situations and alight on particular events? Is there, as it were, a reciprocity between law-governed causes and cause-applied laws. This view is dangerously close to the notion that we have rejected: that laws operate from outside of nature, as if they were external powers. The belief in the need for a causal mediator to attach the laws to actual situations, would presuppose to a prior *de*tachment – the result of projecting the distance between the habits of unfolding nature and the laws of science into nature itself.

At any rate, it is entirely unclear not only in what respect causal powers bring something extra to the party but also why they are required; why what actually happened had somehow to be *made to* happen – typically by prior events or states. Change, instability, the generation of events is, after all, in nature's starter pack, implicit in the Big Bang, and is present in all that follows. Nothing is entirely still. Stasis is an illusion. Mountains are (very) slow smoke. We would not therefore require anything additional – such as causal oomph – to keep the unfolding show unfolding. The habits of nature and the reliable correlations between the manifestations or realizations of those habits are enough.

We therefore return to the view developed in this section already: that it is because events are picked out by a conscious subject that they are isolated and have then to be reconnected with the habitual flow or unfolding continuum of the universe.[51] The picked-out events are not individuated in nature. The grounds for such "picking out" then have to be accounted for. We naturally look to the needs of subjects, of agents, and to the properties of the universe they find themselves in to guide the picking out and to settle what counts as salient.

But the story does not stop there: we are confronted with the larger puzzle of the emergence of subjects with their needs and needs-based interests in an insentient, worldless, subjectless universe. Why or how were the pickers out themselves picked out? This is a question to which neither the present author nor anyone else has the beginning of an answer.[52] Suffice it to say that the so-called causally regulated world seems to be one that has been glued together in the wake of the "smithereening" irruption of an embodied, and therefore located, conscious subject into an overwhelmingly subjectless universe, creating parishes unknown to that universe. The mind that, according to Hume, glues the succession of events in causal connections is also the mind that pulled them apart in the first place in discrete, atomic perceptions.

Beyond Hume, we may note that the pulling apart begins with the global separation evident in the spectatorial distance opened up in, the outside created by, perception. This is what highlights the depth of the seemingly self-evident observation by Thalos that "Causality is connected in philosophical literature with the idea of locality"[53] – the parishes that are the product of dividing "what-is" into "what-is-there" or "what-is-there-for-me" or "what-is-there-for-everyone". In the idea of "parish" is gathered up not only location in space and time but also the scaling and direction and the tuning – courtesy of the senses, wider aspects of embodiment, and a multiplicity of cultural heritages – of awareness. Causes are invoked – and seem to be independent guarantors of the order of the universe – because they represent the habits of nature as they touch down in those parishes that are the shared and separate worlds of conscious subjects. "Law-governed causes" are merely the habits of nature as evident in a certain spot, singular coherence as a reflection of general coherence. Causal powers are invoked to reinsert events into a habit-governed world after they have been lifted out of them by interest-relative attention.

Reference to the interests of the subject in elevating an event to the status of a cause or an effect brings us close to the agenda of the next chapter: goal-driven actions. A cause is a step on the road to a change that someone wants to bring about; a *point d'appui* on the material world; a prior event as a handle to enable an agent to secure delivery of a subsequent event. The agent theory of causation asserts that A is a cause B if A is an effective means by which a free agent could bring about the occurrence of B. Identifying causes is to see where we have to engage with what is out there in order to make things go the way we want them to go.

To invoke the idea of causes as actual or potential handles is finally to give up on the notion of causes as something universal and inherent in nature. The reliable seemingly law-governed succession of events will be transformed into a succession of causes bringing out intended effects only when the former is seen as a possible *means* to the latter. As Thalos expresses it, "causal analysis is best suited to thinking about how to make things happen, at least in the most global way. It's the way to think about how to make things happen when you don't have the engineer's story about how the system is put together from scratch".[54]

Even if one does not embrace a wholehearted manipulative theory of causation, and fear that it might be too anthropocentric to do so, the link between causes and human intervention, or at least the possibility of intervention, is not easily broken. Causation is then seen as the necessary partner of agency and of the exercise of free will rather than its adversary. Of course, events as causes-as-putative handles may not deliver. Magic thinking, which among its other cognitive sins confuses correlation with a causative power, or even singular succession with causation, assigns handle status to many other events than those that will deliver the desired outcome as their effects. And events may qualify equally as causes if they are experienced as obstacles to the achievement of goals.[55] Either way, they are inseparable from the idea of a means of controlling what happens. While agents cannot automatically make events or objects into causes, the possibility of doing so must be connected with goal-directed behaviour. If this is accepted, we can see that causation is not a separate source of implacability in the unfolding of events, additional to the habits portrayed in the laws of science.

One final point – to connect our present concerns with the argument central to this book. It is evident that, as Hume argued, the sense of material necessity manifested in the idea of causation must be inseparable from (sophisticated) consciousness. This demolishes any idea that consciousness itself, beginning with perception and rising to complex mental contents such as intention, can be explained as the effect of causes. The causal theory of perception (and of other mental entities such as thoughts and beliefs) looks even more vulnerable than it did in the Overture where we first introduced intentionality as the key element in our case for the reality of free will.

CHAPTER 4

Actions

4.1 WHAT REAL ACTIONS LOOK LIKE[1]

Our critical examination in Section 1.2 of neurodeterminism and of experiments that supposedly demonstrated that we are the helpless puppets of
unconscious processes in our brains was not entirely a waste of time. At the
very least, it was an opportunity to remind ourselves of something not captured in the neuroscience lab: the nature of real actions in real life. Agency is
not tacked together out of discrete movements, except insofar as those movements are part of something much bigger – as when, for example, I may raise
my hand to vote at the end of a discussion. The exercise of the free will is
typically to be found in large-scale actions that are interconnected with, or at
least make sense in the light of, other actions.

Connected with this, and contrary to what some neurodeterminists seem to
believe, free will is not a matter of trains of atomic urges resulting in twitches.
While actions in the physiology laboratory may be teased apart into separate
physical movements, they are irreducibly compound, being part of, indeed
constituting, the ongoingness of our lives. A combined electromyographic
and kinetic account of what is happening in and to my limbs would give no
hint as to what I am doing, why, and how it fits into my present situation or
long stretches of my life.

One way of putting this would be to say the free will is to be found in a *field*
of volition. It is here that we will find the sense of ordinary voluntary activity,
such as picking up the kids from school, making time to telephone a friend to
offer condolences, or planning a holiday. Such actions weave together countless movements, requisitioned to serve a network of connected purposes. The

field, or world, from which these actions draw their meaning is deep, wide, without a clear-cut boundary, and is often shared with others. In short, no action is an island. Nor is any agent. Voluntary actions are integrated with one another in our individual and communal hourly, daily, weekly, yearly, lives. They are woven into the complex embroidery of journeys that is a life.

It is equally a travesty to conceive of voluntary activity as a linear progress punctuated by binary "left" or "right" decisions. By the time we have reached a fork – and have to choose between A or B – most of the work of choosing has been done. We do not spend our days choosing between the lemmas of dilemmas – either through making agonizing decisions or exercising the empty "liberty of indifference" by tossing a coin. Even on those occasions when we do face a fork in the path, the path has been laid down through a terrain we have in an important sense chosen and may have had a significant role in creating. Though the exercise of choice is an important manifestation of freedom, therefore, our agency is not sewn together out of a succession of discrete choices; rather it emerges out of a nexus of situations we have had a role in creating. These provide the medium from which any clear-cut "A or B" decisions confront us. For this reason, we should not envisage our ordinary, conscientious routines, the discharge of our duties, the pursuit of our interests, and the fulfilment of our many-layered preferences, as being propelled by pulses of volition understood as a kind of force – a mysterious fifth added to the four (gravitational, electromagnetic, strong and weak nuclear forces) recognized by physics.

This is particularly clear in actions that are extended over time. A succession of localized urges or binary choices would not take us from the beginning to the end of medical training or even to a meeting in another city. We saw the deep, complex connectedness in the very actions that made the experiments conducted by Libet and Haynes possible: the actions necessary for the subjects to participate in them and scientists to conceive them, set them up, carry them out, and broadcast their results in published papers. A succession of atomic intentions or discrete urges would not deliver this. In short, the very conditions of the experiments being set up and completed were overlooked by the experimenters when they drew their conclusions about free will.

Distinctive features of real actions

If we are going to address the question of free will, therefore, we should look at real actions in the ordinary lives of real people and focus on their distinctive features.

The most obvious feature is that what agents do is initiated, shaped, or jus-tified by explicit intentions pointing to an outcome that they entertain, even if the actions are performed reluctantly, being done at the behest of others. The goal may not always be present and explicit but it should always be available to agents when they are asked to account for their behaviour – to respond to the question "What are you doing?" in which is embedded the other question "And why are you doing it?".

Let me illustrate this with a personal example that will do a lot of work in the pages that follow: a ten-year campaign, with many others, to establish national standards for the care of patients who have had strokes. It involved much commuting to the capital. My reason for boarding a train on any par-ticular trip – in order to get to London, in order to attend a meeting, in order to make the case for improved stroke services, in order that those stroke ser-vices might be improved, in order that patients should have better outcomes – did not have to be continuously entertained. We don't have continuously to intend our intentions. Voluntary activity is not accompanied by an incessant commentary reminding agents of what is being done and why or a repeated pulse of willing ensuring that they do it. The point of my attending the meet-ing in London is implicitly present in my getting to the station, waiting for the right train, boarding the train, alighting in London, taking a taxi to the venue, locating and walking to the right room, listening to what everyone has to say, and making my contribution to the meeting, having waited for what I thought an appropriate moment. The relevant intentions, reasons, and beliefs are always on stand-by. At any given time, I could respond to the challenge to say what I am doing and why. Every now and then I might have to remind myself what I am doing – inseparable from why I am doing it – though the need for a reminder usually applies to small-scale, trivial actions, as when I go to my bedroom to find something I need for my meeting and forget why I have gone upstairs.

Intentions do not have to be sustained, any more than the reasons or justi-fications that are connected with them. This alone should be sufficient to flag up that they are not quasi-causes that might otherwise have in some sense to be maintained through the course of the action. One way of capturing this difference between causes and, say, reasons or intentions is to think of actions being pulled from a future that lies ahead rather than being causally pushed from behind. The pull-push contrast, while helpful, is over-simplifying, and is misleading; for the future in question exists only in the form of a possibility which we see or imagine and which we wish for: it is not something out there in the material world. (We shall return this in the next section.) It is important not to conflate reasons and justifications – which are visible to ourselves when we stand back from the action or may be evident to someone else looking at it – with anything we immediately experience, like an appetite.

The centrality of intentions to actions was flagged up in anglophone philosophy in the mid-twentieth century by Elizabeth Anscombe and Donald Davidson.[2] Much of the literature in the philosophy of action in the more than half century since then has been directly and indirectly in dialogue with these two thinkers. The most important difference between them was that Davidson regarded intentions as causes and Anscombe didn't.[3] Just how important that difference is will be discussed later in this chapter. (Spoiler alert! Intentions are *not* causes in any remaining sense of "cause" surviving the scrutiny of Chapter 3).

The complex and interacting roles of intentions, reasons, and justifications in action is particularly evident when the goal is long term, such as getting fit or learning to cope with shyness – or setting national standards for stroke care. The numerous physical events brought together in the performance of such an action would have had zero possibility of coming together as a result of the unguided operation of the habits of nature unfolding through a succession of material causes and effects.

Let me illustrate this with another example: going to a gym to get fit. Before I do so, I want to defend the banality of my chosen action. It most certainly would not have been approved by my younger self, preoccupied by the dramatic examples of moral conflict that featured in the writing of existentialists, notably Sartre. Here and in the pages to follow there will be no reference to agonizing decisions between joining the Resistance to fight and staying at home to look after an ageing mother. Nor will there be any discussion of shocking, gratuitous acts – acts that lack reason, motivation or inducement – as a demonstration of the absoluteness of one's freedom. For my concern is with the nature and possibility of freedom, its pervasive presence in the seemingly ordinary complexity of daily life; with the metaphysics rather than the drama of freedom; with the distance between things that are done by agents and things that just happen in the natural world. Hence my choice of the seemingly humdrum example of the project of improving one's fitness. (I say "seemingly" because there is nothing metaphysically humdrum in an embodied subject exercising his body over a long period with the intention of improving the state of said body and, hopefully, postponing its own demise.)[4]

My going to the gym for several years involves freeing up time, making car journeys, buying and wearing appropriate kit, ensuring that the relevant subscription is up to date, and so on. While all these elements are realized in physical movements, they would not have come together had they not been requisitioned by a goal regulating the whole, sustained operation, like a magnet creating a pattern out of iron filings. An extraordinarily heteroge-neous array of physical movements happens, and in the order they do, only because I know what I am doing and why; because they are justified by a goal and requisitioned in order to achieve that goal; because I have the intention – refreshed as necessary – to realize the abstract goal of "getting fit".

It is worth dwelling on some of the movements involved, in order to high-light their heterogeneity. I make a phone call to check the opening hours of the gym. I put my hand in my pocket to check that I have the key to my gym locker. I change to a higher gear in the car in order to speed up my transit to the gym because I have limited time. I move my lips and, mobilizing a minute portion of my knowledge of the English language, inquire which of the gym spaces is open and propel myself accordingly. In the gym, I ride a bicycle going nowhere, my destination being a future state of my body. I repeatedly turn my head in order to consult my watch – to time the duration of my exer-cises and to make sure the activity could fit into the day's timetable that has itself been coordinated with the timetables of others with whom I have shared commitments.

As we dig into each of these elements, we discover more depths, routines and sub-routines, nested and sequential, hierarchically ordered or disordered, interrupted and resumed as external circumstances dictate. Their goals are, most importantly, at different temporal distance from the time at which they take place. For example, when I go downstairs to make a phone call to renew my subscription to the gym for next year, months may intervene between this action and the consequences that I wish to secure. These temporal distances built into actions are different from anything seen elsewhere in nature in at least two respects.

First, the present and future are co-present, the former actual, the latter an envisaged possibility (of which more in Section 4.2). Temporal relationships may be even more complex, as when, for example, I intend an action in the future that will redeem something I have done in the past; for example, I may remind myself to inquire after the health of one of the individuals working in the gym, having thoughtlessly omitted to do so last time. I plan, that is, to do something in future that will not lead to a regret located in a further future; that will head off a future possible backward-looking regret.

Secondly, the temporal distance is quite unlike the fixed distance between links in a chain of material events. The temporal relationship between my current intention and its subsequent realization will depend on opportuni-ties that present themselves and my prioritizing those opportunities. Subject to my inclinations, I can decide when I go to the gym after I have renewed my subscription or whether other activities take priority. I will judge the prioritization. Temporal relationships between flashes of lightning and rumbles of thunder are not open to variations dictated in this way.

All of my actions either explicitly or implicitly involve other actions and other people. The renewal of my gym subscription requires the participation of other parties whose contributions cannot be credibly described as convergent (material) causes. Indeed, the parties encompass an invisible crowd of agents ranging from the person at the other end of the phone to the individuals who had a role in developing the electronic means of payment, the communications systems that support it, the manufacturer of plastic, and so on. This is equally true when I perform seemingly similar short-range actions such as getting dressed, eating a meal, or catching a bus. It is self-evidently so when I work as part of a visible or invisible, defined or open, team.

What is coming into view is the community of minds,[5] shaping the flow of meaning, and understanding, that directly or indirectly supports the most ordinary decisions and actions of our daily life. It scarcely needs saying that, being woven out of many modes of joined intentionality, this community cannot be located in individual brains causally wired into their immediate surroundings. As we enter this community of minds – with our bodies and brains being of course necessary entrance tickets – so we are increasingly (non-spatially) distanced from the natural world and its habits, even though we still rely on those habits to deliver the physical bases of our actions and their outcomes.

We are acknowledging the rather obvious truth that human actions – including the non-dramatic ones of our more or less organized daily lives – take place and happen because, and only because, an individual or a collection of individuals wanted certain outcomes and endeavoured to bring them about – and indeed knew (as it were from within) what she was or they were doing.

It is important to highlight that those purposes have to be *envisaged*: I have to know what I am doing, why I am doing it, in order for it to be done. While it is the function of a seed to unfold into a tree, neither the seed nor the sapling knows where it is going or why, or has any idea of purpose. That knowledge would anyway be unnecessary in order for what is a mechanical process to continue: it is taken care of by programming. Saplings are not impatient to grow. Only metaphorically do heliotropes "seek the sun" "in order to" maximize photosynthesis. Yes, the behaviour of organisms may seem to include the ability to respond to a probable future but it does not require the plant to *entertain* that future in order to behave appropriately; in short, that future does not exist – except in the consciousness of a human observer thinking about the plant. A micro-organism swimming towards a source of energy is addressing its future energy needs but it is not aware of them. Nor does it need to be aware of them since those needs are not bespoke and they can be taken care of by general mechanisms linking general states. The overwhelming majority of animal behaviour is likewise mechanical. (How much, we shall discuss in Appendix C).

Granted, there may be more than a tincture of *telos* in some of the more complex behaviours of animals such as migration, nest-building, and hive-making. The succession of events involved in weaving a nest do not look like the spontaneous unfolding of the material world expressing the most general habits of nature. However, the link between beginning and end of the process is overwhelmingly secured by instinct, modulated where necessary by associative learning. Swallows making their way from South Africa to a particular barn in Herefordshire are effectively animated drones, guided by devices of which they are unconscious. Even if we could talk with swallows, it would be unlikely that they could tell us the address they are heading for. Behaviour such as nest-building or migration is not, and does not have to be, motivated by the specific, singular, bespoke goals that human beings *entertain* for themselves. Human goals, by contrast, make sense in relation to, and in connection with, their own remembered past and an envisaged future. In humans, doing things and knowing why one is doing them (however limited one's self-knowledge in this respect) are connected and the connection – whereby knowledge guides the action – is not (as we shall discuss in Section 4.3) translatable into whatever remains of the idea of causation.

While there may be (biological and cultural) "drives" in the background of any particular human action, the overwhelming majority of behaviour is stitched into a nexus of purposes that are not merely available to the individual taking a particular path through her day: they are indispensable for her to stick to that singular path. (We have only to observe the tragic, hopeless wandering of people with dementia to be reminded of this – if any reminder were required.) The necessary presence or availability of our intentions to ourselves as agents is evident even before we consider more obviously self-conscious aspects of action and the evaluative standpoint – expressed in setting one's own priorities or in first-order or higher-order reflections on one's actions. It is also present in the way we signal to others what we are up to: being noisily "busy" or shaking one's head and looking at one's watch to show that one is not lurking but waiting for someone who is late and so heading off suspicion.

We need to know what we are doing in order to do it. This is the other side of the fact that many of our goals are discretionary, our journeys personalized. This is the most fundamental difference between doings and happenings.

Acting without current intentions[6]

> "As always when you are out on the road, Princess Marya fixed her eyes exclusively on the actual journey and lost sight of its purpose".
>
> Tolstoy, *War and Peace*

Some readers may feel that I am exaggerating the extent to which conscious intention is present in and shapes or directs voluntary action. As a corrective to what they perceive as over-intellectualization of voluntary activity, psychologists have embraced Daniel Kahneman's "dual-system theory" of action and cognition and this has become influential in the philosophy of action.[7] Processes in System 1 are fast, effortless, automatic, and unconscious while those in System 2 are slow, deliberate, controlled, and conscious. While this is acknowledged as a simplification, it has been widely accepted that System 1 processing dominates in everyday activity. As Markus Schlosser notes, "it is often claimed that the great majority of our behaviour is automatic". It has been estimated that only about 5 per cent of our behaviour is consciously controlled.[8]

This would seem to be disturbing since "if one simply claimed that intentional action requires conscious intention, without further qualification, ... and one would ... face the undesirable conclusion that most of our actions are not intentional".[9] Schlosser deals with this concern by introducing the notion of a derivative intention. An action, he argues, can be intentional either "if the performance of the action is initiated and guided by a conscious intention" or "the action is derivatively intention". And an action is derivatively intentional if it is "the manifestation of a habit that has been acquired in some other way and has later been endorsed by the conscious formation of an intention (and this intention is still consciously accessible and would still be endorsed)".[10] He concludes from this most of our everyday behaviour is (derivatively) intentional, even if much of it is automatic.

I share this conclusion. It puts into a correct and non-alarming perspective the fact that most of our actions are indeed built on automaticities and are shot through with mechanisms that seem to happen of their own accord. When I hurry to the station to catch the London train, the voluntariness and goal-directed nature of my action is not undermined by the fact that my capacity to put one leg in front of the other, to duck and weave to avoid bumping into people and objects at the station, and my fancy footwork as I dodge puddles and dog-dirt on the pavement is exercised automatically. Indeed, the thicker the layer of acquired automaticity, the more elevated my freedom.

This is particularly evident in the case of higher-level, hard-won fluency and painfully acquired competence. Honing my skills, learning from experience, self-correction, are ways of adding to my volitional muscle and range. The speed with which I am typing this sentence (matched, I hope, by the speed of thought), such that I am not hunting for and picking out individual letters, was made possible by hours of hunt-and-peck in the 1970s when I taught myself to type. It is a measure of the scale of my freedom not a limit to that freedom. In a practised routine – walking across the road, catching a train, examining a patient, typing a sentence – it is necessary only to keep tabs on what I am doing, not separately to intend every element, every twist and turn of the material events that correspond to the action. Indeed, the sub-routine I am actually performing may be relegated from the headlines, with the latter being grabbed by elements that touch more directly on the larger significance of the action (as when I plan what I am going to say when I get to London while I am sitting on the train) or by a momentary distraction (as when I see someone whom I want to talk to me or worry about spilling coffee on my keyboard).

The fact that deliberate behaviour is dappled, indeed shot through with, the automatic – the habitual, the practised, the triggered – is not, therefore, grounds for shame. We have no need to mourn (to echo the title of Milan Kundera's novel) "the unbearable automaticity of being".[11] It is a reflection of our capacity to choose the appropriate objects and scale of attention necessary to be an agent at the level at which people customarily function in daily life. To perform effortlessly and absent-mindedly actions that once required intense effort and concentration is hardly a cause for shame. As Harry Shearer (the actor who does voices for *The Simpsons*) said, "If you are thinking while you are doing it, you are in the wrong place. You should be doing all your thinking in your preparation".[12]

Moreover, it is a reminder of how agency is inseparable from our temporal depths. Even something as elementary as being able to type without trying is a tribute to the extent to which we are beneficiaries of the efforts of our past selves. Importantly, we are usually available to be woken up out of automatic pilot and hauled back from distractions to the matter at hand. As we take the familiar route to our favourite holiday destination, we can be precipitated out of the conversation, thoughts about what the holiday holds, or the story on the tape, by a car cutting across in front of us. The implicit temporal depth of fluent actions is another element of the case against seeing reason-based action as reason-*caused* action – a step that threatens to gather actions back into a putative law-governed causal network of the natural world.[13] (This is something we shall discuss in Section 4.3).

The orchestrated daily life of the agent

It is easy to forget, and certainly to underestimate, the complexity of ordinary actions and, in particular, the multitude of intermediate steps of different scales, in the realization of our goals. The ways of "becausation" are labyrinthine. I do X in order to be able to do Y; I do A in order to be in a position to do B. I am hunting for the shoe polish and brush in order that I might shine my shoes so that I might look smart and make a certain impression at the meeting at which I hope to make the case for national standards for stroke care. I polish my shoes more vigorously in order that the job might be done more quickly so that I don't (consulting the kitchen clock and reminding myself that it needs a new battery) miss my train, correcting my assessment of how long it might take to get to the station in the light of the likely effect of the wet weather on the traffic or the roadworks you told me about yesterday.

In performing each of these steps, routines and sub-routines, nested and parallel, connected and disconnected elements of the overall plan for the day, I mobilize know-how and know-that, locally informed common sense and general and specialist knowledge, as enacted "becausation" takes me from one step to the next. My complex actions are structured to fit into an orchestrated routine sustained in the face of, or modified in response to, the foreseen and unforeseen circumstances of my unfolding days. And in many cases those unforeseen circumstances may inhibit planned actions. My intention to meet you in the pub to discuss a surprise birthday treat for a mutual friend will be postponed when I learn that that friend is going to join us.

We have already noted how, in the exercise of our free will, we often come at things from a long way off. The contrast between acting, at what is deemed an appropriate time, and merely *re*acting – as would be the case with an organism wired to respond to a stimulus – is profound. Longer-term plans require *refraining* from action, resisting invitations or even pressure to respond, so that one is not blown off the course one has set for oneself. Elective inaction to protect one's availability for other actions is as valid an expression of agency as doing things. In the face of distractions or rival claims to our attention, we may need to refresh the intention – to place it in the forefront of our mind – perhaps by articulating it. ("My God, is that the time?!"). Deliberately reminding oneself (or others) of what one is, or should be, about is an esoteric, and yet commonplace, expression of agency.

This, then, is what real actions look like. Once we see how they are put together, it is clear that they are quite unlike the mindless products of the habits of nature. This is nothing like, for example, the binary choice between pressing a button with a right hand and pressing a button with the left hand observed in the experiments of Libet or John-Dylan Haynes. The daily life of a human agent is not to be understood as a causally driven thread down a succession of forks. The path that is fashioned out of the fabric of the natural and human world is more complex than that. Much, perhaps most, of what we do grows out of a complex network of things we formulate to ourselves and to one another even though that formulation may recede into the background.

Some readers may still be unconvinced that there is a fundamental difference between actions and other happenings in the physical world, and are unpersuaded that we are able to pull rank on the natural world to which we owe our origin and in which we are (to put it mildly) *parvenus*. They may even suspect that the focus on complexities of everyday behaviour is a diversionary tactic to conceal the law-governed causal influences that predetermine, drive, and shape our actions. We need therefore to look more closely at the relationship between actions and something that has no place in the physical world: possibility.

4.2 POSSIBILITY AND ACTIONS

> "A spider conducts operations that resemble those of a weaver, and a bee puts to shame many an architect in the construction of her cells. But what distinguishes the worst architect from the best of bees is this – that the architect raises his structure in imagination before he erects it in reality".
>
> Karl Marx, *Capital Volume 1*[14]

The origin of possibility

I hope the arguments in the previous chapters persuaded you that the "double whammy" of laws and causation is not clearly double and may not be a whammy. Both laws and causes seem less straightforwardly the keepers of a prison in which nature seems to have us locked up, notwithstanding the various ways in which we are a part of nature. Even though causes seem to lack their own oomph and laws do not seem to have intrinsic regulatory powers, we still seem to be faced with the implacable uniformity of the way things go: nature has habits of unfolding that are not negotiable.

And yet it is undeniable that we are able to transform objects into means of requisitioning events in virtue of which they are turned into handles, enablers of, rather than obstacles to, our freedom. We pick up the hammer and bash in the nail, an event that seems likely to occur only in relation to the purpose that we envisage for the item we are constructing. Even more impressively we are capable of exploiting our, admittedly incomplete, knowledge of the habits of nature formulated as the laws of science to magnify our capacity to manipulate the natural world to achieve our ends. How can this be possible?

What makes it possible is our capacity to entertain *possibility*, which is outside of, or beyond, the actual. This capacity is rooted in something that we flagged up at the very beginning: the intentionality of our consciousness. Envisaged possibility is the benign presence that is overlooked in our ability to manipulate the world – either in everyday life or in the more sophisticated and specialized setting of the science laboratory as we discussed in Sections 2.2 and 2.3.

Nature, understood as the physical world, and encompassing the tissues of organisms, is confined – it hardly needs saying – to what-is and to what (actually) happens. By contrast, conscious subjects see *that*, *what*, and *how* things are; and what they see, or think they see, or expect to see, exceeds what they actually, directly experience. They are thereby enabled to supplement the actuality before them with *intuited possibilities* as to how things might be or might become and what they might or might not experience. It is this standpoint outside of nature, courtesy of intentionality, that envisages future states of affairs that are the objects of intentions, and the reasons for actions that transform events into potential handles to bring about possible states of affairs. We are able to cooperate with or, more precisely, exploit the material world to realize ends – states of affairs – that, so long as they are only possibilities, are immaterial.

Intentionality, then, opens up the possibility of possibility.[15] Let us develop this thought because while it may be elusive, it is central to the argument about free will. As we discussed in the Overture, objects of perception are intuited as exceeding what is revealed in experience. It is worth reiterating some of the points made there.

When I see or touch, or hear an object, I am conscious that there is more to it than what is delivered to me through seeing, touching, or hearing. Consider my seeing a cup. I intuit that it is only incompletely revealed to my gaze. It has other possible appearances than those that are presently visible – such as the view from different angles, different distances, and different lights. Beyond that, it has properties that could be uncovered by my other senses and, indeed, that go beyond untutored perception – for example, weight, tensile strength, and so on. There is no guarantee that any given one of the possibilities that I envisage corresponds to actuality. In the overwhelming majority of cases my anticipations will prove to be correct. Nevertheless, what I anticipate, exceeding what is presented to me, may correspond to no reality.

This "full-blown" intentional relationship between the consciousness of a perceiving subject and a perceived object is further supplemented by the sense that there are things "out there" that I cannot at present sense. The visual field, for example, is populated with items that are visibly hidden, because they are concealed by other visible objects. Seeing involves believing more than what is being seen. This has been beautifully expressed by psychologist of vision Richard Gregory: "A nothing can be a clue for seeing, as when a nearby object is inferred from the gap it makes in the background".[16] "Full-blown" intentionality also extends to objects that are being heard but cannot be seen, as when I hear what I assume to be a bird singing in a bush. The well-founded intuition that there is more to things than what we experience of them at any given moment underpins the sense of an infinitely expandible space of possibility around what is actual and present.

The realm of the possible expands as we go beyond a single sense – as when we anticipate how a cup we see will feel to the touch, or imagine the look of a bird whose song we can hear. This is particularly apparent when what we perceive is an item that we have to interact with – an obstacle to be avoided, a tool to be used, something that piques our curiosity (as we shall discuss in Appendix C, all objects are potential "affordances" in this sense). This is brought home to us through the surprises and disappointments that attend our interactions with such objects. The cup that breaks when we pick it up highlights, in retrospect, the assumptions we had about its robustness or the material of whih it is made. Our sense of possibility, although the key to our agency, is also fallible.

Most importantly, full-blown intentionality is supplemented by the joining of intentionality with other conscious subjects – something that we discussed briefly in the Overture. You and I share experiences of a public realm populated by objects, processes, events, and other people, that is present to us and to others. Additionally, you may report and hence share with me experiences that I do not have – as when you see something that is beyond my visual field because you are occupying a different viewpoint. Your indicating to me objects that I cannot see or otherwise sense reinforces the intuition that objects "out there" exist independently of my experiences of them: that they exist in themselves as well as for me – that they are an inexhaustible source of possible experience.

Shared or joined intentionality – mediated through gestures such as pointing and, of course, language – ultimately makes available knowledge *that* such-and-such is, or might be, the case, an awareness that is not directly dependent on sense experience. The virtual outside opened up by knowledge is vastly greater than that which is opened up by our individual experiences.

Factual knowledge is put to use in the pooling of agency, the employment of ever more complex skills, tools, facilities, and institutions through which we act directly and indirectly in and on the world, exerting, and magnifying, our power. Most importantly, knowledge enables us to reach from the present into a future fashioned individually or collectively from an acknowledged past.

Like a true agent, I am getting ahead of myself. The key point is that, courtesy of full-blown intentionality, which takes us beyond what is before us, the world we face is haunted by the possible, by what might be the case. While basic objects of perception, the goods that populate our immediate surroundings, are invested with possibility, as we ascribe to them properties they may or may not have, the entertainment of possibility ascends to a higher order when it is a matter of entities or states of affairs intimated to us through the experiences of others as objects of knowledge. The most capacious bearers of possibilities are what philosophers call propositional attitudes. Propositional attitudes play an important role in the arguments that follow and a pause to examine what they are is warranted.

The term refers to mental entities such as beliefs, knowledge, hopes, fears, thoughts, intentions. When I believe that it is raining outside, I have a psychological attitude (a "belief") towards a state of affairs which can be captured by a proposition ("It is raining outside"). The belief may be directly rooted in experience: I believe that it is raining because the rain is falling on my head. More typically, beliefs are inferences from experience. I hear the noise of drops of water falling on the glass of the skylight and come to believe that it is raining. Many, perhaps the majority, of our propositional attitudes are based not on things we ourselves have perceived or have directly inferred from experience but on what we have been told or has been conveyed to us through writing and other media. Other propositional attitudes grow out of the way in which what we know or believe – how it is with the world and with ourselves – impinges on our needs. Hopes, wishes, and fears, informed by our knowledge and beliefs, provide the platform or soil out of which particular and general, short-term and long-term, intentions grow. I shall embrace in the pages to come the view shared with many philosophers that propositional attitudes are the central vehicles of voluntary action.

We have talked about ourselves as subjects facing the world. Courtesy of intentionality, we have access to that world without being entirely wired into, or submerged in, it. When I see a cup, I do so because of my interaction with it. If that interaction were understood as a causal interaction instantiating the general habits of nature it would not account for my seeing the cup. The habits of nature as revealed by the laws of science may explain how the light gets into my brain but not how my gaze looks out; how I see what has interacted with the light. It is this asymmetrical relationship between ourselves and the material world – we face it but it does not face us – that makes it possible to act upon the world *from a (non-spatial) distance*, initially opened up by perception and then vastly extended in a shared space of human knowledge.

What is clearly evident in sense experience – the world I experience does not experience me – is mirrored in agentive interactions. While there is a degree of *inter*action in any physical action – especially obvious when I lift an object and it presses down on my hand – there is something at the heart of action that is not reciprocated. This lies behind the difference between the half of the interaction that is an action and the half that is not; between the passivity of the weight I am lifting pressing on my hand and the activity of my pushing on the weight to lift it. In that sense action is offset from the material world. The asymmetry is even more pronounced in the case of knowledge: that which I know does not have knowledge of me – except in the rare cases where the object of knowledge is a knowing subject.

My relationship to objects out there is not matched by the (merely spatial) relationship the objects have to my body. In virtue of my being aware of them, they are not only located by me in relation to my body, they are located by me in a non-physical outside or "over there" – handy, or out of reach, or in the way, just there. While the object is "over there" for me, neither I nor my body is "over there" for the object, notwithstanding that the object and my body are two metres from each other. This asymmetry is most obvious in the case of vision; but it applies to humbler senses such as touch. While I sit on the chair, it is not true that the chair squats under me.[17]

The asymmetrical intentional relationship of the conscious subject is not confined to the material participants – to bodies, ships, shoes, and sealing wax. Intentionality opens up a landscape dappled with possibilities that may or may not be actualized. Seeing those possibilities, I am ahead of myself and of the present state of the world. I straddle a realm of material objects and their material surroundings and a realm unknown to them. The realm of possibility not confined to the habits of actuality, that is to say of nature.[18]

Possibility and tensed time

There is another important dimension to the relationship between intentionality, possibility, and freedom. Perception, and even more strikingly knowledge, open up a *temporal* distance from what is thereby established as the present, as "now" opposed to "not-yet". As perceiving, knowing subjects, we advance into a future populated with possible states of affairs we envisage and may wish to bring about or to avert. The landscape of possibilities occupied by human subjects is extended in time. Its most proximate layer is opened up by the ongoing activity in which I am presently engaged: by what I am now doing, that extends towards the immediate future – as when I literally reach for an object or walk towards a nearby destination. But the temporal distance is extended without limit as I envisage ever more remote possibilities that are relevant to my needs, wishes, plans, and dreams. The explicit future envisaged by agents, supplementing the actual present, is informed by a remembered or implicit past.

Without the entertainment of possibility through hopes, fears, plans, and so on, there would be no such explicit future: it is only in a conscious subject that what is happening in time t_1 and what might happen at time t_2 – or some unspecified future time – are side by side. It is only from the prospective or retrospective standpoint of a conscious subject that what happens is seen as realizing one out of several possible paths. In the absence of entertained possibility, there is neither what might happen or might not happen; even less what ought to happen or ought not to happen.[19] Of course, possibilities are not free-floating: they take their rise from our experience of actuality. But they are not part of, even less confined to, that actuality.

Envisaged possibilities, vastly extended by the joining of intentionality in the community of minds, the inner connectedness of the self, of its many-layered past, and various modes of communication with ourselves and others, open up and populate a future available to the present as an object of our hopes, fears, and above all our intentions. And given that agency is about stopping things from happening, about pre-emption, as well as about making them happen, the future contains possible non-events as well as possible events, existing for an agent picking and choosing a path through the world. Things that are prevented from happening – non-events – owe what existence they have to being envisaged. It is a truism that there are no non-happenings in the natural world. And of course, the envisaged future has no obligation to occur. Just because my diary for 2021 is packed with engagements, I am not guaranteed to live past 2020.

In the last chapter, we quoted Peter van Inwagen who asserted that "there is, at any instant exactly one physical possible future".[20] We can now see that this is an overestimate: at any instant in the material world, there is one less future than van Inwagen allows. There are *zero* physical possible futures because possible futures – indeed futures period – exist only insofar as they are entertained. The physical world does not have the capacity to entertain its own future, to project at time t from its state at that time to a future state. At any given time, t there is no state-of-the-world-at-time $t + n$. Future states cohabiting with present states of the material world exist only in the minds of those who (accurately or inaccurately) envisage those states as possibilities that may happen and/or that they wish to bring about. It is the anticipations of a conscious subject that create the openness of what-is to what-might-be. Once the future is possible, more than one future is possible. Even where we imagine a particular future event, what is imagined could be realized by a range of possible events.

We shape the future by making it first exist – however sketchily – as an envisaged possibility before it is present. Where time t_2 exists at t_1 through being populated with possibilities envisaged as being located at time t_2 we have a future. That future is necessarily open, if only because it cannot be defined down to the last discernible detail. That is obviously true when I plan (say) next year's holiday, however careful and successful my planning. Indeed, I will probably be glad of the unexpected seeping through the interstices of my fulfilled plans. But this openness is evident even in the case of something very simple and very close; for example, my anticipation of seeing a dog in the garden, having heard barking. The precise position and state of the dog will be undetermined by the most assiduous act of my imagination.

Hence, when there is any future, there is a range of futures. And when of course many different futures are being envisaged by an individual, and where different groups of individuals are engaged in anticipation, there will be a combinatorial explosion of possible futures. None of them will be realized, of course, if they are contrary to the habits of nature; and they may be pre-empted by current local circumstances.

The physical world is actual and determinate and has no place for the possible that is indeterminate in the sense of having a range of possible realizations. There is thus future in the physical world. The vision founded in general relativity of the universe as a four-dimensional block in which all its states coexist in space-time may seem to be at odds with the claim that there is no future in the physical world. It is not. Different locations in the block universe are neither in themselves past, future, or present. Times are assigned to tenses only with reference to a "now" or present, a temporal reference point that has to be inserted by privileging the viewpoint of a conscious subject. The block is tenseless, as was echoed by Einstein in the somewhat tactless letter he wrote to the widow of his oldest friend that we quoted in Chapter 3. Indeed, the sum total of everything that has happened, is happening, and will happen coexists in this block.

This should not concern us. Given that such coexistence will encompass incompatible states of the universe – such as my not yet being born, my being alive, and my being long dead – this clearly has little to do with the reality in which we live our lives. Indeed, it has little to do with the reality of a universe that does seem, after all, to change. The block universe is a frozen universe. (Not for nothing did Einstein accept the soubriquet "the Parmenidean" from Karl Popper.)[21] That general relativity does not accommodate a world in which there is a real future that is to say, one that is not actual, is a reminder of how actions that occur in order to realize a possibility located in the future have their roots in something outside of the natural world.

There is more, much more, to be said about the shaping of the actual future – or a future actualized as a subsequent present – from the standpoint of a possible future. First, however, it is necessary to appreciate that the possible future is anchored to the present, a present realized in a conscious subject in virtue of whom what-is has presence. Hopes and expectations and the intentions that crystalize out of them are nourished not only by our own individual prior experience: they draw on a shared, even collective, past experience.

As we observed, at a very basic level, a visual field is haunted by absences – supplementing what is seen with what is inferred and hence with a sense of that which might be. Those absences are multiplied and elaborated as we pass from experience to knowledge. The future is populated by many things that will not happen or not in the way they are envisaged. Mistaken expectations, unicorns, and gods testify to the power of nothing, of non-existent entities and never-existent states of affairs in our lives and in prompting behaviour. For a secular humanist, the huge influence the gods have had on our lives, is the most important expression of the power of nothing. If, as theologians tell us, God is the possibility of possibility, then possibility is the possibility of God. The power of nothing would have no place in a causally closed natural world entirely subject to the habits of nature.

Actions, which necessarily take place in the present, look both ways, to futures and pasts. There is a reciprocal relationship between the present, which looks back on the past and forward to the future, and the past and future which define what is ongoing as Now. This applies not only to actions envisaged from without as a whole, as done-and-dusted events, but also to actions experienced from within as ongoing processes. In the latter case past and future have more obviously to be copresent in order that we should know where we have got to, what we have achieved, and what remains to be achieved.[22]

The sedimentation of past and future: post-tensed time

I have argued that possibilities are the link between agency and tensed time. It is important not to underestimate the extent to which possibilities may be shared and entertained jointly or collectively. A striking reflection of this is in the development of projects located in a collective or shared future – stabilized in timetables, diaries, or calendars – that is the temporal partner of a jointly acknowledged past.

These collective futures, set out in a publicly accessible space amount to what we might call "post-tensed" time. I say post-tensed because the locations in the timetable, diary, or calendar, lose their explicit relationship to a present. But that relationship is still potentially there. I can say "See you on 12 May" only because I can say "See you tomorrow"; and I can say "See you tomorrow" because we can each envisage a shared future. That future is, of course, related to and relevant to, the present. The twelfth of May seems tenseless only because its original connection with a present is concealed. It is a mistake to think that clock, diary, and calendrical time are a reversion to the tenseless (or pre-tense) time of nature rather than something built on tensed time.

And yet clock and calendrical time are seen by some metaphysicians to be more objectively real, and closer to physical time, than tensed time. This is a mistake – because post-tensed time is mathematized or in some other way formalized tensed time – though an understandable one. While the sharing of futures and pasts results in a sedimentation through discourse of tensed time into something that appears to be objective, this does not mean that they have been returned to the time of the natural world. Calendars, etc. are a collectivision of tensed time and depend on the latter and hence on modes of temporality which are not to be found in nature. There is no calendrical time outside of human consciousness, any more than there is a 5 o'clock on the sun (to steal an example from Wittgenstein).[23] Clock, diary, and calendrical time are as much a product of human consciousness as "yesterday" and "tomorrow".[24] They are an aspect of the extraordinary journey taken by humans from personal memories to a realm of semantic memories – the realm of facts.

The significance of post-tensed time is that it provides a stable, communal scaffolding to which future possibilities can be attached, an exoskeleton organizing the individual and shared past and future which the plans of agents can draw upon. The public future of the calendar and its more local expression in for example appointment books enables a vast expansion of the scope of cooperation, of shared agency, between individuals and between groups, of the joined activity to realize possibilities.

Post-tensed time supports our endeavours to prepare ourselves to act more effectively at some future time. We create the circumstances in which this is possible. Such positioning may encompass not merely assuming a literal vantage point but something much more long term. It may involve rehearsal, practice, and training for some action or opportunity I anticipate in future:

the enabling conditions I establish are both within and outside of myself. I am, or we are, given notice which permits us to prepare ourselves. Practice in December with others in the nets provided for us all enables me to catch the cricket ball that comes my direction one afternoon the following May. What may seem the work of a moment is the fruit of months of preparation.[25] The months that are allowed for my preparation are the children of tensed time, the sedimented structure of shared possibility.[26] They provide an exoskeleton to help us to organize our lives and to maximize opportunities for coordinated activity in which we pool our agency. And they vastly extend our capacity to bind ourselves to each other (and indeed to ourselves), through the fundamental human activity of making and keeping promises and appointments.[27]

Some philosophers of a naturalist persuasion might insist that the entertaining of possibility is a capacity widespread through the animal kingdom and even beyond. Much animal and plant behaviour, they will argue, can be explained only in terms of what *will* happen. That is, of course, true. What is happening now in a seedling makes sense as part of a journey to a full-grown tree. The pursuit of a prey by a predator is in the service of a future state of satiety and the capacity to generate progeny. None of this disproves the uniqueness of human agency or the vital role of entertained possibility in the activity of agent. For the forward-pointing behaviour in plants and beasts does not require a particular future to be envisaged or articulated by the organism in question. The seed does not have to imagine the tree to be motivated to grow. The predator does not have to articulate the benefits of eating the prey in order to be prompted to chase it. The cooperation of beasts does not depend on meeting by agreed appointment. The parallel realm of as yet invisible, but sharply-defined future possible events, illuminated by knowledge or hope or fear, and bespoke to the life of the individual, that underpins human actions, is not available for non-human animals. We humans can see the direction things are going for animals, the purposes various mechanisms or automatisms serve; but the animals do not need to entertain the ends understood as future possible states in order to progress towards them.

A final thought to take away. Post-tensed time has so deeply entered our social life that something as biologically (as well as socially and culturally) fundamental as mating is entangled with – "dating."

Conclusion

Agency is rooted in a sense of possibility and possibility arises out of the intentional relationships of human consciousness to what is experienced as being "out there". Actions are the realization of possibilities: they are possibility-led, conjured into being by the idea of an envisaged, wished-for future, something that does not otherwise exist. In this fundamental respect they are unlike happenings in the natural world, which are actuality-driven, growing out of an (if unacknowledged) actual prior state of the world.

Physical actuality, as described by physics, cannot, of itself, give rise to possibility, though it will license what we envisage as realistic or realizable when we anticipate or make plans for the future. The material world is what it is and it cannot transcend itself to give rise to what is not or what might be. For the latter, we require the distance opened up by intentionality. From such a distance, manifested in hopes, expectations, desires, and thoughts, the actual may be realized possibility.

Possibility is what is common to intentions, hopes, fears, wonderings (idle and otherwise), speculations, and other propositional attitudes, to the tentacles reaching into an as-yet non-existent but envisaged future, that define and motivate actions. Perhaps it is for this reason that some philosophers of a materialist persuasion deny the existence of propositional attitudes, of these bearers of more-or-less articulated possibility.[28] For propositional attitudes cannot be identified with material events in or material states of the brain, since there is nothing in neural activity to sustain the intentionality of items of consciousness of any sort. Neural activity wired into the material world cannot reach back to its causal ancestors to reveal them as those ancestors or more generally as objects "out there".

Others, appreciating the implausibility of denying the existence of propositional attitudes, grudgingly accept such entities. They endeavour to mitigate the threat they pose to their materialism by claiming that propositional attitudes are "realized in", or identical with, material, specifically neural, events – a view we shall examine in the next section. For the present, we note that, if this were true, propositional attitudes would lose their distinctive nature; indeed, they would be superfluous. Actions would be placed on a level footing with other material events and consequently be captured by the physical world and its unshakeable habits. There would be nothing to supplement actuality with possibility. Hence agents would not be independent players in the world in which they live – a result that some who find it difficult to accommodate agency in a hard-line naturalist view of the world may welcome.[29]

We may summarize the burden of this section in a sentence. An action is an event that happens only because it has been entertained as a possibility to be realized by a subject that desires and intends it.[30]

4.3 ACTIONS, CAUSES AND PROPOSITIONAL ATTITUDES

Donald Davidson's theory of action

Actions are distinguished from other happenings by virtue of the fact that they typically occur because someone wants or intends them to happen: they happen for a reason explicitly embraced by an agent; they correspond to a possibility that someone wishes to be actualized. For these reasons, the very idea of an action does not fit into that of nature unfolding mindlessly according to its universal and immemorial habits. Even so, many philosophers of a naturalistic persuasion, notwithstanding the difficulties associated with the very notion of a cause, try to naturalize actions by treating their intentions and reasons as causes understood in the traditional pre-Humean way, as something that connects elements in the natural world, such that any given element is necessitated by certain predecessors and in turn necessitates its successors.

Donald Davidson in his classic paper "Actions, Reasons, and Causes", that set much of the agenda for the philosophy of action in the second half of the twentieth century in analytical philosophy, argued that the *reasons* for actions operate as their *causes*. "[R]ationalization" he maintained "is a species of causal explanation".[31] Davidson elaborates his thesis as follows: "the ordinary notion of cause which enters into scientific or common-sense accounts of non-psychological affairs is essential also to the understanding of what it is to act with a reason, to have a certain intention in acting, to be an agent, to act counter to one's own best judgement, or to act freely".[32]

Davidson's defence of this view is seemingly straightforward: if reasons are *not* the causes of actions, he argues, then doing something because of a reason removes the explanatory value of "because".[33] If actions are not explained by causes, they are unexplained. "Becausation", it seems, is a species of causation – otherwise it is redundant.

If propositional attitudes really are the causes of actions, then we must assume that they in turn are the effects of other causes. And, if we overlook the rather elusive nature of propositional attitudes, this story seems to exorcise the magic or mystery from actions. By being causes, reasons and the like are re-integrated as entities in the natural world. Davidson makes this explicit: "Cause is the cement of the universe: the concept of cause is what holds together our picture of the universe, a picture that would otherwise disintegrate into a diptych of the mental and the physical".[34]

Davidson's position – that, when I act for a reason, the reason causes my action – has been variously refined and attacked in the half-century or more since he first articulated it. Nevertheless, the papers in which he first advanced it remain a useful, because lucid, account of a profoundly but interestingly mistaken theory of action: one in which the central, distinctive elements – propositional attitudes such as beliefs, reasons, and intentions – are causally embedded in the world from which the action arises and upon which it acts. The true nature of actions – as realizations of general possibilities that are entertained before they are actualized – is consequently lost.[35]

In this and the following section I want to argue that to think of intentions, reasons and the like as causes radically misconstrues propositional attitudes. It does not reflect their nature as the bearers of the possibilities in whose realization the essence of a voluntary action lies. It thereby travesties actions and, most importantly, removes what it is that makes doings different from other happenings. As a consequence, it reduces the agent to a mere conduit for events passing through his body. Farewell, freedom.

Propositional attitudes as effects and as causes

What follows is not meant to veto the use of the concept of causation when we talk about what people do in everyday life – plumbers and neurosurgeons. But we need to be more circumspect in philosophical discussion, particularly since, as we saw in Chapter 3, there is very little of the idea of causation that stands up to critical scrutiny. Causation, and causes as events that makes other events happen, wilt in a sustained metaphysical gaze. Causation is stripped of its status as an "occult force", as a path for the passage of oomph, or even (to pick up on Davidson) as "the cement of the universe". Counterfactual and statistical accounts of causation do little to restore its explanatory power after the Humean assault. What little remains of the idea of causation does not seem likely to survive extrapolation from its home territories (billiard balls, lightning-and-thunder, noises caused by swinging doors, and cigarettes and cancer) to propositional attitudes and whatever it is that prompts actions, especially the complex actions out of which we weave our daily lives. (We shall return in Section 5.2 to address the concerns of those who see whole agents as causes – indeed for whom agency is the true and only home of causation.)

Let us therefore scrutinize the idea that actions are the *effects* of propositional attitudes such as beliefs and intentions and that those propositional attitudes are the effects of external events:

External Events (input) → Propositional Attitudes → Actions (output)

A favourite example used to support this account of agency is a rain shower (input) causing me to have the belief that it is raining and that belief in turn causing me to behave in a certain way, such as telling someone that it is rain-ing or picking up my umbrella before I leave the house (output). The example is suspiciously simple and simplified – not the least because it overlooks the need to invest a subject with a viewpoint to single out and unify items such as "rain showers" and organize the multiplicity of propositional attitudes that may be involved whenever someone acts. But its very simplicity helps us to see more clearly the misrepresentation of actions that results when we invite causation into the heart of agency.

It will be useful to examine separately the input phase and the output phase.

Inputs: the supposed causes of propositional attitudes

A description of a shower of rain as causing a belief, or a subject to become the bearer of a belief, that it is raining fails for the same reason that the causal theory of perception fails. The rain cannot be an entity that has as one of its effects something, namely a belief, that points back to itself, that which justifies it, namely the rain. Yes, the rain could directly make my head wet or indirectly cause me to catch cold. But there is nothing inherent in the rain as it is understood in physics, or in its interaction with a material object such as a brain, that can cause a belief about itself: a belief that the shower exists "out there" and that it belongs to a general category of event captured in the sen-tence "It is raining". There is nothing in the interaction of one material object (a rain-shower) with another (a brain) to account for one object becoming explicit to the other; or not, at least, if both objects are subject to the habits of nature as captured in the laws of natural science.

This failure of the rain as a material cause to explain the belief that it is raining – a failure that is no less complete even if we forget the Hume-iliation of the very idea of causal powers that we discussed in Chapter 3 – touches on something more basic than belief. It is the dubious assumption that the rain is an adequate cause of the sight and sound of itself courtesy of the brain activity it triggers. This assumption passes over the means by which its characteristics becomes audible and visible. The sight and sound of the rain is fundamen-tally different from any (intrinsic) properties of the rain, if we identify those properties as what is seen in the gaze of natural science. There is nothing intrinsically audible or visible in drops of H_2O. This is why, since Galileo, sights and sounds have been downgraded to the status of secondary qualities. They are mind-dependent and there is nothing in the world, seen as being com-posed entirely of physical stuff as defined by natural science, corresponding to science.

That is the first, most obvious, and most fundamental problem with the idea that propositional attitudes are caused by that which they are about. But there are others. The claim that the rain implants the belief *that* it is raining by standard causal mechanisms looks even less plausible when it is acknowledged that beliefs are remote from what eyes can see and the ears can hear, even where they are ultimately justified by what is heard and seen and otherwise sensed. They are fundamentally different from anything that is experienced: beliefs lack visibility and audibility, as is evident when they are acquired indirectly through verbal communication. That is why it is acceptable that the sound associated with your telling me that it is raining has no resemblance to the sound of the rain; nor, of course, does it need to.

This difference is a manifestation of something fundamental and, perhaps for that reason, elusive. There are many ways of capturing it but one way of doing so has the virtue of succinctness: it is the difference between "what-is" and "that what-is is"; or between matter and "thatter". Propositions – and propositional attitudes insofar as they include assertions or assumptions or beliefs or pieces of knowledge – are distinct from what they are about, from what they propose, or what they entertain as a (necessarily general) possibility. The distance between propositions and what they propose, in virtue of which they may have a truth value, cannot either be opened up, or crossed, by the kinds of causal connections as they are typically ascribed to the material world. The belief that it is raining belongs to a different order of being from a shower of rain and consequently, unlike the wet pavements, cannot be understood as an effect of the shower analogous to wet pavements and wet heads.[36]

The problems with a causal theory of propositional attitudes go beyond the difficulties of the causal theory of perception. These additional problems are relevant to understanding the distinctive nature of action.

Firstly, the belief that it is raining does not track the rain – either its place or its duration. I do not have to locate the rain in space nor in time. I can continue to believe it is raining even though it has stopped. A four-hour rain-spell does not sustain a four-hour belief that it is raining, even though that belief remains true throughout that time. And when the belief is translated into a statement such as "It rained for four hours yesterday" (justifying your further belief that it might be hard-going walking in the countryside this afternoon and your choice of footwear) the disconnection between the temporal duration of the belief and that of the event whose occurrence is believed in is complete.

Indeed, there is a sense in which beliefs (and other propositional attitudes) do not "happen" in the way that events such as rain showers happen. This is more obviously true when the belief is instilled in me by someone else reporting that it is, or that it may be, raining. At the very least, there is a lack of physical proportionality between putative cause and putative effect. In short, the belief that it is raining, unlike the rain, does not occupy a definite portion of space-time. By contrast, causes, as understood in the basic sense of individual events causing other individual events, do occupy stretches of space and time.[37]

Secondly, the belief, unlike any actual rain, is cast in general terms. While the assertion "it is raining" is implicitly singular in its reference to a particular rain spell, and singular when it is thought at a given moment, it is general in form. My belief extracts and retains from all the singular features of a particular sustained shower of falling drops only the general notion that it is raining. As we shall see, this generality also extends to the output – the actions that I plan in response to the belief. "It's raining, so I'd better take an umbrella" can be realized in a wide range of ways. And at the risk of too much anticipation, there is a lack of proportionality between input and output in voluntary actions. Consider what can be achieved through a wink or a smile. Or settling down to sleep early with a view to improving one's performance on the following day's tasks.

We shall return to the output question presently, but let us stick with the input relationship. The belief that it is raining, even when it is connected with the sound of actual rainfall, has an openness that is reflected in the fact that it can be justified, seen to be true, by a wide range of actual rain showers, a range that has fluffy boundaries. There is an intrinsic vagueness in the idea of a rain shower and *a fortiori* the criteria to be met to justify my going to the trouble to find that bl**dy umbrella that has the irritating habit of hiding itself and to take it with me when I go out.

That a belief that it is raining does not map on to something that has certain spatio-temporal extent and other physical properties is clear in those cases where I acquire it as a result of being informed by a trusted source. I do not require her to give unique specification of the meteorological phenomenon in question. The fit is even looser when what I am told is something like "it's a bit wet outside".[38] And looser still when my informant tells me that there is a good chance of a shower today.

Thirdly, the belief that it is raining has properties that we do not associate with physical events: rational consequences and logical entailments. For example, I cannot believe that it is rainy and sunny, or that it is raining heavily and lightly, in precisely the same place and at the same time. And I can make a rational connection along the lines of "It is raining so I ought to take my umbrella", though this will depend on my estimate of the heaviness of the rain, the availability of alternative ways of protecting myself, and my valuation of the bother of locating an umbrella compared with that of getting wet. What's more, another person may make this connection for me: "It is raining so you had better take your umbrella".

My conclusion that I had better take an umbrella, and my consequently doing so, do not map onto the physical event of the rain in the way that effects are supposed to map on to causes. The disconnection is even more obvious as when my knowledge that the country I am travelling to has wet climate prompts me to believe that I ought to pack an umbrella in my luggage.

Finally, propositional attitudes are individuated and unified in ways that do not correspond to the coherence of states or objects or processes in the material world. A belief can gather up disparate items in a manner that is only tenuously connected with the spatio-temporal coherence of objects and events seen in the natural world. Things that are physically next to an item of interest, or (to be a little technical for a moment) are located in the same light cone, may not belong to the target of a belief relevant to it, while other things that are remote from that item may be collected together. My disposition to believe that a sound is that of the rain rather than of fluttering leaves may be increased by someone telling me last week that it was likely to rain today. The telling and the belief are hardly next-door neighbours either to each other or to the sound that I am interpreting as rain.

The widespread assumption that beliefs (and other propositional attitudes, notably the intentions and reasons that are so important for actions) are the effects of external events and that they are "realized in" or "caused by" neural activity, itself caused by that which they are about, therefore has nothing going for it.[39] Physical events happening throughout nature typically just happen: they are neither true or false. Beliefs specify possibilities that may or may not turn out to be the case. I may imagine it is raining as a result of mistaking the sound of fluttering leaves for that of falling drops or because someone misinformed me. In short, beliefs can propose events that have not occurred: it is not mandatory, though it is of course desirable, that the belief that it is raining should be justified by actual rain.

All of this undermines any claim that propositional attitudes are effects of the things they are about and that as such they are themselves material events. The acquisition of a belief "that X is the case" cannot be merely an effect of a pre-existing X impinging on a sensitive surface. The "aboutness" of a belief distances it from any sequence of causes and effects – even if we were to entertain the pre-Humean belief that the very idea of causation refers to anything inherent in the material world.

Outputs: propositional attitudes as causes

So much for the input and the looseness of the connection between external events and propositional attitudes. Let's now look at outputs: what work propositional attitudes are supposed to do; in what way they work to change the world to align it more closely to the wishes of agents. In what sense of "cause" that survives after the critique in Chapter 3 do they have causal power?

Let us stick with the belief that it is raining. Is the reason this gives me to look for my umbrella and take it with me when I leave the house anything like a physical cause? The answer is no. There is nothing comparable to the tight fit – based on a spatio-temporal continuity – between physical events and their effects. This becomes even more evident when we think of my taking an umbrella as being the result of a *decision* that takes account of the fact that it is raining, mediated to me by my belief that it is, and which has also weighed up the bother of looking for that umbrella which seems to have an extraordinary capacity for hiding itself.

The lack of fit becomes even more obvious when we consider more radical rain-avoiding behaviour, such as deciding not to leave the house and instead curl up with a book that someone has recommended me to read. My decision to stay at home, justified by my belief that it is raining, justified in turn by the rain, is influenced by the value I place on not getting wet compared with (say) honouring a promise to see a friend whom I agreed to meet at the far end of a journey through the rain. The value I place on honouring that promise will in turn depend on many things: my assessment as to how my friend will respond to, interpret, judge, my no-show; my sense of obligation to him and how important I feel it to be not to upset him; his and my previous track record of keeping appointments; and so on. Between my being apprised that it is raining and my decision as to how to act on this there may be a process of deliberation where I identify the options, weigh them, and evaluate and compare possible futures. We are a long way from the paradigm examples of causal connections ascribed to successive events in the natural world. What is more we have exposed an assumption that is not justified even in this simple example: that propositional attitudes are not free-standing nor discrete, something to which we shall return.

I have just mentioned in passing decision-making as an element of voluntary action. It is, of course, a huge topic. Indeed, for some thinkers, decisions are the heart of agency. It is true that they draw on and feed into propositional attitudes. And they can be agonized over, embraced, altered in the light of further reflection. The paths by which we arrive at them – active recall of previous experience, the appeal to principles or to what someone else would expect, a reasoned defence of our reasons for actions, and so on – and the paths leading away from them – may be very winding indeed. They are yet another aspect of ordinary actions that place them at a distance from the flow of events as they are seen in the material world.

In the case of behavioural outputs, the lack of localization we noted in the generation of propositional attitudes such as beliefs may be even more obvious. The intended or desired action is not specified as to the physical movements it involves, even when the action is something as simple as arming myself with an umbrella. It includes (for example) reminding myself to take the item – any umbrella that is available – hunting for it, after having racked my brains as to where it might be, or having asked you if I might borrow yours, and so on. In short, the specification of the action is only that it should realize certain general characteristics, not that it should have certain definite physical characteristics.

At this point, we may run into an objection. The response by *any* organism to some physical event is not readily mapped on to the features of that event. When a dog howls for hours because someone has trodden on its paw, there is no congruity between the input and the behavioural output. This objection, however, holds up only in cases where, as in the case of the dog howling, there is no mediation by propositional attitudes. The example of the action I take in response to a shower of rain is designed to expose the fallacy of thinking of actions as being *causally* driven by propositional attitudes that are themselves the effects of the physical impact of external events on the nervous system of the agent. If this is offered as to how it came about that I took my umbrella on hearing the rain, then the disparity between the rain and the propositional attitude and between the propositional attitude and the action of taking an umbrella becomes relevant.

If the problems with the idea of actions being causally driven by propositional attitudes are evident in something as simple as taking an umbrella in response to the belief that it is raining, they are even more apparent in the case of much of the behaviour that fills our daily life. The specification of the goal can never be complete down to the last detail nor does it need to be. While elements of the goal have to be realized in some physical form – for example the displacement of my body from my home to a committee room in London where I hope to make a case for better stroke services – my attending the committee is not defined by a connected succession of physical events. You could not discern, in a physical description of the movements involved in realizing such a goal, anything of what Donald Davidson has described as "the features, consequences, actions that the agent wanted, desired, prized, held dear, thought dutiful, beneficial, obligatory, or agreeable".[40]

What is more, as we have already noted and will discuss further presently, "becausation" is embedded in a complex network of propositional attitudes. Part of this is a quasi-logical network – if you want this you must do that. In order to attend a meeting in London, I must of course go physically to London – though even this physical requirement is waived in the era of Zoom and Skype. (There remains, of course, a physical requirement – being in front of a screen.) Typically, for my views to be heard in London, those to whom I am speaking need to be in the same room as myself. But this hardly amounts to a specification of a physical outcome of a propositional attitude understood as a physical process.

There are many other reasons why to describe an action in the language of physical events – movement, momentum, charge, etc. – misrepresents its essential nature. For example, raising one's hand to vote, raising one's hand in greeting, or lifting one's flattened palm to see whether it is raining and lifting one's flattened palms to beg, may be very similar physical events but are fundamentally different actions. And, to avoid any misunderstanding, the difference between my raising my arm to vote and my raising my arm to greet is not just a question of choice of description. Descriptions in terms of physical movements and forces on the one hand and descriptions in the language of intention, wishes, are not simply two vocabularies applied externally to the same event. The difference between a physical movement and an action lies *within* the action rather than being a feature of its external surface or any putative law-governed causal connectedness. What distinguishes the two almost identical physical movements such as greeting and voting are what the agent intends to signify through them, which in turn will account for the very fact that they are happening. And those intentions are best captured through further propositional attitudes that also cannot be reduced to physical events.

Behind any given propositional attitude – intending to greet or to vote – is a vast hinterland. That hinterland has developed within a temporally deep person facing what-is-there as their world and consciously engaging with it, alone or, more typically, in conjunction with others. My voting, for example, is embedded in the larger action – which will encompass among other things my over-used journey to London – of attending a meeting where the vote will be counted. This will in turn be part of a larger project of bringing about improved stroke services.

From this it follows that, while actions may be composed of interwoven sequences of vast numbers of bodily movements, what is essential to the relations between the successive elements are not spatio-temporal connections but connected intentions. I rush to the station (Part 1) in order to catch a train (Part 2) in order to attend a meeting (Part 3) in order to persuade a committee to support a particular decision (Part 4) and so on – these elements do not stand in a relationship of cause and effect but of "in order to"; a becausation that cannot, *pace* Donaldson, be reduced to causation in any sense of the term that did not wilt in the gaze to which it was exposed in Chapter 3.

The profound heterogeneity of the various components of the action that makes it possible for me to make my views heard and count by casting a vote also underlines how spatio-temporal proximity, or relationship to a particular force field allowing influence at a distance (as when the moon's position governs the tides), are irrelevant for uniting its parts. The very notion of putting oneself into a position to be able to perform an action includes many things. They range from moving to a particular place (such as travelling to London), to "clearing the decks" in order to make time for the meeting, to acquiring a variety of skills, such as the capacity to give a persuasive presentation and creating and using the slides that will support it, that aims to be sensitive to the interests, concerns, and patience of the audience, and the knowledge and expertise upon which it is based. While I may have to be in, or in communication with, a particular room to deliver my case for improving stroke services, the strength of my presentation of my case will depend on other things – the extent to which I know what I am talking about, the fluency of my presentation, the quality of my slides, and my reading of my audience. It will be this that will determine – or so I believe – the proportion of those present who raise their hands at the crucial moment to signify their agreement with me.

The irreducibility of actions to physical events of which they are comprised is particularly obvious in the case of those actions which can be, indeed may have to be, interrupted and resumed. Or by an action is postponed to a later time, such that the intention and the realization are widely separated: "I'll sort that out tomorrow … next week … next year … when the war is over". Earmarking future dates for particular actions, drawing up a timetable to ensure that there is space for different jobs, resisting being blown off course, prioritization of tasks, regretting that the urgent has yet again driven out the truly important – all of these perfectly ordinary features of everyday activity have no place in a world sewn together by anything meant in natural science by law-governed causation. It certainly has little relation to paradigm examples of causation such as lightning causing thunder where the two elements are contiguous (or connect by a force field that permits action at a distance by bridging the gap) – where locality is all – and proportionate, such that the size of the effect may be quantitatively related to the size of the cause, allowing for dampening and amplification.[41]

Action: the holism of propositional attitudes

Beliefs, desires, fears, intentions are connected with, indeed impregnated by, or make sense only in relation to, one another. The "holism of the mental" as it is called has been flagged up by many philosophers, including Donald Davidson himself, who, notwithstanding his belief that individual mental states are identical with (presumably discrete) physical states and in the causal role of propositional attitudes, correctly argued that holism is without limit.[42] As Ned Block has expressed it, "the identity of a belief content (or the meaning of a sentence that expresses it) is determined by its place in the web of beliefs or sentences comprising a whole theory or group of theories".[43]

While this may seem an overstatement in the case of a simple singular belief such as that it is raining – though it becomes far from simple and singular when it plays a role in actions – it underlines how a given belief is part of an ever-shifting mindscape, which explains how actions, rational or irrational, make sense to the agent, how they fit into her life and understanding, and may be intelligible to any observer. And beliefs are connected not only with other beliefs but also with knowledge, reasons, intentions, hopes, goals, fears, and so on when they are implicated in agency. Even actions seemingly prompted by discrete beliefs triggered by external events are part of, and make sense only in the context of, a whole person and for this reason may indeed be detached from the immediate physical surroundings or, at least, have very little to do with them. Think of the difference between a baby being woken up by the sound of rain and crying and my deciding on hearing the same sound to cancel a planned visit. While we may seem to have discrete reasons for doing A or B, our decision to do A rather than B will depend on the different weights we grant to these reasons. These weightings in turn will depend on many other considerations informed by a sense of priorities, beliefs, desires, and so on.

The background knowledge influencing action is often quite elaborate. While the vehicles of this knowledge are physical events – spoken utterances, written statements – it is not their physical properties (the weight of the paper on which they are written, the colour of the ink, etc.) but the meanings extracted from them that count as what is transmitted and the influence they have or are intended to have. When I act in the light of knowledge, I am not responding to knowledge as a quasi-physical stimulus. When, aware that a toddler is visiting my house next week, and conscious from bitter experience also of my own absent-mindedness, I mobilize my knowledge of the toddler, of her perhaps all-too-relaxed parents, and of the fragility of glass, and remove the glass out of harm's way now ("before I forget"), the complexity of my action is not reflected in the idea that I am "responding to a stimulus" or even "a shower of stimuli" understood as inner causes in turn triggered by external causes. Although I may have been in receipt of the relevant knowledge at a particular time and place – the visit was fixed up on a phone call – its content is timeless. What is more the knowledge that informs my action – the possibility that the toddler might break the glass – has no definite spatio-temporal location. Indeed, this is the very reason that it is applicable to a range of situations in which the toddler might encounter the glass. The boundaries even of a discrete piece of knowledge about a physical state of affairs are semantic and are not tethered to a specific region of space and time. The decision to move the glass out of harm's way on catching sight of it is fundamentally different from responding to a crash with a jump. The hinterland of the decision is one of the markers of the distance between action and mere reaction.

And, of course, no piece of knowledge, or act of mobilizing a piece of knowledge, is genuinely discrete, an island unto itself. The information we receive is rooted in a terrain of the unspoken, of implicit understanding and presupposed knowledge. As with beliefs, the intentional object of knowledge – say, "London", or "a journey to London" – leaves much that is unspecified. When I go to London, I do not go to all of London and I could not anyway say what all of London was. There is a variety of ways of fulfilling the intention to go to London in this necessarily under-specified sense in order to attend a meeting. That is one of the many reasons why knowledge-guided action envisages and can be satisfied by an entire class of possible futures that can be instantiated in many different ways. As a manifestation of this, sentences describing propositional attitudes – intending-that, believing-that, knowing-that – both fall short of and exceed any kind of imaginable physical causation that might be envisaged as inimical to genuine agency: the outlines of their meaning simply fail to be congruent with the lineaments of a cause as generally understood.

The reminder that beliefs, intentions, knowledge and so on are interwoven reconnects us with our critique of neurodeterminism in Section 1.2, when we emphasized how the operation of free will in a real world is not a discrete succession of urges or pulses of willing. It is exercised in a *field* of possibilities. The field may be visible as in a landscape before us, that we intuit as seething with possibilities; it is, however, most often invisible or, indeed, insensible, being presented to us in the form of descriptions filled out with memories. Even where the field is a range of visible options, those options qualify as such only in the light of many things that are not visible. My concern for the glass that makes me move it to a safe place in anticipation of a visit from a toddler is heightened by my knowledge of the frailty of glass, how much sentimental value the items has for you, the general properties of toddlers, and the capacity of broken glass to lacerate the skin.

That propositional attitudes do not operate separately – with each making a discrete contribution – is thus a major barrier to thinking of them as causes in any sense of "cause" that has explanatory value. The holism of the mental reflects a coherence utterly unlike the manner in which the material world hangs together or appears to be organized.

Let us return to a seemingly Donaldson-friendly example of my behavioural response to becoming aware that it is raining. In order that this should result in my carrying an umbrella when I leave the house, several, perhaps many, propositional attitudes may be mobilized. I have to: know that there is an umbrella in the house; envisage my journey; assign greater positive value to my not getting wet over the hassle of searching for, finding, and carrying an umbrella – an assessment that may be altered if I think the chances of the rain easing off, or being light, are high or if I am concerned that an umbrella will be a pest in a high wind that I might also anticipate. The hope of tracking causal connectedness and causal forces through this nexus of heterogeneous but connected propositional attitudes seems even more forlorn than the hope of cashing single propositional attitudes such as beliefs into causal connections linking incoming experiences and outgoing actions.

It may seem that we are unfairly loading the dice against a causal under-standing of propositional attitudes by taking as the implicit paradigm of causation the spatio-temporally localized interaction between events, reduc-ing causation to the relationship between billiard ball. This is a criticism we have already anticipated. There are, so the criticism would run, other causal interactions that we accept as real in everyday life that are remote from such a model; for example, those that are invoked to explain the way history unfolds. Historians might tell us that a rise in chauvinist sentiment whipped up by demagogues causes wars. Such examples, however, are on the far side of the localized agency that we are talking about. Historical, social, and economic trends are built on what is established in individual and small group behaviour. Yes, voluntary individual and small group behaviour may add up to something that no-one intends; but this does not cancel – or indeed deny – the agency of the actors. The fact that my switching on an electric fire to keep me warm may inadvertently contribute to global warming does not remove the free will from my action. Explanations in history and the social sciences that are framed in the form of non-localized causation are based on a narrative "becausation" that is remote from causation as it is mobilized in scientific or common-sense accounts of what is happening in nature. The "causal mechanisms" that, for example, connect chauvinism with wars between nations are built out of the complex, entangled, connected attitudes of agents. Yes, causation may be employed in other contexts, outside of the natural world seen through the lens of natural science: in history, in economics, in everyday talk about why people behave in ways that seem surprising. As we do so, however, we drift ever further away from the authority of natural science, from mechanisms, the seeming implacable force of "causation", and the inescapability of the regular patterns of the succession of events that make actions predetermined. By the time we have reached individual human action, the notion of causation has lost any connection with the paradigm cases that seem to give the idea of causal connection any kind of sense, even if the Humean, empiricist critique is not accepted.

So we can acknowledge that the idea of causation is deployed in contexts that extend far beyond billiard balls banging into each other or other push-and-shove examples but it is not clear how much explanatory force "causation" then retains. Our critique of the supposed causal relationship within voluntary behaviour between external events, experiences, propositional attitudes, and actions, is to demonstrate that little – indeed, nothing – is retained, even if there were any in the first place.

Causation understood counterfactually might seem to fare better. I would not have formed the belief that it is raining had it not been (physically, actually) raining. Nor would I have decided to take my umbrella. Or (to take a statistical view of causation) I might have been less likely to have formed that belief on a dry day or to have sought out my umbrella. As we saw in Chapter 3, however, counterfactual and statistical theories of causation seem to empty the notion of the essential idea of material necessitation; in short of anything that embeds actions in a causal nexus where events are glued to their predecessors or are pushed by them into being. Counterfactual causes such as "not watering the flowers" are non-events that belong to the realm of possibility rather than that of nature.

If causation fails to capture the becausation of actions that are as seemingly straightforward as responding to the belief that it is raining, what of other propositional attitudes that play into the holistic mix that is the mental state of agents? It is easy to overlook the complexity of the different kinds of relationships between desires, beliefs, intentions and reasons. While there are problems with seeing any of these as causes of actions, some are even more remote than others. Wishes, as the saying goes, are not horses, but desires at least seem to have the shadow of an "oomph" that is lacking in (relatively) abstract reasons. Indeed, those that are closest to appetites, while not identical with or reducible to physiological events (such as rapid heartbeats), do seem more red-blooded, and to have one foot in a place occupied by the agent's flesh as a source of force. While reasons may justify the movements that comprise actions – or connect parts of actions with other parts – they do not seem to drive them. The hotter propositional attitudes, may therefore seem to have more oomph. Nevertheless, they grow in a medium of something paler, such as reasons. Lichtenberg's joking observation that he often grew angry "on his own advice" is a reminder of the extent to which reflection shapes our attitudes, chooses those we acknowledge, embrace and approve of or resist, and regulates their expression in action. While reason may often be the slave of passions, passions are not infrequently stoked up by reasons. And we frequently ignore our passions because our reasons insist that we fry other fish. I don't abandon my hurry to catch the train to London in order to have a time-consuming blazing row with someone who has jumped ahead of me in a queue for a coffee.

As for the reasons we may have, or believe we have, for our actions, their difference from anything that could be described as physical events with causal powers and connections as they are traditionally described is reflected in the extent to which the propositional component of propositional attitudes may be separated from any emotional directedness towards a goal. While "the heart has its reasons that reason knows nothing of", reason has its rationale that is often closer to the space of logic than the chambers of the heart. At any rate, it does not seem qualified to carry out the double duty of justifying the action – making it what it is as the realization of a goal – and of being a physical cause making a physical event happen; of ensuring both the why and the how.[44] Reasons, in short, even when they are instantiated in a token thought that occurs at a particular time, do not seem like material events that could bring about other material events such as the movement of the arm in voting.

It is also worth reflecting on what we might call background, or continuant mental states such as being irritated, angry, jumpy, afraid, bored, outraged, cheerful, smug, content, or well-disposed. Whether they count as propositional attitudes or as the medium in which propositional attitudes are brewed or, again, as modulators of other attitudes is a question to which there is no strict answer. For example, they may or may not have definite intentional objects. I may be bored period – so that I find everything boring – or I may be bored with a lecture. Contrary to the claims of philosophers such as John Searle, even such states of mind have intentionality. Irritation, nervousness, boredom and so on may support an intentionality that butterflies from object to object; or they modulate the way the intentional object is experienced. I mention this only as further support for the general point that propositional attitudes are extraordinarily complex and interwoven and they are not reducible to anything we would recognize as causes with a *point d'appui*.

We typically designate propositional attitudes as "that"-clauses: "I thought that", "intended that", "feared that", etc. Something more subtle, however, is needed to do them justice, capturing what they are at a particular time, their rapid succession over time, and their co-presence at any time. What prompts us to storm out of a meeting or sheepishly zephyr back into it is not reducible to anything captured by single propositions. The causal status of propositional attitudes is further undermined when we acknowledge that their triggers and intentional objects may not correspond to anything "out there". Action, as we discussed in the previous section, is inspired by possibilities – by the not-yet existent. Imagination, giving birth to beliefs, expectations, etc., is a pervasive, necessary, though admittedly often unreliable presence in the mind of the agent.

The abstract face of intentions, reasons, and so forth further undermines the notion that they are, or even requisition, a discrete portion of kinetic or other energy. Their force is argumentative or persuasive and is carried through their general meaning or significance. They have a purchase on the agent only insofar as she classifies her present situation and the desirable way forward as being of such and such a nature. Without this, nothing in a reason as some-thing articulated or potentially articulated to one's self would deliver a direc-tion of travel. If this does not seem as obvious as it should, it may be because we use metaphorical terms such as "motivation", "motive" or "motivating con-siderations" to herd reasons into an enclosure shared with other more clearly energetic entities such as emotions.

There is a dimension of the propositional attitudes that we have not touched on but we should not ignore; indeed, it deserves much more than the passing glance of a paragraph. It is the hierarchical relationship between them.[45] I may wish to have a coffee on the train but decide not to because the last time I did so I spilt coffee on my keyboard and I rate the risk of doing this higher than the anticipation of pleasure that ignites my desire for a coffee. Or, noticing that I am passing through Watford, conclude that there is insufficient time to buy, transport and consume a coffee, before pulling into the station. I prioritize getting to my meeting and doing what I had set out to London to do over having a coffee and, anyway, risking burning my mouth as a result of drinking it in a rush.

These are small-scale but telling manifestations of the coherence or integ-rity of the self who hosts propositional attitudes and resists what would count as getting blown off what she decides is her course, her chosen path, the day's schedule. The prioritization and comparative valuation of the objects of prop-ositional attitudes is central to our agency and to a life that is not merely a succession of responses to events, a pinballing through our days. This hier-archy of wishes is a manifestation of something wider: our regulation of the propositional attitudes that prompt and guide our actions – exemplified in how we reject or endorse desires, test our beliefs, and set out in advance to acquire knowledge that we feel may be of value.

When we think of the mélange of thoughts and feelings, sentences and memories and emotions, of momentary reflections and longer-lasting states of mind that unfold in the stream of consciousness, "holism" sounds too polite or tidy a term. The extent to which the pell-mell of successive moments of the mind is disconnected from, as well as connected with, action is often over-looked. Out of the torrent of reasons, beliefs, hopes, fragments of knowledge, only a minute proportion are acted upon immediately or in the longer term rather than merely hosted. We do not, in this sense, take the most of our mental contents seriously enough to translate them into action. We dismiss some of them as silly and much else as merely idle. The idea of a cause that would have its effect only if it were taken seriously either by itself or by its material context reminds us how far we are away from any use of the notion of "cause" in respect of propositional attitudes that account for actions.

Action: the holism of the physical

As we have seen in the case of Donald Davidson, it is possible for philosophers to acknowledge the holism of the mental and still to adhere to a causal account of agency and stick with the claim that propositional attitudes such as reasons, beliefs and desires, themselves caused by external events, are the causes of actions. To reinforce my argument against this view, I want to switch attention from the holism of mental states to that of actions.

It will be clear from what was said earlier, that actions are not simply iso-lated events or isolated chains of events. Just as their reasons are not defined by discrete events with clear-cut spatio-temporal boundaries so what counts as their desired outcomes, as fulfilling our intentions, are likewise not speci-fiable as events with clear-cut spatio-temporal boundaries. For example, my going to London to attend a meeting to change a committee's mind and its public position on, say, the appropriate care of stroke patients has as its *raison d'etre* something that does not have the lineaments of a physical event, though any realization of it may incorporate a vast number of events that are brought together. The goal it is intended to fulfil is not usefully described as an event, or a determinate collection of events, if by "event" is meant something analogous to an occurrence that takes its place among other physical events such as the fall of a stone or the rising of the sun.

To develop this point, it might seem more helpful to examine separately (a) the background to my action of going down to London for the meeting; (b) the action itself; and (c) the goal to which it is directed – though for reasons that tell us something about the unique nature of action, it is impossible to disentangle these three holisms. Unlike prior causes, the background that permeates the beliefs, wishes, reasons, etc. will explain my particular trajectory on the day I go to London for the meeting. Those background beliefs, etc., unlike causes, will also define what counts as the arrival at my goal and hence as the intended effect of my action. This overarching "super-holism" highlights what is distinctive, indeed unique, about voluntary activity. Nevertheless, I will endeavour separately to tease out some holisms relevant to my action.

The myriads of events and circumstances that are in the background of my going to the meeting, will encompass such nebulous – but real – items as my objective professional responsibilities, and my take on what those responsibilities require of me, expressed in my desire to shape medical policies. The trip to London, therefore, and my attending and speaking at the meeting, draw upon large numbers of experiences (including many actions) in my own and others' past that make sense of my present concerns, and go some way towards explaining my wish to pursue them at this meeting, and my capacity to do so.

That background also permeates and shapes the actions outside of my trip to London that I count as belonging to an ordinary day's work as a doctor. From it, I could pick out numerous propositional attitudes that justify those actions and, what is more, keep them active and connected over several hours of that day in London and over the days in which I prepared for this meeting. Those reasons, etc. would justify my attention, concern, and efforts being directed away from many of the events that I encounter en route to, and in, the meeting room prior to my securing the committee decision I seek. Throughout the day, a tentacular network of in-order-tos will downgrade my surroundings into a mere substrate for my actions. My surroundings will be populated with items that will be classified as irrelevant to the narrative of my attending the meeting. This notwithstanding, I will always have to be prepared to respond to occurrences only peripherally relevant to my aim – such as avoiding oncoming cars, greeting other members of the committee, engaging in small talk, including sympathizing with someone's bad luck, or declining the offer of a cup of coffee in case I am taken short when I need to present my arguments. The brushwood either side of my chosen path includes the many incidental occurrences that arise out of the material world that continues on its broad front, faithful to its habits, as I stick to the straight and narrow of realizing my intentions – though the straightest line that connects my present circumstances with a distant goal may be very winding. The selectivity of my attention and of my responses to events is a reflection of the complex interconnectedness of the various propositional attitudes that are implicated in my day trip.

What is more, the process and outcome of my action – my trip to London and the responses to those responding to me at the meeting – will necessarily have many physical effects and social consequences, large and small, that are not intended and do not count as part of my achieved goal. I will, for example, add to the crowdedness of the train; my footfall will echo in the building where the meeting takes place and perhaps distract someone in an office that I pass; my shadow may be cast on the pavement; I may annoy a stranger by not catching what he said when he asks me the time. The shadow of my pen dancing across my page, the creak of the seat as I lean forward, will remind me that my chosen path is abuzz with unchosen consequences of my steps along it. And consequences will ripple out from these unchosen events which have no bearing on whether my wish has been fulfilled and my meeting is a success.

So much for the background to the day's work and the path to completing it. What of the goal, that which I would have given as the reason for my action, to which my hopes and desires are directed? That this can be summarized in a sentence: "I wanted to get the committee to agree to support improved stroke services" is deceptive. Unlike the sentence, the material actualization of the goal is not discrete or in any sense sharp-edged. The committee's agreement to my proposal is not defined by the physical properties – just as my journey to London is not just the displacement of a human body from A to B. Moreover, the realization of a possibility that I want to see actualized cannot be specified solely in terms of a particular arrangement of the material world being reached at a particular time or a particular place. The obverse of this is that a wide range of physical states of affairs could count as a realization of my goal though none of them alone could count as this achievement.

The lack of a purely physical definition of the goal of an action follows in part from the fact that propositional attitudes envisage goals as possibilities and possibilities are necessarily general. Even if the committee's decision depended on something as specific as a show of hands, the posture of the hands, exactly when they are raised and in what order, and any incidental material events such as the shadows cast by the raised arms, are irrelevant. It may be that, because of a fire alarm, we have to move to another building to finish the meeting so any hand-raising takes place outside of the room that was scheduled for the meeting. Nevertheless, the goal would still be achieved. Likewise, if the Chair decided that, in view of the disruption caused by the fire alarm, members of the committee could send their votes in by post, my intention could still be fulfilled but through different physical events. And the goal could be achieved in many other ways; for example, the Chair agreeing that the committee should support my proposal but giving anyone who (on second thoughts) disagrees, the opportunity to write in to oppose what I have suggested. The physical features of the event or events that constitute the goal would not be ill-defined, even irrelevant, if what was to be achieved was an outcome defined in purely material terms, as would be the effect of a material cause.[46]

It is worth noting at this juncture that the outcome – a majority of attendees at the meeting signaling support for my proposals – may be arrived at by an extremely circuitous route. I may in advance circulate position papers and make phone calls and send emails to those who have voting rights to persuade them of my case. The physical content of these actions, their timing, and the order in which they take place, will reflect the opportunities that are available to me to communicate with those whom I wish to encourage to support my case. My judgement as to the availability of the recipients of my canvassing and when I might be least likely to get an unsympathetic hearing will influence the timing of my actions. I won't, for example, phone any of my fellow committee members at a time when they might be watching the final episode of *Line of Duty*. Thus, the path to the apparently simple goal of achieving a majority of hands raised in support of the motion. Appearances, of course, deceive, because the raised hands deliver what is wanted only because they are signs whose meanings are dependent on a vast, largely unstated, hinterland of shared meanings and human purposes.

The absence of a physical specification of the goal envisaged in a propositional attitude that informs an action is even more striking when we consider ultimate, as opposed to intermediate, goals. Behind my wish to get the committee to agree to supporting the improvement of stroke services is a vision of what those improved stroke services might be. They would encompass better prevention, timelier and more effective treatment, and comprehensive, high-calibre rehabilitation services. There is no way such an outcome, and the manner in which its countless elements fit together, could be specified in physical terms, though they would have to be realized in physical events: "improved stroke services" does not correspond solely to an altered distribution of mass and energy in a specified quarter of space-time. The verso of this recto is that there is a multitude of ways in which the elements of such services could be successfully delivered to patients. The philosopher's cherished notion of "multiple realizations" hardly cuts it. And what that realization consists of coheres in ways that are not seen outside of the human world.

The nearest neighbour to the agreement of the committee to my proposal is not something physically close to it – for example, the next event that takes place in the room, such as everyone helping themselves to coffee or the increasing sound of the rush-hour traffic. Rather it is the disagreement of the committee; or perhaps an agreement by a narrower or wider margin than proved to be the case. In short, its neighbourliness in this context belongs not to the space of nature but to the space of reasons[47] – more specifically to the space of (shared) propositional attitudes. Items in that space are not connected in the way that items in the material world are connected; or even in the way that material items are disconnected, as the clouds floating outside the window while I type this are disconnected from the sound of typing.

While Davidson correctly acknowledged the holism of the mental, he did not fully appreciate its significance and its fatal consequences for any causal theory of action since action, too, is holistic.[48] One important aspect of this holism is that it does not make sense to think of propositional attitudes occurring at a certain time. It would be rather odd to say such things as that "My intention came on at 4 pm and lasted for two days". This hardly fits, for example, my intention to persuade the committee to change its position on campaigning for better stroke management. It is equally ill-fitting for something less high-flown, such as my intention to take a holiday sometime next summer. Desires reduced to simple appetites may have a time of switching on and switching off, though the desire may not pervade or be present as a driving force in all the steps necessary for its satisfaction. They are not of course reducible to appetites. (While I may desire that such-and-such may be the case, I do not appetite *that*. Desires narrate themselves, observe themselves, and connect with other propositional attitudes in the way that biological appetites do not.) Other propositional attitudes – hopes, fears, and thinking that such and such is the case – do not have clear start and finish times.[49]

The returning ghost of determinism

The reason for emphasizing – perhaps labouring – the distinctive nature of actions is to lift them beyond the reach of any physical causal explanation and to discredit the notion that mental events such as propositional attitudes are causal intermediaries linking inputs into an agent with her outputs of action.

Many who are committed to such an explanation identify propositional attitudes with sets of brain events. If it could accommodate the distinctive features of propositional attitudes, this way of understanding actions would do determinists' work for them. It would obliterate the fundamental difference between actions and other happenings in the natural world. Reducing "becausation" to common-or-garden causation would reinsert actions into the causally closed physical world. The essential step is to identify propositional attitudes with brain states.

Davidson does this, asserting that, since all events are physical, "Mental events are identical with physical events".[50] Acknowledging the difficulty of accommodating events such as propositional attitudes in a physicalist world picture, he tries to get round this by arguing for what he called anomalous monism. According to this position, individual, token mental events are identical with individual, token physical events. A particular episode of a particular belief is realized in a particular pattern of neural activity. This token identity notwithstanding, there are no psycho-physical laws connecting the mental and physical realms. We should not expect every instance of a particular belief to be realized in the same pattern of neural activity. Hence the "anomalous" (not law-bound) nature of his identification of mental events with physical events in the brain.[51]

Davidson's central claim that what makes a mental event identical to a physical event is that the mental event also has a physical description seems wrong. If the physical description in question is of a pattern of neural activity, then the intentionality of mental entities such as propositional attitudes is unexplained. This would be true even if propositional attitudes did not have additional awkward features we have discussed – for example, their holistic connectedness and the lack of physical specification of their intentional objects.[52] Neither an intention nor its goal is defined in space and time in the way that a set of neural discharges must be defined in space and time. As we discussed in the Overture, being *about* anything such as an event or a material object, seems to lie beyond the reach of any physical event; but to have the aboutness of a propositional attitude seems to be even further beyond its reach. Neural discharges are inside the skull (spatial location) and last a certain period of time (temporal location) that could be measured by the clock. This is entirely different from that which prompts, justifies, rationalizes actions which are defined by envisaged possibilities that are not spatio-temporally circumscribed or in other ways defined by physical parameters.

Denying that mental contents such as propositional attitudes are causes in any sense of the term used in other contexts, has the additional advantage of avoiding the so-called "exclusion problem", which troubles philosophers who accept that mental and physical entities are different.[53] The exclusion problem arises when "philosophers want to say both that everything is determined by the physical, and that certain mental entities cannot be identified with any physical entities. The problem is to make these two assumptions compatible with the causal efficacy of the mental. The concern is that this physicalist picture of the world leaves no space for the causal efficacy of anything non-physical. The physical, as it is sometimes said, *excludes* anything non-physical from doing 'any work'".[54]

A popular way of dealing with this problem is to assert that mental entities are "constituted by", or "realized in", physical entities.[55] Does this justify ascribing additional causal powers to events in virtue of their being mental as well as physical? If it does seem to justify invoking such double causal powers is this owing to the slippery nature of terms such as "realize". The meaning of the term is typically unpacked using the example of a lump of clay that is also a statue: the statue is *realized* in clay. This single item can thus be legitimately thought of as two items with different causal properties. While the lump of clay may have effects – casting a shadow, being heavy to lift, blocking the view of what is behind it – due to its physical properties, the statue has quite different effects due to its aesthetic properties – giving pleasure, prompting admiration.

Not so fast. This apparent duality of causal power is possible only in virtue of someone assuming more than one viewpoint on the object: to be two objects it has to be recognized in two ways. It is not two objects for another piece of clay with which it is interacting or for a slug crawling over it or even for a human being with agnosia. In the absence of a conscious subject, it has only one set or type of material interactions. Any multiplicity of viewpoints on a single item must be downstream of, indeed presuppose, consciousness. Without consciousness, there are no viewpoints or descriptions, never mind more than one viewpoint on or description of a given item. The lump of clay/statue analogy does not, in short, explain how a physical process such as a shower of neural discharges generating other neural discharges could also be a conscious experience such as a belief having the consequences a belief may have.

The endeavour to make propositional attitudes more respectable as "real" entities by identifying them with neural activity in the brain therefore fails. Which is a good thing from the point of view of anyone for whom intentions and beliefs and the like are the clue to true agency. If they were identical with nerve impulses, they would have no causal power except insofar as they were physical entities and that power, if it amounted to anything, would simply be the inherited power of effects of extra-cranial physical causes. Any supposed mental aspect of brain activity would seem to be a causal passenger and bring nothing new to the party. Actions, notwithstanding that they seem to be situated by reasons and other propositional attitudes in the life of an agent, would be happenings like any other. There would be no fundamental difference between my walking down the stairs on the first leg of my journey to London to persuade my colleagues to support national standards for stroke services and my falling down the stairs by accident.

All of this would be true even if the very idea of causal efficacy were not problematic; if it were not something that is invoked by a mind projecting a sense of necessity into a material world. It will be recalled that in Chapter 3 I radicalized this Humean critique of causation and argued that – irrespective of whether causal connectivity is seen as "oomph" or as "glue" – any connectedness it delivers repairs discontinuities opened up by the conscious subject "smithereening" a continuum into fragments, fragments whose independence, whose borders, are consolidated by descriptions. To apply the notion of causation as a means of connecting elements of the mind such as propositional attitudes to each other or to the physical world is therefore inappropriate. Causal connectedness is downstream, rather than upstream, of the mind. It is created in the mind. The failure of mental items to have their own causal powers is not a lack; rather it is a reflection of the mental origin of the very idea of causal connectedness, irrespective of whether it is conceived as glue or oomph.

This is why it is a simplification to locate the difference between mere happenings and genuine actions in the distinction between events whose (physical) causes push from behind and events whose (mental) causes – possibilities entertained in propositional attitudes – that pull from in front. We can now see that the contrast is misleading because it places physical causes and mental entities such as reasons on a comparable footing, though the difference between a push from the past and a pull from the feature captures some aspect of the difference between events that merely happen and actions that are performed. Events that have not yet happened, states of affairs that have not yet come into being, do not have any influence, even less a specific influence, on the material world but the idea of them is central to action.[56] Actions owe their character and the direction in which they unfold to the *possibilities* of states of affairs that are located in an as yet non-existent future. Nevertheless, it is grossly simplifying. Behind the distinction between the push-from-behind of ordinary happenings and the pull-from-in-front of "becausation" – energized by motivations and the unfolding intentions and reason arising out of them – of voluntary actions is something much more profound than (say) any putative difference between physical and mental causations. While humans may have to deploy brute mechanical force to lift the building blocks of a temple, the construction is driven by the idea of the completed building and, behind this, its function as a place of worship. That driver is in no way comparable to any putative causal influence – push or pull – supposedly delivered by nature and its forces.

Where the buck starts: beginnings and endings

It is time to reintroduce another feature of actions: *initiation*. It is true that, once we are embarked on actions, we are – inasmuch as we are material bodies – subject to the habits of nature and the democracy of material interactions: things we push against push back against us, though their reactions are entirely innocent of any intention, even the intention to frustrate us or to make us work to achieve our goals. But the origin of those visible actions is not to be found in some quasi-causal ancestry.

Indeed, there are no starting points in the unfolding of the natural world, whether or not its successive states are causally glued. The true source of our actions is to be found elsewhere than what is already in place: we are genuine initiators because, as we discussed in Section 4.2, our actions realize possibilities *we* have entertained, possibilities that nature has neither entertained nor would, without our involvement, actualize.

It is this that lies behind our capacity to elevate moments in time and their associated states of affairs to the status of beginnings and endings – beginnings, which mark the start of journeys large and small, linked to endings that are ends in the sense of goals – in a universe that is continuous and ongoing and has no beginning after the Big Bang and no ending before the Big Crunch. Our actions, with their beginnings, are in this respect unlike mere successions of material events, whose individual elements do not have the status of first and subsequent steps. And, while the material consequences of our actions – as of any physical events – are endless, the realizations of our intentions have endings defined by those of its consequences that count as the fulfilment of their envisaged goal.

The sense of the beginning, the middle, and the end, of starts, stops, and the ongoing, of interruptions and resumptions, and of the arrival, shapes, defines, and pervades actions. Our waking hours are a cauldron of initiations, continuations, and conclusions. This fundamental character of our lives is sometimes obscured since, at any given moment, we may be initiating one action, be part way through another, and nearing the end of a third. The different timescales of our actions, obliges us to be multi-taskers: getting dressed, checking our diaries for the day's engagements, clearing up a misunderstanding, planning a new project, studying for a profession, saving up for one's old age may all be happening at once, though they have different timeframes. Training to be a doctor does not require one to be so single-minded as not to be able to focus on finishing a meal.

What counts as a beginning is not defined physically, even though an action may have a physical beginning. Take something as simple as going for a walk.

Before the first step, there is the journey to the starting place; before this, there is the getting ready; before this getting dressed; before this getting out of bed; before this, waking up in response to a pre-set alarm. And yet we still see the first step of the walk as a beginning.

Beginnings, that is to say, are stipulated. Likewise, endings. Both are defined by an implicit or explicit goal or goals. To some extent this fundamental truth about the action-based nature of beginnings and endings – and their absence in the material world in which actions are performed – is concealed by narrative. "Yesterday, I went for a walk" gives the action misleadingly sharp edges, offsetting it from all that is happening before, after, and during it, as if there were no need to account for the sense of a beginning. Indeed, the reason why we enjoy narratives so much is not only because they have defined beginnings and ends but because those limits are not blurred and the elements between are illuminated by the glow from both limits. I am tempted to say that "In the beginning – and the end – of agency was the word"; or two words – the words "beginning" and "end".[57]

In daily life, outside the realm of story-telling, there is a mixing of actions and other events that provide their context and ripple out from them as incidental consequences. Consider my going to my car to fetch an item I had left in it. The elements include: (a) my walk to the car; (b) the sound emitted by the gravel under my feet; and (c) the passage of a cloud overhead. The first is a genuine action. The second is an unintended consequence of my action. The last has nothing to do with me or my action. All are events that seem to be physically connected but the latter two are defined by those physical connections while the first one is not: it occurs in virtue of a rational choice, a preference for one outcome rather than another. It is a passage from a beginning to an end. Even so, our voluntary actions are cast into an ongoing world that is largely indifferent to them. As Rogers Albritton has expressed it "What we propose to do is up to us, if our wills are free. But what the world will make of what we do is, of course, up to the world"[58] – at least, to some extent. Our stories surface out of, float in, and disappear into, storyless chaos.

The simplicity of our chosen example of walking to the car is deceptive. Our initiations enter a sea of ongoing activities that are at different distances from their hoped-for destinations. Any action has to hold itself together not only in the face of unfolding nature, natural noise, but in a seething medium of volition – our own and that of others. And it exploits the sedimented shared agency expressed in institutions and has given rise to the multiplicity of artefacts large and small (buildings, roads, clothes, knives and forks), of standing possibilities of action, that pave our passage from beginnings to ends.

In more complex actions, there are relays of beginnings and ends, chains of "in order to" – with a multitude of routines and sub-routines. As the chains get longer, so the journey of the agent towards her goal, realized in physical events, deviates ever more widely from anything that can be described in term of the physical characteristics of those physical events. Its trajectory parts company from the sequences of events that surround it in a world left to itself.[59]

Concluding thoughts

Actions are conceived, shaped and guided, and modified in a virtual world of possible futures whose origin is in the intentionality – individual and shared – of human consciousness. This is the space from which agents are able to exploit what they know of the world to serve their ends and, where necessary, to exploit the habits of nature to shape the direction of some events. They do so, of course, without needing to break those habits in exploiting them or in getting into a position to do so: the outside-of-nature from which the habits are exploited is the same as that from which nature was manipulated to uncover its habits as the laws of science.

Reasons and other propositional attitudes are a key part of that outside. To see them merely as intermediary physical or quasi-physical causes between an input of experience and an output of action is to lose the distinction between actions and other happenings; to make an agent a mere conduit; and to reduce the exercise of free will to the operation of a mechanism. In short, to remove any possibility of agents deflecting the course of events and being in an impor-tant sense the source of that deflection.

In order to accommodate the possibility of genuine agency we have to accept that the laws of science, which look past the conscious subject in order to arrive at an objective image of the natural world, are not the last word on all that there is and how things happen. There is, in short, room for events – actions – that exploit the habits of nature. And those actions, most strikingly, include those that enabled us to reveal the laws of science or, pre-scientifically, to see how "the world" or nature "works".

CHAPTER 5

The human agent

5.1 ALTERNATIVE CANDIDATES FOR A CAUSAL PARTNERSHIP UNDERPINNING AGENCY

Final dismantling of event-causation of action

It will be obvious from the previous chapter that any "causes" I mobilize to bring about "effects" that count as the goal of my action will not be discrete spatio-temporal stretches of happening such as those who have a realist view of causes imagine are served up by the physical world innocent of the intentions of agents. Crucially, the goals of successful actions will not be defined in terms of their physical properties – which is the other side of the fact that intentions can be realized in a multitude of ways. There is no satisfactory physical description of the fulfilment of an intention to go to London to make the case for improving stroke services, let alone a unique or definitive one.

This is signalled from the beginning. In the initial conditions that we set off from to our goal, we exploit events and states of affairs that we single out in relation to a *situation* which demands something of us in order that we shall achieve what our interests require of us or (more tellingly) we require of ourselves. This situation transcends discrete, demarcated events that tradition and common sense classify as causes and even their surrounding conditions; indeed, what brings about our actions is not something that weaves itself out of material events. Where there is a so-called cause of our action, it figures as an *opportunity* which, notwithstanding its physical reality, is gathered up or unified by an idea, a unification that is delivered in part by a future possibility equally defined by an idea.

In short, nothing essential to voluntary activity is captured in the idea of material responses to material stimuli, in which the former are discrete physical effects of the latter understood as discrete physical causes. Replacing "material causes" by "mental causes" does not help in the slightest for reasons set out in our previous discussion of propositional attitudes.

Of course, there are some elements of human behaviour that seem to be mere responses to stimuli understood as biologically mediated causes – as when I withdraw my foot having stood on a sharp object, duck as a missile comes towards me, jump at a loud bang, or absent-mindedly scratch an itch. Even such primitive responses may, however, be entangled with higher-order considerations. I may resist scratching an itch if it is in an embarrassing place until I have an opportunity to do it discretely. Or I may disguise a response. When I was a child, I used to develop a stitch when hurriedly walking to school too soon after breakfast. I felt embarrassed to stop and wait for the pain to pass, so I would pretend to be sorting out my shoelaces, tying and untying them until the stitch passed.

As agents, we do not typically begin from a standing, or single, start. At any given moment in our lives, *nous sommes embarqués* – on a multitude of voyages in a fleet of vessels of different sizes. We wake up in the morning with a to-do list, and our days are already pre-filled with tasks, duties, responsibilities, and plans for work and pleasure. Our volitions grow out of the immediate and long-term results of other volitions. For this and other reasons, unlike material causes, beliefs, desires and other propositional attitudes that set goals are not therefore events occurring at time t_1 or even standing states enduring from t_1 to t_2.

Our engagement with the world, and the platform from which our engagement takes its rise, is therefore on, and from, too broad a front to be spoken of in causal terms where causes are understood as events. The link between what happens and what I am prompted to do in response to it is nothing like the thin, linear trickle of "Event A causes Event B causes Event C". This is on top of the fact that events do not have the capacity to assume the role of a beginning and independently to shape what succeeds them.

At any rate, our discussion has taken us a long way away from an event-causal chain where something in the environment (a rain shower) causes a propositional attitude (a belief that it is raining) which in turn causes an action (to take an umbrella). This model does not fit even relatively simple actions. Supposing I want to nail together two things that have fallen apart. I may have to go to the chandlers to buy the right kind of nails and this will depend on my setting aside time to make the journey, and identifying a space in a nearby street to park my car. I will need to mobilize my knowledge of the location and stock of different kinds of shops. Finding the hammer may involve racking my brains as to when I last used it – or when someone else last used it – to determine where it is likely to be located.

Employing a hammer is a straightforward example of events generated by an agent – or if they occur spontaneously, requisitioned opportunistically – to use as handles that manipulate the world. But it also reminds us that even events transformed from spontaneous, mindless occurrences to handles are caught up in a complex network of agency.[1] The scale and direction of our attention will highlight and bring together the relevant elements in our surroundings. They will not be defined in terms of their physical properties or spatio-temporal location. The hammer in the kitchen is more closely linked within agency to the nails thought to be in the chandler's shop and the broken fence that is to be repaired than to the kitchen drawer in which it is presently hiding from my gaze. Of course, scaling up and down, and directing and re-directing, our attention are not events on all fours with the events and objects that are thus picked out as the mediators of our agency. (Appendix B examines the role of attention and our control of our own attention in the exercise of free will.)

Alternatives to event-causation of action

All this notwithstanding, philosophers who accept the reality of free will may still be reluctant to abandon the belief that actions, and what is achieved through them, are the law-governed effects of prior causes. The idea may be dead but it won't lie down, perhaps because the alternative – actions being somehow outside of a putative nexus of causation – may seem like magic thinking. And it may seem inconsistent. If my raising my hand in order to vote cannot be seen as the effect of causes – of, for example, reasons understood as causes – is it not a bit rich to expect that action to have its desired effects – at the very least that the teller should see my vote? There is more work to be done, therefore, to unlock the tenacious hold that the idea of law-governed causation has on the initiation of action and, indeed, to abolish causal talk altogether from the philosophy of action, though it may still have a (non-metaphysical) place in the legal and moral allocation of blame. And, indeed, in the discourses of plumbers and neurosurgeons, as Smart sniffily suggested.

Some philosophers look to something plumper to capture the nature of our agency in action, connecting means with ends. It seems to demand something more weighty than material events to be the initiators, continuers, and concluders of actions. That something has to have the capacity to host a multi-dimensional parish-wide unfolding *gestalt*, that gathers up distant and disconnected places and distant and disconnected times.

Leaving aside the problems with the very idea of causation as either the transmission of oomph between discrete events or as an adhesive, binding together discrete events, could other kinds of causal partners deliver something closer to the reality of agency?

Object-causation

There is no shortage of candidates of items plumper than discrete events on offer in the philosophical literature. Front-runners include states of affairs, properties, and material objects or portions of stuff. We can set aside states of affairs – successive slices through the world or relevant parts of the world. They do not seem to have the wherewithal to gather themselves together and act as one. Their status as unitary items is clearly dependent on the viewpoint of a subject and the scale and direction of her attention; to depend on the synthetic activity of a mind.

What then of objects as causes – items that occupy a certain quantity of space over a certain period of time?[2] They seem to have one clear advantage over events: namely that they are self-standing.[3] Unlike events, they do not rely on anything else in order to exist. A clap of thunder, for example, requires air and ears to be heard; a collision of billiard balls requires billiard balls. By contrast sticks and stones and indeed billiard balls simply *are*. Moreover, the status of objects as single, coherent entities, again unlike that of events (and *a fortiori* states of affairs) is apparently inbuilt. They seem to have a natural unity, courtesy of their continuous boundary. By contrast, an event such as a rumble of thunder or even a collision between billiard balls may seem to be self-bounded in time but does not have a space of its own, even though we could say where it took place. And even the temporal limits are not intrinsic to many events. After all, the duration of a rumble of thunder depends on the presence of, and the sharpness of the ears, of hearers. And there is no point at which we can regard the vibrations that constitute a thunder clap to have been sufficiently dissipated. And this lack of intrinsic boundaries is even more obvious in the case of events such as a war or a bout of depression. What unity such events have is due not to an enclosing border but to a description that freezes an item of attention so that it seems to have a stability comparable to that of an object.

Objects, therefore, seem the least unpromising alternatives to events, particularly as agents are, in some respect identical with objects; namely, in virtue of their bodies or parts of them. When I bowl a ball, there is a sense in which my body bowls a ball. When I play the piano, my fingers, supported by my arms, my trunk, and my head, play the piano. This is taken quite literally by some philosophers. For example, Quine: "We can say of John's body not only that it broke a leg, but that it thinks it sees how to prove Fermat's Last Theorem".[4]

This example, however, reduces the idea of agents as object-causes to absurdity. One would like to know whether it was all or part of John's body that was engaging in higher mathematics and, if only a part, which part. The standard answer (alas!) would be a certain part of John's brain but that item, standing alone, would not engage with the realm where the very question of proving Fermat's Last Theorem arises. It is equally absurd to ascribe thoughts (or indeed any propositional attitudes) either to all of the body or to part of it. Thinking seems to belong to the first-person not to something that has a third-person, or no-person, status. And this exclusion applies to all objects, whether or not they are human bodies.

So while body-as-object-cause is encouragingly plumper than, say, propositional attitudes, it seems to have the wrong kind of plumpness to fill the role of being the cause of action. Besides, there is another reason for resisting the general idea of object-causation and it will take us to the heart of the nature of voluntary action.

In the material world, an entire object could not be involved in the causation of any particular event. Take an example that should be particularly friendly to the idea of objects as causes: the collision between billiard balls. There are properties of the balls that are relevant to what happens in, and as a result of, the collision, and that are not localized within only parts of the balls – for example mass (to which all parts of the ball contribute) or velocity (with respect to which all parts of the ball are as one). But there are other properties, such as colour, which are irrelevant to the effect. And there are intermediate properties that are only partly involved. The elasticity of the balls is key to the transmission of momentum from one to the other. It need not necessarily be uniformly distributed over the surface of the ball, while it is only the elasticity of those parts of the surfaces actually involved in the collision that determines what happens.

There is a deeper problem with the notion of an entire object counting as the cause of an event: it is the principle of proportionality. If the whole of an object, rather than an event in which it is engaged, is a cause, we might expect something more than an event to be its effect. Perhaps even an entire object. This is clearly not possible, otherwise every cause would result in an effect that was the replication of the material involved in the cause. The universe would be a universal 3D printer. This unwelcome consequence – that effects, too, are objects – would also follow from the fact that effects in their turn become causes: and having become causes, they, too, must be object-causes generating objects as their effects.

This argument from a principle of proportionality may be resisted. After all, non-linear effects are seen in certain circumstances: a small change in initial conditions may, if the circumstances are right, result in a vast difference in outcomes. This, however, does not match the kind of difference we are concerned about here: between an object as an input and an event as an output. At the very least, this concern should prompt questions about what we mean when we are talking about objects as causes. Even if we leave aside the question of the description-dependency of what counts as a single object – a landslide or its component stones – there remains an important unresolved issue. To bring this more into focus, we need to reflect on the nature of objects.

There are two (at least) schools of thought among philosophers as to what objects are.[5] Those who subscribe to "endurantism" maintain that an object is wholly present at each moment of its existence. There are many difficulties associated with this, not the least of reconciling different states of the object at different times of its existence if they have somehow to be co-present. Some philosophers have, therefore, suggested an alternative, "perdurantism", according to which an object is a succession of time-slices. Bertrand Russell embraced this view and expressed it with characteristic lucidity:

> Each of these [items such as tables and chairs] is to be regarded, not as one single persistent entity, but a series of entities succeeding each other in time, for a very brief period, though probably not for a mere mathematical instant. A body which fills a cubic foot will be admitted to consist of many smaller bodies, each occupying only a very tiny volume; similarly, a thing which persists for an hour is to be regarded as composed of many things of less duration. A true theory of matter requires a division of things into time-corpuscles as well as into space-corpuscles.[6]

This is sharply different from the idea of an object as something that "occupies a certain quantity of space over a certain period of time". It endeavours to address the difficulty of trying to envisage an object as occupying "a certain period of time" *at* any particular time – particularly if it is changing. It cannot pack its life-history into each moment of its existence. That paradoxical skill is, as we have seen, reserved to conscious subjects who can reach from any given moment backwards and forwards in their life.[7] (This will be central to our understanding of the embodied subject as an agent in the next section).

If we look carefully at what happens in a paradigm causal interaction such as the collision of billiard balls, what we actually see is one object participating in an event – a collision – followed by an event in another object – a movement. It would appear then that "object causation" is in fact "event-in-object causation" – with an event-in-object-effect. Or, more precisely (taking account of the discussion we have just had) event-in-time-slice-object causation.

If there is any role for the idea of object-causation, it is when objects are used as tools. When I hammer a nail, I hold the entire hammer – by means of a part – and by means of another part the head of a nail to drive the entre nail into the wood: the interaction appears to be between objects. This however is an illusion. The real business is an interaction between the movement of the hammer and the movement of the nail. It is the process of hammering, not the hammer, that drives in the nail and the consequence of the hammering is not an object but a displacement of an object. It just happens to be convenient to describe what is happening in terms of the participating objects rather than the events that are taking place in those objects – especially as I, the agent, manipulate the entire object and my target is the entire nail whose position I want to settle once and for all.

Actually, something more profound than mere convenience is in play here. An object has many successive states and it is clear that only one of those states can be engaged in an event taking place at a particular time. There is an important exception to this, when the object is the embodied subject that is a person. The I who reaches for the hammer is – or rather *am* – extended in time *at* a time. The objects I exploit in the furtherance of my agency, borrows some of this temporal depth that have as an agent. The hammer I reach for has a temporally extended place in my life – most obviously as a possession – and consequently I curate some of its states additional to those engaged in present hammering. This co-presence of time-slices of the object is, however, possible only courtesy of a conscious agent who is an embodied subject.

We shall return to this in the next section.

Other alternatives to event-causation of action

Another relatively popular candidate for an alternative to events as causal partners is the salient property of an object. Property causation overlaps with the notion of tropes, changing values of variables, powers, dispositions, and capacities as causally efficacious. As Sidney Shoemaker has expressed it, "what makes a property the property it is, what determines its identity, is its potential for contributing to the causal powers of the things that have it".[8]

For some philosophers, such as Stephen Mumford, identifying causes with these standing propensities of objects has the advantage of effectively disposing of causation altogether, and hence promising "to offer a solution to or dissolution of, the problem of causation".[9] In short, a place to go to after the Hume-iliation of causes discussed in Chapter 3. For Mumford, the universe is not composed of Humean "loose and separate" entities. According to this alternative view of causation, it is not "an asymmetric, external relation, between *discreta*".[10] The causal relata will not primarily be events but "the powers and properties of things, the universals that particular objects instantiate". It is these, Mumford claims, that underpin the necessary connectedness of the universe that Hume rejected because he could see no evidence of it: "The powers ontology accepts necessary connections in nature, in which the causal interactions of a thing, in virtue of its properties, can be essential to it. Instead of contingently related cause and effect, we have power and its manifestations, which remain distinct existences but with a necessary connection between".[11]

As will be evident, it is not entirely clear whether the appeal to "powers"[12] and "properties" and the like restores causation to its pre-Humean status or bypasses the requirement for causal necessity connecting discrete events to reassure us that the world will continue behaving in future as it has in the past, placing induction on a secure ground. For Hume, "powers" and "necessary connections" are explanatorily vacuous. Additionally, there is the unmet challenge – analogous to the one we encountered with (whole) object causation – of managing the descent from standing or continuant properties, powers, dispositions, and capacities to the episodic relationships between occurrent events. It might be argued that properties will translate into events, and powers, dispositions, and capacities will deliver effects, if and only if the surrounding circumstances are appropriate. For example, the solubility of sugar crystals will not be manifest until they meet a solvent. The encounter with the relevant circumstances will be contingent. The loose and separate entities – say, sugar cubes and water – will remain loose and separate. This is still true even if the powers, etc. are translated into something scientifically respectable such as forces and fields. In short, it will not be possible to restore pre-Humean material necessity. Instead, contingency and looseness and separateness will simply be differently distributed: contingency will be found (for example) in the distribution of properties over objects and the encounters with other objects; and separateness will return in the separation of objects and the intermittent, accidental nature of their encounter.

Conclusion

So much for the alternatives to event-causation. Notwithstanding that they seem more substantial than events, objects and properties (powers, etc.) do not seem to deliver what is required to address the peculiar nature of actions. Yes, they are more substantial than a linear trickle of events but it is not clear, if we accept them as real, what they deliver that event-causation does not. Object and property causation do not have the capacity to generate beginnings – points of departure – or endings – points of arrival. We cannot get anything corresponding to the realization of goals out of causal relationships, however plump the partners are.

What it amounts to is this: actions, doings, are above and beyond the temporal succession of mere happenings. Becausation requires that what is happening now – what I am doing – should be explicitly rooted in what has happened before and what will come about as a result of my action. Actions aim at an envisaged outcome; at the realization of a possibility.

Notwithstanding our rejection of objects and properties as causes, this discussion has not been a mere digression. Thinking about objects has brought us nearer to seeing the nature of the human agent: an entity – an embodied subject – that is substantial and that, at any given time, extends out of that time; that is in contact with its successive time-slices.

5.2 PERSONS AS AGENTS

> "Surely my actions aren't merely caused by things happening in my mind; rather, they are caused by me. It is *I*, and not the mere goings on in my head, who ultimately determines whether or not I make a cup of tea".   Helen Beebee[13]

Agent causation: law-governed causation's last stand

The state we have reached in our inquiry is captured in this engaging passage from the American philosopher Richard Taylor:

> Now this conception of activity, and of an agent who is the cause of it, involves two rather strange metaphysical notions that are never applied elsewhere in nature. The first is that of a *self* or *person* – for

example, a man – who is not merely a collection of things or events, but a substance and a self-moving being. For on this view it is a man himself, and not merely some part of him or something within him, that is the cause of his own activity ... Second, this conception of activity involves an extraordinary conception of *causation* [emphasis added], according to which an agent, which is a substance and not an event, can nevertheless be the cause of an event. Indeed, if he is a free agent then he can, on this conception, cause an event to occur – namely some act of his own – without anything else causing him to do so".[14]

We have come to causation's last stand – agent-causation in which causation is claimed mysteriously to arise out of its own ruins. The appeal to agents-as-a-whole as causes has the obvious attraction; it is, after all, agents – aka people – who do things. It is agents who know what is being done and why. They are the indispensable hosts of the intentions, reasons, hopes and desires, that motivate actions; and intentions, reasons, hopes, and desires – that are often weighed up in competition in advance of a decision – are not the kind of interactions or processes that we have in mind when we think of a material cause bringing about a material effect. Such hosts have a life history in virtue of which they can see what they are doing and why and are prepared to account for their behaviour and even to defend it in the light of that life history and their knowledge of it.

To say that it is *people* who do things is hardly controversial, though it will require some clarification, as we shall discuss presently. But this is not the same as to propose that there is something called *agent-causation*. The latter is an awkward hybrid as revealed by this definition: "According to agency theory, at the core of every free action is an *ontologically irreducible causal relation* between a person and some appropriate internal event that triggers later elements of the actions".[15]

The two partners in the first part of this account – a person and an internal event – seem ill-matched. If a (whole) person has to be the cause of an event in that same person, or in their life, the top-down direction of causation from agent (actor) to event (action) seems top-heavy. And the nature of the partners in the second part of the account – "some appropriate internal event" and the "later elements of the actions" that event triggers – is unclear. It is not obvious what an "internal" event is. Presumably it is not literally internal – such as an intracranial neural discharge. If it is something like a reason, or other propositional attitude, it is not evident what it is that prises it out of its shell ("internal") and enables it to have the causal power to bring about as its effects "the later elements of actions" – presumably the externally visible events such as my moving my legs, cracking a joke, or raising my hand to vote.

Agent-causation seems to inherit all the problems encountered when event-causation is proposed as the connection between a propositional attitude and an action, problems that we have discussed at length. The most pressing problem is the mismatch between the goal or aim of an action, a possibility envisaged in a propositional attitude – which is general and does not correspond to a spatio-temporally, or more broadly physical, state of affairs – and the supposedly local and determinate nature of "an internal event". In short the problems that beset Davidson's account of action.

It may seem possible to mitigate the asymmetry of the link between the person-as-agent and the action, envisaged as a possibility, by appealing to a component of the person, such as a disposition, as the proximate source of the action. Suppose I am disposed to be generous towards my fellow citizens. This may be expressed in many different ways – for example, greeting strangers in the street, donating to charities, choosing a career because it might bring benefit to society. Dispositions seem close to capacities, inclinations, and character traits.

Mobilizing the word "disposition" is not as helpful as might seem. We have already seen the problems associated with dispositional (properties, capacities, powers) interpretation of causation in the physical world. They are even more acute in the present context. The appropriate causal transition from a general disposition – understood as a standing feature of myself – to such a variety of specific behaviours as listed above will be dependent on many other things; for example, my gathering up certain physical circumstances into a situation and my interpreting that situation as an opportunity to be (for example) generous. This is quite different from the supposed connections between dispositions and events that we observe in nature – for example the brittleness of glass and its subsequent breakage. Consequently, it is difficult to see the use of dispositions in this context as anything other than metaphorical. At any rate, narrowing the idea of agent-causation to agent-disposition-causation does not add to the explanatory force of the notion of agent-causation.

The impression that "agent-causation" is the product of an unhappy attempt to marry the language of agency to that of causation grows stronger. The reluctance of philosophers of action to give up on causation expresses a striking stubbornness. Nevertheless, it is understandable: it is motivated by a worry as to what we might be letting ourselves in for when we identify (whole) agents as the source of actions. Is the agent some kind of little *deus ex machina*? Is she importing a fifth force into nature additional to gravity, electromagnetism, and the weak and strong nuclear forces? Is she nipping in between causes and their usual effects, frustrating the law-governed unfolding of the material world? Is she creating causes *ex nihilo* to produce an effect? Are actions material physical happenings driven by immaterial mental happenings?

An agent construed in any of these ways would soon run into trouble. She would need to be quarantined from, or absolved from obedience to, the material world with its habits captured in the laws of science such as the conservation of energy and, at the same time, to be able to act effectively within or upon that world and wittingly or unwittingly exploiting those laws. Intermediaries such as intentions would seem to have to be uncaused while themselves having intended effects. Moreover, such items, weightless and difficult to localize in space, are ill-suited to the localized, sweaty push-and-shove grunt-and-groan that many actions involve.[16] If the agent were a cause and her actions were effects, and if she were truly the origin of her actions, her causal powers would have to be uncaused. In short, the conception of causation be both embraced and rejected.

Rather than resuscitate causation on its death bed by offering it a role in agency, it is better to reject it entirely. To hold causation in reserve solely for things that really *are* made to happen (by agents), is to drain it of any explanatory force. If "causation" does no work – and indeed is discredited – outside of agency, it is not going to do any work in helping us either to explain agency or to see its unique place in the order of things; or to understand the deliberate ordering of things by agents in the unregulated natural order. The endeavour to make agency respectable by regarding it as a causal power is doomed, particularly if causation outside of agency has ceased to be respectable.

Embodied subjects as agents

The criticism of object causation in Section 5.1 should guard us against reacting to the unattractive notion of the agent as a ghost by making the opposite mistake of thinking of her as some kind of solid object, specifically a material object such as a body or a brain. We have already noted the problems with object-causation, additional to those already identified with the event-causation of actions. How are we to interpret "object-as-cause"? Is it the whole object over time over time; or a time slice of the object? Neither, we concluded, because objects do not divide themselves into slices or, alternately, add themselves up to their entire history such that they are at time t the whole object that endures from t_1 to t_{1000}. If the source of an action were not an event but an object there would be a mismatch between the continuant cause (an object) and the occurrent effect (an action).

It is this that lies behind C. D. Broad's famous critique of agent causation: "How can an event possibly be determined to happen at a certain date if its total cause contained no factor to which the notion of date has any application? And how can the notion of date have any application to anything that is not an event?"[17] We shall return to this argument presently for it points to what we require of agents in order for them to be the true authors of actions.

While the agent's body may satisfy the need for something more substantive than a mere event such as a propositional attitude to host, to give birth to, actions, its candidature comes with additional problems. Where objects are causes, it is through the forces they exert, most obviously mechanical forces, but those forces are interactive – between one object and another on a democratic basis. So, while an object is more solid than, say, a succession of propositional attitudes (which seem closer to mist than muscularity) it does not seem to be "the right stuff". It has, as we have said, the wrong kind of plumpness. Nevertheless, we still seem to need something more substantial than a mental event (if propositional attitudes are even that). Reasons alone cannot make things happen. We need to move from the guest to the host for reasons to be situated and to be influential. It is agents with their reasons who make things happen. "I did this" does not translate without loss into "My reason brought this about".

To get a clear view of the agent, we need to remind ourselves what human beings are: not ghosts, certainly; nor simply material objects. They are embodied *subjects*,[18] who bring to the field of volition a unified material body with substantial pasts and futures that are actually present; who gather up the past, present, and possible futures of a part of the world into platforms for action. The embodied subject is a whole that affirms her own unity. In this respect, her unity is unlike that of a pebble that owes its status as a spatial whole, as opposed to part of a heap (of pebbles) or as two separate halves, and its temporal unity over the period of its existence, to the synthetic activity of the consciousness of an outside observer. Her bodily unity at and over time is reaffirmed in temporally extended action: all hands – and feet, and breathing chest, and so on – on deck; and on deck over minutes, days, weeks, and years. Her working day draws on her past and points to her future, no-longer and not-yet, that are to a significant degree co-curated with her fellow human beings – most explicitly in the sedimentation of tensed time in calendrical, historical, post-tensed time.

We can now address Broad's critique of the idea of agent-causation: his concern over the temporal asymmetry between an action that takes place at a particular time and an agent who does not "occur" at a particular time. This mismatch is resolved when the first entity is not to be understood as a material object but an embodied subject in whom the past, present, and future, are co-present and their co-presence is necessary for an action that makes sense to the agent, in her life, and to her world.

The embodied subject is a self-unifying whole that exists at times and over times. It is implicitly and explicitly the same body that is a third-year medical student, an intern, and a retired consultant, and the connections between them that make sense of her actions at any given time. That is why the embodied subject is able to contain: the link between the intention and that which justifies it; the link between the intention and the goal that realizes it; and the link between a particular goal and an over-arching aim or ambition. The body that endures and is, say, transported from beginning to the end of a journey to London or over the trajectory of a medical career is a body that unites itself at a time and over time from beginning to end.

The embodied subject seems to span or reconcile the perdurantist (succession of time-slices) and endurantist (whole-life) ways of seeing objects. We may get a handle on this by speaking of the temporal transparency of the embodied conscious subject. My self, my state, at any given time can be accessed by my self, my state, at other times: I am not a succession of distinct, mutually exclusive, time-slices. This is strikingly highlighted in the case of autobiographical memories. I can be in my study as I am now, and yet capable of recalling (in my mind seeing) myself walking down a favourite street in Prague. There are many other modes of temporal extendedness through all the varieties of individual and shared memory. It is this extendedness through time at a time that is presupposed when I intend a meaningful action that will take place over time.

The temporal depth of the lived body is projected into the world surrounding the agent. Hence, when I pick up a hammer, I am aware of picking up more than a hammer-time-slice; and the same applies to the nail that I am driving into the fence which I am repairing and also to the fence into which I am driving it. My home with its familiar rooms and clutter of objects acquires temporal depth along with me: it has cohabited with me. The very idea of being the owner of a "possession" is inseparable from that of my having a temporal depth. The sense of the persistence over time of what is out there and its status as the theatre of our agency, are inseparable from our being embodied subjects.[19]

Persons as agents are not (merely) bodies nor (merely) trickles of mental events such as propositional attitudes acting as causes. They are self-unifying embodied subjects who, at any given time, are extended over time. It is such subjects, making sense of their world, who are the source of actions. To say this still leaves work to be done. The body embraced by the subject as herself will not be identical with all the material from the scalp to the toe-nails: there is, as it were, an *a la carte* menu of parts and the array of parts lived by the subject will vary from moment to moment. Bodily experiences such as itches and gut sensations may bring otherwise absent parts into the light of consciousness. The most important determinant of the scope of the currently lived body will be determined by the activities in which it is engaged.

The agent in action

It takes something as plump as an embodied subject, or an embodied self, in part sustained by a community of selves, to entertain the possibilities, the motives, and the reasons, that lie behind any genuine action, even a seemingly trivial one. A self that harvests the achieved goal – which can often be quite abstract as when we secure the agreement of others to support a particular policy – filters out those things that are irrelevant to it from the countless physical effects that follow from the actions, the physical movements, that constitute the process of realizing the goal. It is the same self that separates the proximate "here" from the more remote "there", that which matters from that which does not, and knows which among those things that are relevant can be ignored as neither contributing to nor frustrating the achievement of the goal. It is this that sees an action through from its conception to its conclusion.[20]

Agents seen correctly – as embodied subjects – are capable of being the source of date-specific actions as in "I lifted this hammer at 12 noon". But neither the agent nor the meaning of the action is confined to that date and time. I am not confined to the present state of my body that is presently interacting with the material world. Raymond Tallis whose body is interacting with the hammer at 12 noon is explicitly aware of the past and anticipates the future towards which the present is pointing. Insofar as it is engaged in an action that necessarily draws upon a past and a future, particularly since the latter is specified in general terms and, until actualized, the embodied subject is timeless. The embodied subject is a point of intersection between the time of the physical world and the timelessness of a consciousness that reaches into a not-yet-existent future and a no-longer-existent past.

We are able therefore to respond to Broad's concern about the mismatch between a timeless agent (or an agent not confined to a particular time) and her actions which take place at a particular time and engage with the material world at that time. While the action understood as a sequence of material events does take place at a certain date, it is not embedded in a nexus of events caused by other events taking place at a certain date. I, the agent, do not "take place at a certain date"; for I am extended over time. Yes, of course, I am co-present with my action but the I that is presently hammering a nail with the aim of fixing a fence, delivering on a promise to my neighbour and on the wider aim of clearing a backlog of tasks, is not confined to the moment at which I take hold of the hammer. My skills, my sense of what a hammer is and what it can do, the task for which I am using it, the purpose of the task, where it fits into larger purposes, etc. add up to something that extends far beyond that moment. Far from being a barrier to agency, to intervention in the world, the apparent temporal asymmetry between an action that takes place at time t and an agent who is in no sense confined to time t is a necessary condition of agency. It would be a barrier to agency only if actions were construed on analogy with causation.

What goes on in active agents is nothing like causation, in which an entity is confined to its present state and engages surroundings confined to their present state (which are entirely unaware of their being "surroundings"). A personal past, present, and future are implicitly or explicitly involved in any endeavour to bring about a future state of some part of the world that the agent envisages and sees as desirable. Human agents, in short, are not reducible to, or identifiable with, large, oddly shaped, well-dressed, articulate, self-conscious, billiard balls. Nor is their agency reducible to the properties, powers, or capacities thereof of such objects understood as the sources of causes in turn understood in terms of the universal habits of nature as reflected in the laws of science.

The agency of the embodied subject is inseparable from its capacity to gather up a world – including its own body or parts of it – as its situation, and as the locus of goals, or the means to achieve them. As many philosophers have pointed out, events, objects, processes, places, and the body are united in the evolving situation of the person. They are not, of course, united by being rearranged so that they are side-by-side or glued together; rather through being located in a multi-layered conscious field and, beyond that, fields of interest, concern, or of preoccupation – fields that are interconnected within the agent's life and, indeed, beyond the agent: with other individual agents, bounded and boundless groups of others, drawing on a collective history, via connections that are extended almost without limit into a virtual realm opened up by post-tensed time. It is from such a world and a standpoint adopted in it that we expend effort in voluntary action and negotiate with the forces of nature.

While embodied subjects bring something new to the world, therefore, this is not because they are a source of additional causal power, a fifth force jostling with the other four – gravity, electromagnetism, strong and weak nuclear forces. When the psychologist Daniel Wegner asserted that free will was a feeling but not a force he was entirely right, though he drew the wrong conclusion from it. The fact that it is not a force does not imply, as Wegner believed it did, that free will is therefore an illusion and that our actions merely happen to us.[21]

The key point is that selves as agents are not causes of effects if causation is understood as being analogous to whatever it is that connects successive events in the natural world. Voluntary action is not a passage from cause to effect but from situation to situation. It is agency that makes the room, as opposed to the individual objects in it such as tables and bottles of printer ink, into a whole, or part of a bigger whole such as a house or a district.[22] As we have noted, much of our lives as agents involves creating the conditions for certain actions to be possible; for the relevant circumstances to be available; and for certain events in them to be exploited as handles. Positioning and niche construction are the relatively stable background of our capacity for voluntary action. We operate in a multitude of environmental niches – which may be described in physical, biological, or social terms – that we have individually and (more often) jointly created to support us in the fulfilment of our needs in actions. What agency draws on is a long way from the interactions that we typically associate with causation in the natural world. The kinds of pressures that agents exert do not have defined surfaces of contact with the material world.

What is drawn upon when we are the originators of our actions is not confined to the time of the commencement of the action but incorporates a past which we have had a significant role in shaping, and which has in part created the present circumstances, the self that faces them, and the future which seems to require them. Our freedom is not realized in a series of episodes motivated solely by contemporary circumstances and the needs, reasons, and desires arising out of them. We own – and should own up to – our present actions because we own the depths, the presuppositions, that makes sense of them for us.

And so we should resist the notion of selves-as-agents as being kinds of causes and henceforth avoid all talk of "agent-causation". If we take agency seriously, we should accept that, while it uses what it sees as causal connections in the world as means of manipulation, it is not itself a cause or a generator of causes – a *machina ex machina*.

Farewell to causes[23]

Some philosophers have argued that the idea of causation still has a home in our capacity to manipulate the world and that this justifies thinking of agents as causes. The position developed in this book argues that agents are cause-makers, transformers of events into causes, or requisitioners of events to be causes, rather than themselves being causes. This may seem a distinction without a difference but the difference is real. As we have already discussed, if we allow agents to be characterized as causes, then we are in danger of looking to parts of, or events in, agents to cause particular actions. Before we know what has happened, we are back in Donald Davidson territory and (for example) seeing propositional attitudes as causes, identifying causes of those causes, and as a result stitching actions into the wider network of a causally closed physical world. We should accept the full implications of the fact that the ascription of causal connectedness to the natural world is inseparable from our experience of ourselves as agents. We project into nature at large our ability to shape things and consequently see natural events as having a quasi-agentive power. This is an expression of what Hume termed (as cited in Chapter 3) "to spread itself on external objects".

We might be tempted to rescue the notion of agent-causation and, indeed, causation by suggesting that agents are the source of meta-causes that cause the transformation of events into causes. This is a desperate attempt to rescue a notion that, after Hume, anyway has little going for it. It is best, therefore, to lay aside the idea of causation completely. Any reluctance to do this could be dealt with by listening to the message delivered by the progressive attenuation of the seeming explanatory force or intuitive appeal of causation as we move from billiard-ball collisions, to the pairing of thunder and lightning, to lung cancer and smoking, to the behaviour of the stock market, to the supposed operation of causation in world history. This attenuation is completed when we reach agency. The transformation of events into causes-as-handles is not a process that is accurately or even usefully described as "causation", the term typically invoked in our understanding of the coherent unfolding of nature.[24]

Which is, of course, to be welcomed. Any endeavour to translate agency into causation as it is understood from informal or scientific observation of nature will trap them in the causal nexus. This is true even when we appeal to freedom-friendly items such as propositional attitudes if they are seen as causes of actions. Given that anything that qualifies as a cause must itself be an effect, it is not possible to channel agency through "internal" causes without reinserting agents into a causally wired material world and thereby stripping them of the power to initiate that is essential to agency. Seeing propositional attitudes as quasi-physical causes – necessary for them to have a spatio-temporal point of application – is inextricably caught up with the notion that they are identical with (or to use the slippery term we have dis-credited "realized in") brain states. This erases the fundamental fact – arising out of the intentionality of their consciousness – that agents *face* their worlds. We are creatures who transform what-is into "my circumstances" or "our circumstances" – as those things that "stand round" us. We insert localities into the universe as our individual and shared worlds – a process, as we have seen, that begins with intentionality and is upstream of any ascription of causal connectedness or government by laws.

The idea of an agent as a cause, or as a source of discrete causes, unpacked by breaking down agency into mental events that boil down to physical (brain) events, located in physical space-time collapses the space, essential for agency, opened up by intentionality and subsequently expanded by the sharing of intentionality within a self over time, between selves, and across communities of minds. We lose that which is central to agency; namely, that that in virtue of which an agent is a *genuine point of departure for* events that comprise its actions. Causal chains, if they have any reality, do not have beginnings or ends any more than do any sequences of events conforming to the habits of nature. Any powers agents have must be at least to some degree originate with them, rather than simply being powers that are propagated through them. Those powers, as we have described them, are not special extra-physical forces. Rather, they amount to a capacity to mobilize the habits – which may look like powers – of nature, to deliver envisaged ends. If there is a connection between causation and agency, it is not because agents or propositional attitudes they entertain are causes; rather because they are that through which events, states of affairs and objects may be co-opted as means to ends. They are points of departure in the world in virtue of which (beginning with the perception) intentionality bends back against the flow of events, making the conscious subject a point of arrival (or reception) and of departure.

The capacity of agents to connect events is rooted in their ability to pick them out. One key to this is the ability to regulate their *scale* of selective attention – focusing on something as small as swatting an annoying insect or as large as completing training for medicine (see Appendix B). The conscious subject facing the world, highlights those things that are relevant to its needs, purposes, hopes, ambitions, projects and values. These are deeply interwoven aspects of ongoing self-expression and self-affirmation. Additionally, the agent plays an important role in creating and maintaining the cognitive and material infrastructure to support its own agency – in rigging the odds to secure a certain outcome. The exercise of our freedom is rooted in the self-curated depth and breadth of the self.

The relevant depths may even extend over many years, or – as in the case of the artefactscape we have built up to serve our individual and collective needs – have tentacular roots that reach deeper and spread wider than our own lives. The outside from which individual agents act, the leverage they have on the natural world, has been in part constructed over many years directly or indirectly by billions of fellow humans. Think of what and who is involved in making a phone call. The circumstances that made it possible began to be created with the scientific revolution of the sixteenth century and drew on other, subsidiary, revolutions in, for example, materials science and solid state physics.

The identification of the embodied subject with the agent points to a middle course between too ethereal a concept of the agent – in which its engine is a succession of mental events – and too material a concept in which it is composed of physical events in a body subject to the habits of nature. As organisms we have to engage physically with the physical world. We are immersed in the push-and-shove of things but we are not dissolved in them and absorbed into nature. Our interaction with the natural world is not a dialogue of equals. As I choose to sit on a chair to give myself what I consider to be a well-earned rest, both the chair and I are subject to the equality of action and reaction, but the chair's being sat on is not equivalent to my sitting on the chair.

Our embrace of our bodies as ourselves – the existential intuition that "I am this" – is what ultimately makes us the source and initiator of some of its happenings. Our human being is "amming". Our status as "beings whose being is an issue for itself"[25] imports "becausation" into the universe and this cannot be reduced to causation. Because our being is an issue for itself, so too is the present and future state of the world in which we have our being. As its states, or some of them, and the conditions of its continuation, define our needs, translated into appetites and desires, so the actions they justify become events of which we are the source. Our unique mode of being identified with our bodies is the necessary condition of our being agents acting upon the material and cultural world from a virtual outside. Agency in turn supports my plans, projects, and short- and long-term goals, individual and shared, that reinforce my sense of who I am and, hence, *that* I am.[26] It is in cooperation with ourselves and others we grow into beginnings, into sources of events.

It might be thought that setting aside causation should commit us to setting aside other concepts that Hume (see Chapter 2, note 6) discarded, such as power, capacity, and so on. In this case, however, while causation is irredeemably contaminated by its association with the idea of necessity built into the material world, in using these other terms, I am merely returning them to the place where they belong. That people exert power, have capacities, face the world, etc. are things that we can see and feel. We are led to doubt this evidence only by a misunderstanding of the authority of a scientific worldview that embeds humans in the material world and assumes they are entirely subject to the government of laws and causes. As we have seen, the very existence of the scientific worldview is the most striking expression of our not being defined by it.

5.3 FINAL THOUGHTS ON AGENCY

My underlying aim has been to separate actions – what people do – from nature conceived of as a nexus of law-governed causes of what merely happens in the physical world. The causal theory of action – that an item of behaviour counts as a voluntary action, indeed as a genuine action, in virtue of being *caused* by a mental state such as an intention – fails either to do justice to genuinely free actions or indeed to explain how they are possible. Any causal account of what prompts and sustains actions and the nature of the goals that make sense of and justify them fails to capture how purposeful behaviour is fundamentally different from the dynamism of nature. It overlooks what is central to action; namely the *possibilities* that agents aim to actualize and the co-presence of past, present, and future which lies at their heart.

The argument made in Chapters 2 and 3 (and further developed in Appendix A) that neither the habits of nature depicted as the laws of science nor the law-governed causes we pick out of the flow of events are inherent in the natural world should refute Daniel Dennett's claim that actions can be accounted for "using the same physical principles, laws and raw materials that suffice to explain radioactivity, continental drift, photosynthesis, reproduction, nutrition and growth".[27]

The very fact that we undoubtedly exploit the habits of nature to realize possibilities in order to serve envisaged ends – not the least when we are engaged in discovering those habits as the laws of science – is a powerful demonstration of the capacity of the human agent to be *ex machina* and of how actions are not reducible to mere happenings, stretches of self-stitching chains of token physical events.

To round off our defence of free will against determinist claims, let us focus on the fact that, in the absence of a (human) being that *faces* a world that is *her* world, there are neither outsides nor (since they are defined by being outside of outside) any insides. This is highlighted by the fact that our relationship with our own bodies, or parts of them, fluctuates between that of their being an inside with respect to which everything else is outside or themselves being part of an outside. I can inspect parts of my body as objects out there, including as objects seen in the eyes of others. I can even, with the aid of a mirror, make my own eyes an object of vision.

Action is made possible by spaces – parts of an Open – that do not belong to the space and times of the physical world. This space has been variously named and explored in different ways by philosophers. One of the most well-known acknowledgements of this space is owing to Heidegger, for whom it was central to his thought. It was "a clearing in which entities can be, a space or realm of illumination in whose light things can show or manifest themselves to people".[28] It is in this space that rational agents have – limited but nonetheless significant – powers to direct the course of events.

The pessimistic notion that we are the helpless spectators of our lives, of events that take place within and around us, looks straight past the fact that we *are* spectators and in this there lies hope. Our freedom is made possible by the spectatorial distance between ourselves and the universe. We lose sight of this when we see the world through the eyes of natural science because the spectator is side-lined in scientific enquiry, most notably in measurement, and is progressively erased in pursuit of what Thomas Nagel called "the view from nowhere". And yet, ironically, there could be no more striking expression of our individual and collective freedom, our spectatorial distance from the natural world, than those activities that lead to the discovery of the laws of science and to their exploitation in the technologies that have transformed our lives.

The transition from a law-governed physically connected universe to the "becausation" of human agency that, among other things, exploits those laws, cannot be explained by those laws. It is an expression of the irreducible gap between a (typically material) state of affairs X to "*that* X is the case" – or to "might be the case" or to "ought to be the case".[29] This transition is not secured by, nor a product of, the laws of nature that common sense intuits or progressively defines and refines with the advance of science. There are no physical laws by which the habits of nature become the laws of science that guide and hugely amplify our powers – so that, for example, I can converse with a particular individual in Australia without even raising my voice.

It is hardly surprising then that neither whatever we identify as the prompt for an action (for example an intention, a desire, a belief) nor whatever we may single out as its goal, a state of affairs it aims to bring about, maps tidily on to the kinds of causes and effects we pick out from nature, notwithstanding that, as we have seen, those are untidy and fluffy-edged enough.

If agents were themselves causes, they would be strange causes that adopted an attitude towards themselves; that embraced, and chose, and approved or disapproved of, themselves and their effects (or a subset of them) defined in very general terms. Moral exhortation cuts little ice with causal chains as usually construed, even if they pass through a body or a brain, as those chains are incapable of responding to guilt or shame or generating guilt or shame at themselves. What survives of causes after Hume-iliation would have even less moral accountability.

While what I am, and the circumstances in which I act, are to some extent given, they are also things I have chosen, embraced, and cultivated, as I exercise complex preferences rooted in many instances of prior choices through which I have shaped myself. The situation that requires or justifies my action is something I have had a hand in setting up. It is in this sense that freedom is self-expression – and why we own, and should own up to, our actions.

As agents, we are initiators. There are no points of origin in unfolding nature – leaving aside a putative initial act of creation such as The Big Bang. Any particular event is a beginning only from a viewpoint that envisages an end to which it is connected. The state of the natural world becomes a point of departure when a subject, with her point of view, creates a point of reference and transforms tenseless time into the present and time t becomes "now" pointing forward to a future and backwards to a past. It is this that connects the very idea of causation with our ability to intervene and to exploit what is "now" in order to create a future that satisfies a need inherited from our past.

Our wide margin of freedom is disguised from some philosophers by the fact that everything we do involves our body. Indeed, it is the primary instrument of our agency, the most proximal means to chosen ends.[30] It is an item that we for the great part have not chosen and on whose functioning we have a limited influence. And yet, within the constraints of the habits of nature there is an irreducible distance between the biology, chemistry, and physics of our flesh on the one hand and on the other the first-personhood and agency of our "ambodied" being.[31]

Let us, by way of farewell, remind ourselves of the difference between the unfolding of the physical world and the paths of agents by deploying an immemorial example: the difference between a voyaging sailor – using wind and water to tack through currents to a remote destination – and other items floating with the currents. It is a difference that has elevated the most enduring habits of the air into "trade winds". The sailor uses his boat and acquired skills to transform mindless winds into the motor serving his purposes, even to the point where it is possible to tack against the wind. The habits of nature are recruited to deliver ends that have no place in the natural world. This is but one example of the action-from-a-distance that has pitched the vast, multilayered tent of human civilization on to the face of the earth. The sailor's journey to a destination that nature has not prescribed, for purposes connected only indirectly to those implanted by biology, is part of the singular narrative that is sewn together as his life, itself part of his shared culture.

The virtual place from which human agents exploit the laws of nature is vast and ever-expanding. Staying with our sailor for a moment, consider the accumulated expertise of many generations in the construction and use of boats, expertise that feeds in so many ways into the challenge of turning the restlessness of the air into trade winds propelling sailors along routes maintained for millennia. How remote from the forces that propel the boat across the ocean are the labours, interrupted by meal breaks and nights' rest, of the boat-builders, realizing the plans of the naval architect. Equally distant are the processes by which naturally occurring materials – coal, cotton, bananas – are transformed into goods to be bought, transported, and sold. Yet how relevant they are to the voyage. As are also the treasure chests of manufactured tools and the implicit and explicit contractual agreements between boat-builders and the seamen. The transformation of a tree, stripped to a trunk and connected with other pieces of wood, in order to function as the mast to support a sail, is hardly to be understood as comparable with the law-governed energy exchanges observed as the boat interacts with the sea. Equally impressive is the transformation of the movements of the stars into a means of navigation that has been developed over centuries and expressed through evolving technology and expertise handed down from generation to generation.

All of these things belong to an outside in which, or from which, the voyage as a joint enterprise is envisaged. This space where possibilities are entertained and are in the process of being actualized is held open by human consciousness, individual and shared. Our freedom, and its extent, will be entirely overlooked if we focus exclusively on the instantaneous forces at work in a sailing boat, looking at the physical elements of the sailor engaged in his craft, rather than at the voyage, its purpose, and what made it both necessary and possible; in short, if we overlook the big picture of individual and shared agency and focus on individual pixels of physical movements.

The distance between consciousness and its objects marked by intentionality, from which it was possible to see – or see better – how nature "works", is the distance from which the laws of nature are exploited and from which we make nature work for us. Poking and prodding what is out there to arrive at a clearer picture of the lines along which it unfolds enables us, as Mill said, to align ourselves with one law (or habit) – intuitively appreciated or scientifically articulated – in order to use another law (or habit) to carry us to our chosen destinations. The formalization of such poking and prodding in applying calibrated pressures to aspects of the world in controlled conditions and using the measured response to adjust those pressures progressively enhances our capacity to suborn nature in the service of our own ends.

And there we have it: agency understood as the use of events, dissected out by our interests, and the exploitation of the habits of nature revealed to common sense and to science, as the servants of our intentions. Therein lies the irreducible difference between physical actions on the one hand and, on the other, mere physical interactions. The difference is rooted in a distance opened up by one partner to the interaction whose spectatorial stance, made possible by the intentionality of consciousness, creates the seed of her freedom.

The seed is not, of course, the whole story. We are not simply, or even primarily, spectators, not the least because our actions, our lives, are ongoing. This is what those who embrace "enactivism" and "embodied cognition" wish to emphasize and their views are discussed in Appendix D. The fact remains, however, without the virtual distance created by intentionality, there would not be the kind of outside from which true agency is possible.

CHAPTER 6

The limits of freedom

My concern has been with the very possibility of human freedom, not its extent; with the metaphysics of freedom rather than, for example, the local realities of political freedom or specific freedoms from certain constraints. For this reason, it may be necessary to head off a misunderstanding: I am not claiming that our freedom is boundless. On the contrary, it is subject to many restrictions.

The most basic and universal limitation arises from the fact that we do not create the most fundamental condition of our freedom: our very existence. We are the products of a universe evolving before our birth and, most crucially, of our parents' choices – most obviously to have a child; to permit a missed period to mark the beginning of a life.

Aldous Huxley highlights a mind-stretching accident built into this choice:

> A million million spermatozoa
> All of them alive;
> Out of their cataclysm but one poor Noah
> Dare hope to survive.
>
> And among that billion minus one
> Might have chanced to be
> Shakespeare, another Newton, a new Donne,
> But the One was Me.[1]

And we have, in most cases, as little choice over our death as over our birth. Exercising that choice in gratuitous suicide – freely cancelling the accident of our freedom – has been claimed as the freest of all acts. But the one-off freedom to bring our freedom to an end does little to offset the limitations of our freedom.

The extent to which we can exercise our freedom, or have any freedom to exercise, between the usually unchosen limits of our lifespan is contingent on the tickets we draw in the lottery of life – our natural, chance-given gifts, our health, and on the health of our relations with others and of the political system in which we live. While we may elect to make the best of our talents, or allow them to go to waste, their direction and scale do not lie within our gift. And my capacity to do many things is dependent on circumstances I have not chosen: as certain philosophers would put it, "cans are constitutionally iffy".

Failure to achieve our chosen goals is as much a feature of life as success. This may be less evident than it might otherwise be because we often pre-empt failure by accepting our limitations in advance of any endeavour to push against them. I do not encounter, even less fret at, my inability to fly without wings, to run at 50 miles per hour, to play the cello, or to lead my country.

While I can mitigate the play of chance by planning, by preparing myself and my surroundings in the widest and deepest sense, taking precautions, acting with care and foresight, and so on, sooner or later I will revert to the impotent state of the intrauterine creature I was – not so long ago in the scale of things – when I suffered, rather than enacted, the process of coming into being. Nature's implacable habits are upheld and I return to those elements out of which, by processes I knew not, I was gathered into me: "At death you break up; the bits that were you / Start speeding away from each other for ever / With no one to see …".[2]

I have emphasized the extent to which our freedom resides in our capacity to create the conditions in which we act. The passage from neonatal helplessness to full-blown agency is not sudden but gradual and it runs in parallel with the emergence of selfhood, inseparable from our gaining control of, indeed, possession of, our own body. As the self accumulates experience, so its temporal depth increases: its future extends and becomes more complex as a mirror of an extending and ever more complex past. Jean-Paul Sartre expressed this with a certain characteristic exaggeration: "A human being is a project that is formed step by step. Hence, he defines himself by the sum of his acts".[3]

Our potential freedom is realized with the assistance of the experience, knowledge, wisdom, techniques, and technology of the many collectives to which we belong at different times of our lives. This dependency on others is not a limitation because it is mutual: we contribute to, as well as draw upon, the collective enterprise that makes it possible for us to pursue our individual goals. To take a banal example that has been worked to death in this volume,

I rely on the train service to get me to London although I have little idea what is involved in running such a service. I do, however, pay my fare and make my contribution elsewhere in society.

Our interdependence goes very deep; indeed, it goes all the way down. "*Ubuntu*" – a Bantu term for humanity – captures this. It has many translations but the most arresting – "I am because we are" – seems to be closest to the truth. We are crucial conditions of each other's lives as free agents. For this reason, we have the capacity not only to liberate each other but also to limit each other's freedom. Hence the prominence of physical and psychological oppression – from the domestic to the political – in the history of humanity. We have little say in our position in society or, indeed, in history. Slaves in ancient Egypt, early-modern peasants living a life permanently on the edge of starvation, and children worked to death in factories, hardly chose these social positions or their constricted life chances. The limits imposed on our freedom do not merely surround us: they may penetrate every nook and cranny of our lives.

The fundamental point, however, is this: bad luck, imprisonment, servitude, frustration, disappointment, unintentional blunders, failure, the limitations imposed by physical and mental illnesses, the grip of unconscious forces, etc. have meaning only against the background of non-illusory possibility of genuine agency. In the physical world as described in natural science, there is no conception of either failure or success: what happens happens, end of story. Those who try to import the idea of success into nature by talk of "evolutionary success" seem unaware that this does not apply to the individual organism. We are not, after all, inclined to congratulate bacteria on their ubiquity or credit them with being at the beginning of a process that led to primates. Success is relative to an ambition harboured by an individual aiming at some goal, at the realization of an *envisaged* possibility.

So, yes, our freedom, though real, is circumscribed. And it may perhaps be more circumscribed than we appreciate. Psychologists delight in experiments that seemingly demonstrate that we may imagine events over which we have no control are actions that we have performed voluntarily. We can even be fooled into believing that we have, for example, moved our limbs when they have been moved by an external force. And psychologists take equal pleasure in showing how our choices are often influenced by stimuli of which we are hardly aware.[4] It does not follow from this that we are *always* fooled and our decisions are *always* shaped by subconscious influences. If we were permanently deceived, it would not require ingenious experiments to demonstrate this and the findings of the experiments would not cause such a stir. Evidence of unconscious influences highlights by contrast the overwhelming majority of occasions when we really do something deliberately for reasons of which we are aware.

Acknowledging the limits to our freedom highlights rather than obliterates the fundamental difference between things we do and things that merely happen; between my closing the door and the wind slamming it shut; between my falling down the stairs and my walking down the stairs purposefully as the first part of a journey to London for a meeting. Were there no fundamental differences between things we do and happenings that have nothing to do with our intentions, there would be nothing specific corresponding to moral luck, unintended consequences, and failure. If there were no freedom, there could not be degrees of freedom; we could not be freer under certain circumstances rather than others. Nor indeed could there be servitude: avalanches may not have any freedom but neither are they oppressed. Disempowerment would not be real or even possible if our powers as agents were not real.

The all too visible limits to our agency – most notably our mortality that demonstrates that we cannot dig ourselves out of the determinist hole indefinitely, or the single blow on the head that causes an irreversible collapse of our distance from the material world – confirm that, within those limits, agency is real. The total impotence of corpsehood is a testament to the freedom lost in the ontological downgrading we undergo when we die.

Besides, if freedom were boundless, there would be nothing for it to achieve: no distance would separate agents from their goals; there would be neither beginnings, nor means, nor ends, neither departure nor arrival. Action with its often-unchosen contexts, with all its hazards and frustrations and disappointments, with its potential for being derailed and its unintended consequences, would be unnecessary, perhaps impossible. If freedom is to be exercised, it has to be attached to specific purposes. It must therefore be local in its application and in this respect at least of limited scope and consequently constrained. Boundless freedom would have no agenda: the expression of freedom must in part be justified by unchosen as well as chosen circumstances if there is to be something for agents to do. If there are to be choices and those choices are to have meaning, meaning must be local.

This addresses a seemingly unanswerable argument against moral responsibility articulated by Galen Strawson.[5] Nothing, he points out, can be the cause of itself. However, in order to be truly morally responsible for one's actions, one would have to have been the cause of one's self and the agency it exercises. From this it follows that nothing or no-one can be truly morally responsible.

Setting aside the questionable use of causation in this – or indeed any – context, we can now see where this argument goes wrong. Strawson relies on the intuition that we cannot be free if we have any given, as opposed to chosen, characteristics; or, indeed, if we haven't freely brought ourself into being. Even if bringing ourselves into being were logically, never mind materially, possible (which it manifestly is not), it is difficult to see how the primordial act of self-generation could be the basis of freedom, even less its necessary condition. To bring one's self into being one would have to be an ontological Baron Munchausen, pulling one's self out of nothingness by one's non-existent bootstraps. What's more, the action of self-generation would be entirely random, since there could be no grounds for choice – for choosing one's self and choosing one self rather than another.

And without some unchosen context, freedom would have no content nor would our actions have specific, that is to say any, meaning. Actions can hardly be denied to be free on the grounds that they have meaning. Freedom has to have a platform to operate from, a place to head for; in short, givens of self and circumstances. Without starting points there could be no goals, no journeys towards them.

We are close here to the reason why Sartre has not figured more prominently in our discussion of the roots of freedom. My emphasis on intentionality, the possibility of possibility, and the virtual outside, may seem to bring my thinking close to the Nothingness in which the (relatively early) Sartre of *Being and Nothingness* located the possibility of freedom. This is no place for a full-blown exposition and critique of his account of freedom. A few comments, however, are in order.

For Sartre, our freedom lies in the distance opened up in Being (or Being-in-itself) by Nothingness (Being-for-itself) that is consciousness. Humans – who, he claims rather enigmatically, are what they are not and who are not what they are – are beings through whom Nothingness, as a revelation of Being, come into the world and in that world continually make themselves. While we seem to be faced with an obdurate natural world with properties of its own, a world into which we are thrown that includes our own bodily being, the nature of that world is as a *situation* or series of situations for us, revealed to us by the distance opened up by Nothingness.

And here we arrive at what Sartre calls "the paradox of freedom": "there is freedom only in a *situation*, and there is a situation only through freedom."[6] He illustrates this with the case of a mountain that I want to climb but find that I am unable to do so. My inability to climb a mountain is not an intrinsic property of the material world or determined by it. It is only in relation to my desire to climb the mountain that it becomes climbable or unclimbable and hence a marker of the limitation of my freedom. It would seem, therefore, that the apparent limits on my freedom are the results of free choice and hence not limits at all. It is "the intentional choice of the end which reveals the world, and the world is revealed as this or that ... according to the end chosen".[7] It would seem, therefore, that there are no limits to freedom except in relation to our freely chosen intentions, our ends.

In his later writings, Sartre disavowed this implicit belief in the boundlessness of freedom, a position he was now unhappy to share with Descartes who asserted that "the will is so free that it cannot be constrained".[8] As many have pointed out, while my inability to climb a particular mountain may be revealed by my desire to do so, that inability remains the result of the respective properties of the mountain – its height and inclination – and of my body, neither of which fall within the scope of my freedom to determine. It may be I who transform a brick wall into an insuperable obstacle in my path but that makes it no less a constraint on my expression of my freedom insofar as it aims to reach a goal. To deny this can lead to the palpably absurd claim that, even when I am totally paralysed (say by curare) I remain free and my inability to do anything is defined as a limit only by myself.[9]

The later Sartre made a rather more modest claim: "I believe that a man can always make something out of what is made of him. This is the limit I would today accord to freedom: the small movement which makes a totally conditioned social being someone who does not render back completely what his conditioning has given him".[10] He acknowledged that we act from a particular place in space and time – in the physical world, in society, in history, and in our own lives and those of others. We do not choose many aspects of that place, except insofar as it is embraced by us as the substrate of our concern.

This correction is perhaps an over-correction and the margin of freedom Sartre allows may be too narrow. To some extent, it reflects Sartre's shift from an ahistorical metaphysical approach to freedom – which does not accommodate degrees of and limits to freedom – to an historical approach which finds it difficult to grant individuals any freedom at all. The historicist (Marxist) Sartre was "scandalized" (his own word) by the ontological phenomenologist of his earlier writing.

Nevertheless, there is something morally appropriate about this overcorrection. When we consider the limitations imposed on the freedom of many of our fellows – by hunger, destitution, unremitting drudgery, pain, persecution and like terrors, childhood neglect, physical and psychological domination and abuse, and the many modes of bondage and incarceration – affirming metaphysical freedom seems heartless, sickeningly complacent. Listening to the unbearably anguished cries of a new-born child of a drug-addicted mother as it experiences the engulfing horror of opiate withdrawal is a salutary reminder of how little comfort we should draw from the fact that all human beings are points of origin in the world and blessed with agency. The lives of children born to unmarried mothers in Ireland that ended, after years of abuse, in an early unmarked grave, is another reminder of the many whose agency has been subordinated to a mere fight for survival. Even those who lived charmed lives may create their own prisons out of lust, unrequited love, disappointed ambition, greed, resentment, shame, grief and guilt. "Mind-forg'd manacles" may range from major psychoses to small-scale obsessions or just permanently finding things irritating.

We may concede that mere metaphysical freedom, evident even in the self-concern of the most oppressed individual, is a poor, bare thing. Nevertheless, it is the foundation, the necessary condition, of the freedom that makes a rich life possible for some. It is a reminder of the fundamental moral truth that the most important exercise of our own freedom is to enhance the freedom of others, directly or indirectly helping to liberate them from unchosen circumstances which may crush their life chances. How that is to be realized – either individually or politically – is the theme of another book.

With free will comes responsibility whose boundaries are impossible to define, if only because we ride so much on shared agency which has shared consequences. The more our conquest of nature looks like a despoliation, such that nature threatens to return to the unalterable habits' of an uninhabitable planet, the more urgent are our responsibilities though it may sometimes seem difficult to know how to act upon them.

Between birth and death, we have to varying degrees the power to choose and follow our path through life and to regulate our own choices. That power, which originates from the distance opened up by the intentionality of consciousness, may be extended in many ways, though we never come near the omnipotence envisaged by the early Sartre.[11] Our power to choose the circumstances revealed to us as our world, or the needs which shape our interactions with it, has its limits. We can, however, extend that power through the life-long projects of positioning ourselves, projects that are assisted by the agency that originates in collective activities, the technologies and institutions, from which we benefit. We can increase the distance between our day-to-day activities and unchosen, notably biological, needs that we have to satisfy. From this distance, our needs can be elevated to a source of recreation, and an exercise of our freedom. Hobbies, pastimes, sports, socializing, arts, and the pursuit of knowledge for its own sake, are different expressions of that distance and of celebrating the freedom that it permits us.

Art is a particularly striking expression of this. The landscape painting in the gallery requires nothing of us than that we should look at it. Our interaction with its contents – that mountain, those sheep, those clouds – is remote from the interaction that is demanded of the farmer, or even the hiker, never mind the man on the run. Music, which may be about nothing at all, requires only that we should savour sound for its own sake, relish structures being built, and enjoy the passage from beginnings to endings that are motivated by the joy of transition, a virtual journey through a soundscape of connotation where, in the case of programme music, "Spain", "Youth", "The Countryside", "Love" or even "God" are gathered up in a succession of chords, of motifs, in an order that delivers a satisfaction of its own. And then there is literature which allows to us to observe, to engage with, a world on our terms.[12] As Sartre expressed it, art is the world grasped by a freedom, or by one human freedom addressing another.[13]

And so, while we acknowledge that freedom has its limits, not the least being those marked by our unchosen birth and death, we also embrace the pursuit of greater freedom for all as a truly honourable aim. That aim has become more complex as our individual search for freedom and for that of our fellows threatens the very conditions in which human life is possible.

Coda

I have described freedom as an "impossible reality". Its origin is not to be found in the material world and the habits of nature portrayed in the laws and causes of natural science. There are two possible conclusions to be drawn from this: either that our belief in freedom is an illusion; or that natural science, and the simplified metaphysics we take from it, are incomplete accounts of the world and, importantly, of human life. This volume has been devoted to arguing for the second conclusion, not the least because I do not think we should deny the reality of something just because we cannot understand how it is possible when we look at the world through the lens of objective, quantitative science.

That the scientific gaze cannot accommodate free will is to be expected. Science seeks fundamental, underlying, unchanging patterns beneath all change and must therefore look straight past or through the realm where freedom is exercised. It cannot accommodate the perspective on nature that a subject has, even less account for the transformation of what-is into a *situation* which requires action, or into initial conditions that are the platform for such action. There is equally little place for the sense that the present moment, far from being an involuntary inheritance we are stuck with, is a starting point, a point of departure to a chosen future, not predetermined by the habits of nature.

As many philosophers have pointed out, natural science has progressed by removing from its interpretation of the world precisely the subjective consciousness and its intentionality that makes agency possible. The consciousness of human subjects is also that which makes science, its search for laws and causes, possible. If we were not able individually and collectively to approach the habits of nature from without, those habits could not have been discovered and exploited to create the technology by which we are able to predict and manipulate the natural world with ever-increasing power. If the world were the physical world, and the physical world that which is revealed through physics, there would be no physics to reveal it. Physics cannot explain physics. Not even those thinkers wedded to a deterministic world picture rooted in scientism will doubt that there is such a thing as physics.

Our lives as agents are profoundly connected with our sense of purpose, the transformation of appetites and needs into values, and occasionally the search for an overall meaning in our lives. As science ascends to ever wider, impersonal, quantitative generality, however, the last tincture of *telos* is eradicated from its portrait of the universe. Values, meaning, and purpose – central to action – have no place in a reality defined by laws that apply with equal precision to living and non-living entities, to insentient matter. The impossibility of finding agency in the material world drained of "becausation" is consequently entirely unsurprising, as is the absence of whatever it is that motivates physicists to comprehend the universe and gives them the capacity to do so.

This last point is worth dwelling on a little more. Possibly the most illustrious (and profound) of all philosophical determinists was the seventeenth-century Dutch thinker Baruch Spinoza. In his *Ethics* he asserted that: "men think themselves free simply inasmuch as they are conscious of their volitions and desires, and as they are ignorant of the causes by which they are led to wish and desire, they do not even dream of their existence".[1] In saying this, Spinoza overlooked the mysterious process by which he came to this conclusion; the distance from those causes of which he speaks that enabled him to speak of them.

The causes-and-laws deterministic case against free will starts to wilt as soon as we look critically at the nature of causes and laws: when we acknowledge that events seem to be discrete and requiring to be glued together by causation only insofar as they are singled out by the interests of the subject from the continuous unfolding of the physical world; and when we appreciate that the processes leading to the elucidation of the laws of nature do not fall within the scope of those laws and could not be accommodated by them. The causes-and-laws case against free will is further weakened when we acknowledge that actions – even one as simple as raising my hand to vote – are not defined by the physical events of which they are composed. Nor are they embedded in the time and place in which they occur. Actions that take place in the material world draw on the (physically) absent and yet present past and are motivated by possibilities (irreducibly general) that are located in the as yet absent future. To this extent agents are not solely the products of material events but requisition them – as the product of objects that are exploited as handles in a variety of simple and complex ways – to bring about other events.

Thus, we dismantle the arguments which make freedom seem impossible. We allow ourselves to accept the evident truth that it is a universal feature of daily life. It is real. To assert the undeniable reality of human agency is not, however, to deny its mystery. As H. D. Lewis has remarked "If I could lift the spoon at the far end of the table by just willing to do so, instead of walking round and picking it up in the usual way, this would be no more remarkable in the last resort than the control I usually exercise over my own body".[2]

This is echoed by Richard Taylor:

> No one seems able ... to describe *deliberation* without metaphors, and the conception of a thing's being *'within one's power'* or *'up to him'* seems to defy analysis or definition altogether, if taken in a sense which the theory of agency seems to require. These are, then, dubitable conceptions, despite their being so well implanted in the common sense of mankind. Indeed, when we turn to the theory of fatalism, we shall find formidable metaphysical considerations which appear to rule them out altogether. Perhaps here, as elsewhere in metaphysics, we should be content with discovering difficulties, with seeing what is and what is not consistent with such convictions as we happen to have, and then drawing such satisfaction as we can from the realization that, no matter where we begin, *the world is mysterious and the men who try to understand it are even more so.*[3] (emphasis in original).

The most "formidable metaphysical considerations which appear to rule them out altogether" are those which defer to natural science as the nearest we have to the last word on what there is. As we have observed, if what science tells were the whole story, then there would be no science. Human freedom, like science itself, is, and will always remain, a metaphysical scandal if the universe is seen through the necessarily deterministic lens of natural science where, methodologically, no room is or can be allowed for discretion exercised by a part of the whole in shaping the succession of events in other parts of the whole. Agency is real and so, too, is the mystery of agency and the intentionality that makes it possible. The fact that it is real does not make it less mysterious and the fact that it is mysterious does not make it any less real. We are not obliged to deny the reality of something that no-one sincerely denies in daily life.

Free will is not, of course, unique in being at once real, actual, and yet impossible to understand. It shares this character with the universe, which neither could have come out of nothing nor have existed forever (given that there are no actual infinities).[4] And, centrally to our argument, the consciousness in which freedom is rooted is also impossible if we begin with the material world as seen through the lens of science. Nobody, however, doubts, or could sincerely doubt, the existence of the universe or of intentional consciousness. My appeal to intentionality as the origin of the distance that enables us to act on nature, using the laws of nature, and indeed on ourselves, as if from without, does not "solve" the mystery of freedom; rather it moves it to the place where freedom has its origin.

The dark heart of that mystery is our unfathomable ability to *see* the light, to see or *know* how things are, and *face* a world revealed, by literal light or the light of knowledge, to a self-revealing self. Facing the world in this fundamental sense is not an action but the necessary precondition of any action. There is nothing in natural science that gives us any insight into how it comes about that there is something in nature that transforms the anterior surface of the head into something that confronts it, describes it, gives it a name, and puts that name in inverted commas thus: "Nature". *Pace* St John, it was not the Word that was the beginning; rather it was Man, the Explicit Animal whose words transformed what-is into that-it-is; whose gaze illuminated what lay near to hand and reached to the distant stars, bringing them down to earth to be uttered in voices and captured in libraries.

Were we entirely organisms wired into nature, it would not be possible to explain how we could lay down beginnings in the world, initial conditions which provide the platform for actions. Our being true points of origin is something we import into the seamless flow of things, singling out certain events as causes and others as effects, and the present state of things as a jumping off place from which they may be shaped in accordance with our wishes. Perhaps this was what Augustine was referring to in the arresting final sentence of his *City of God* when he said that "God created man so that there might be a beginning in the world".[5] The thought reflects the nature of the human agent as one who, far from being dissolved in the flow of events, intervenes in them, creating fresh starts and (no less mysterious though often overlooked) fresh endings; who has a discrete path through the world, that counts as her own path, rather than being just part of the great universal unfolding.

I shall end where I began – with my teenage self. In this book I have set out the arguments that have persuaded me, in the succeeding decades, that my teenage determinism, which was only intermittently sincere, was also wrong.

Whether I have simply found "bad reasons for what we believe upon instinct"[6] is not for me to say. I can only hope that you have found my arguments persuasive. As for the teenager, I would like to think he would have been converted by this book to a belief in free will, but he disappeared over half a century ago, and so I can't ask him.

APPENDIX A

From the habits of nature to the laws of science

REALISM AND ANTI-REALISM

In an attempt to free the idea of the laws of nature from something that has legislative or regulative power – a hangover, perhaps, from pre-scientific intuitions of God-ordained fate – we have spoken of "the habits" of nature, with reference to the uniformity of its manner of unfolding. The habits are not distinct from nature and hence are not imposed on it. Things don't "obey" their own habits. If those habits are universal and unalterable, however, they are no more open to negotiation than would be the most rigid and "pushy" laws.

But an important point remains: if we close the distance between nature and its patterns of behaviour by replacing "laws" with "habits" we correspondingly widen the distance between nature and the laws of science. At the very least, the laws of science are laws *about* nature and so cannot be identical with the latter. The question therefore arises as to whether, or to what extent, the laws of science are, or could ever be, undistorted articulations of the habits of nature. Are they faithful portraits of how nature fundamentally "goes" and of the stuff in which those habits are expressed; or are they merely useful instruments – cognitive tools to assist us to predict and manipulate the natural world? There are reasons for favouring the latter – the so-called instrumentalist or anti-realist interpretation of the laws of science.

The most obvious come from reflection on the history of science which suggests that all laws hitherto discovered have proved to be provisional, approximate, incomplete, or sometimes plain wrong. They are up for endless revision or replacement. To this process, there seems to be no end in sight. The incompatibility between the two most powerful and fundamental scientific theories

– quantum mechanics and general relativity – is a striking challenge to faith in a gradual progression towards an entirely realistic portrait of the habits of nature. The increasingly desperate but unsuccessful attempts to unite and reconcile those two grand theories – of which 10-dimensional string theory is only the most absurd and inconceivable – gives ammunition to the instrumentalist position.

For instrumentalists, the laws of nature count as true only to the extent that they are useful. Theories are mere tools enabling us to predict and manipulate the future. That they may have astonishing empirical adequacy and enable strikingly accurate novel predictions are not sufficient to prove that they are true in the sense of corresponding to that which is real, independent of human interests or methods of inquiry. For a more effective engagement with the natural world does not require an entirely uncontaminated revelation of what it is in itself, though some may think that the increasing power of its applications is evidence that science is getting closer to how things are in themselves.

Instrumentalists are, furthermore, agnostic about the status of the hidden entities that science talks about. Some are happy to leave it open as to whether, for example, elementary particles are discrete, self-subsistent entities or something more elusive such as the mode of excitation of part of a field. Nevertheless, many physicists and not a few philosophers believe that the most powerful, universal, and basic of the sciences, namely physics, delivers metaphysics, revealing the fundamental truth about nature.

While science is becoming ever more powerful in terms of scope, explanatory reach, the range, novelty, and precision of its predictions, and practical application, it is evident that the multiplicity of its laws reflects the histories of the multiple disciplines of science, whose boundaries may also be construed as historical accidents. As we noted in the main text, laws seem to be tied to scales and direction of attention, to presuppositions that frame enquiries, to the pre-positioning established by prior investigations, and to extra-scientific sources of human interests. The boundaries are consolidated by specialization that separates the work of (for example) physicists, chemists and biologists and the development of further specialisms placing experts into subdisciplines, in different silos. So, experts in optics, acoustics, electromagnetism, electronics, solid state physics, quantum mechanics, work with different laws, though there is considerable overlap and cross-fertilization. Nature herself would not countenance such specialization any more than she could accommodate different funding streams.

The history of science, therefore, with its changing, evolving, and discarded laws and its growing multitude of specialties each populated with their own laws – notwithstanding much cross-border borrowing and unification

– suggests that the laws of science are far from being a direct and undistorted image of the habits of nature.

While for anti-realists, laws are judged true insofar as they work – in the sense of enabling us to make successful predictions and informing technologies that extend our powers – for realists, laws work because they are true. Much discussion in favour of realism was prompted by Hilary Putnam's catchily titled "no-miracles" argument alluded to in the main text.[1] It would be a miracle, he said, if the increasingly empowering laws of science did *not* approximate ever more closely to what is going on in nature and did not connect with real entities and real forces in the real world. Realism is the only philosophy of science that doesn't make the spectacular success of science – pragmatic (delivering what is needed) and epistemic (delivering predictable results) – inexplicable.[2]

One of the most crucial interventions in this debate, in support of the anti-realist position, was Thomas Kuhn's *The Structure of Scientific Revolutions*. Kuhn pointed out that the progress of science was not data-driven in a simple way. There were institutional drivers – and barriers – to the production and revision of theories. This is, of course, what might be expected, given the unnatural nature of natural science.

To Kuhn's dismay – he described himself as not being a Kuhnian – his book was embraced by those who wanted to cut science down to size and to challenge its claim to providing objective truth about the natural world or even to epistemological superiority. His book was appropriated by those who wished to privilege the social dimension of science over method and quality control. The so-called Strong Sociology of Scientific Knowledge relativized the laws of science to "interpretive communities" and made theoretical entities such as atoms and gluons the progeny of laboratories and their parent institutions with their conventions. For Richard Rorty, "truths are … judged only by interpretive communities on the basis of persuasiveness".[3] The objective power of science to help us predict and manipulate the world was ignored or taken for granted.

It is true that the search for laws has often been driven by the need to solve certain technological problems and are hence anchored to human interests and the institutions that serve them. But the great scientific revolutions – the growth of terrestrial mechanics out of celestial mechanics, of electromagnetism out of scattered observations of magnetic behaviour and electricity, and the origin of quantum theory – were not shaped, or centrally determined, by immediate needs; and institutional constraints and group think came further down the track. If scientific inquiry had always been narrowly interested and always constrained by those narrow interests, it would have been closed off from the very sense of possibility that has led to the great breakthroughs, which have ultimately delivered so much. Giving up on the impure alchemical dream of transmuting base elements to gold in favour of understanding those elements has delivered practical riches beyond the dreams of the most avaricious alchemists. No alchemist could have imagined the devices that enable me to see and converse with my friend on the other side of the world by pressing on a few buttons.

THE HIERARCHY OF LAWS: PROGRESS AND UNIFICATION

Nevertheless, those realists who are persuaded by Putnam's no-miracles argument have to confront awkward facts that suggest a gap between the laws of science and the habits of nature. The most striking are the ones that we have referred to already: the exuberant multiplicity of scientific laws. The example, discussed in Chapter 2, of two laws – Boyle's and Charles's – identified as operating at the same place in nature illustrates this. Pressure and temperature are not separated in the natural world: no gas can have a pressure without a temperature or a temperature without a pressure. The two characteristics are different, of course, but as with volume and location, they are both obligatory. Nor does nature differentiate between, and keep apart, dependent, independent, and controlled variables. It is we who do the differentiating in our manipulation of nature to extend our knowledge and understanding of its habits and to exploit that knowledge and understanding in our daily life.

The laws of gases exemplify the distance between the habits of nature on the one hand and on the other the methods by which the laws of science are discovered, and the laws uncovered by these methods. They illustrates the distance between human action (in this case experimentation) and nature, and reveals a margin of freedom available to humans that seemed to have been ruled out by the idea of our being entirely subject to putative laws of nature. We may see the multiplicity of laws as contributing to the case against realism, supporting the belief that the laws of science are not an uncontaminated revelation of the habits, dispositions, and stuff of nature, and challenging the faith that, while science indeed progresses as measured by important criteria, this progress is not a story of ever closer approximation to nature herself. The very idea of pressure or temperature as independent properties in themselves is clearly not sustainable – something that the kinetic theory of gases makes clear.

Notwithstanding the anti-realist case, there is a widespread realist assumption that some scientific laws are closer to nature than others. Those that are further from nature – for example the laws invoked in what are called the special sciences (for some this means all sciences other than fundamental physics) – are, in fact, disguised expressions of the more basic laws, and are in theory deducible from them or will be at some unspecified time in the future. There is, that is to say, a hierarchy of laws and an arrow of explanation that connects the laws at different levels in the hierarchy.

This is captured in a passage from Nobel-prize winning physicist Steve Weinberg: "The explanatory arrow points downwards from societies to people, to organs, to cells, to biochemistry, to chemistry, and ultimately to physics. Societies are explained by people, people by organs, organs by cells, cells by biochemistry, biochemistry by chemistry, and chemistry by physics".[4]

Two features give the laws of fundamental physics their special status. Firstly, they are assumed to be universal. There is no part of the universe that does not at least in theory fall under them. Secondly, and connected with this, it is possible – or thought to be possible in principle – to reduce the laws of the special sciences to those of fundamental physics. The former prove, or will one day prove, to be local expressions of these general laws. Progress in science would be manifested in the convergence of disparate laws to a unified theory of everything, perhaps captured in a handful of equations describing the universe as a single field.

The notion that everything will be reducible to physics of any sort, never mind fundamental physics, is difficult to take seriously. No-one would suggest that the Schrodinger wave equation has much – or indeed anything – to say about the principle of the survival of the fittest or the law of supply and demand. Even if, *per impossible*, it did have something to say, what little it said would remove distinctive content from those laws and from the phenomena falling under them. Removing distinctive content may be what is needed to cancel out the exuberant proliferation of sciences with their own laws that seem to be hostage to the scale and direction of attention, not to say interest, of the relevant science communities and those who make use of their methods, findings, and theories. But it would be a strange kind of progress. The consequences have been wittily summarized by Jerry Fodor when he pointed out that the belief in the ultimate unification of the sciences in physics would have "the peculiar consequence that the more the special sciences succeed, the more they would disappear".[5]

At any rate, the more general and abstract the laws we are working with, the more work that then has to be done to re-attach them to singular, complex, concrete – in short actual – states of affairs. Indeed, as has often been pointed out, scientific laws do not predict actual results (never mine experiences) without the aid of other hypotheses, background assumptions, and specification of initial conditions and of the apparatus being used. The "other things that had to be made equal" (*ceteris paribus*) for laws to be extracted from the unfolding of things have to be unequal. What is described as the "underdetermination" of laws and theories by observations has as its obverse the artificial tidying up of observations to reveal the laws – and requires addition to the laws to deliver actual observations.

It is perhaps not surprising that the laws judged to be most fundamental and closest to nature-in-itself are most explicitly mathematical. Such laws seem not to be dependent on the vagaries of the direction of attention. There is no gaze implicit in numbers or in the connections between variables reduced to quantities, as in say, $E=mc^2$. Equations are ahistorical, non-local in their application, and disconnected from any interests; or, rather, any application and connections with human (or inhuman) interests come later. They are, of course, in addition uncontaminated with the secondary qualities that since Galileo have been regarded as suspect. Light, for example, is represented by its colourless velocity.

This in part explains the privileging of physics but also exposes the irreducible distance between physics and actuality. And it also exposes a questionable assumption: that laws dealing with the very big (indeed the biggest, such as relativity theory) and the very small (indeed the very smallest, such as quantum mechanics) are privileged in the sense of being most liberated from the accidents of the curriculum and of the history of science insofar as it has been determined by human interest and the influence of its own past.

Of the two, it is the science of the very small that has been singled out for especial privilege. A cynic (such as Raymond Tallis) would say that they are closest because specific content has been traded off for scope and reach. Nothing in particle physics would give a hint as to the nature of the world we live in. The Theory of Everything looks like The Theory of Nothing in Particular. That it excludes meaning and value and secondary properties such as colour, experienced warmth, and other contents of experience, is hardly grounds for criticism: it is deeply connected with its extraordinary predictive power. But there is a greater barrenness: it has even been suggested that at the fundamental level there are no discrete entities. As it has been expressed by James Ladyman and others: "fundamental physics for us denotes a set of mathematically specified structures without self-individuating objects".[6] "Everything must go" (to echo the title of Ladyman's book) and be dissolved into mathematics: "fundamental physics has nothing to do with putative tiny objects or their collisions".[7] Farewell the objects, forces, and collisions of classical physics. Hello mathematical structures.

This is a high price to pay for privileging micro-physics as the science that aims to be closest to what nature is in itself. The gradual unpeeling of the veil of appearance seems to result in wholesale dis-appearance. While writers such as Ladyman are aware of, and accept, even welcome, that price, many philosophers who invoke physics – or "micro-physics" – as the ground floor of truth revealing uncontaminated reality seem to have little idea of what they are signing up to.

Consider this passage from John Searle: "Since all of the surface features of the world are entirely caused by and realized in systems of micro-elements, the behaviour of micro-elements is sufficient to determine everything that is happening".[8]

The special sciences – non-fundamental physics and disciplines ranging from chemistry to economics – are confined to what Searle calls "surfaces features": only fundamental physics can see into the depths and this is where (we are to accept) reality is to be found. Any unification of the sciences and progress towards a complete, objective, truthful account of the world, must therefore take the form of an extreme, even perverse, reductionism according to which gluons are more real than swans.

We have repeatedly observed that the laws of science do not explain how they themselves have been extracted from the habits of nature. Privileging the *micro*physical scale makes this failure even more visible. The most obvious problem is that of explaining how the laws of nature are discovered, and indeed have to be discovered, by *macro*scopic beings, using *macro*scopic instruments in *macro*scopic laboratories. Even less does it explain how what is discovered could be sufficiently close to reality to be able to be exploited – as it most certainly is – by the same macroscopic beings using macroscopic technologies in a macroscopic life lived out in macroscopic worlds. Quantum mechanics has changed our lives by being utilized in devices we can see and handle.

This notwithstanding, the prejudice in favour of the microphysical level – that ultimate truth is to be found in atoms or the fields that have replaced them – is so widespread as often to pass without challenge. When physicist Steven Weinberg proclaims that the "explanatory arrow" points downwards from societies to physics, he seems merely to be speaking secular common sense. This is the kind of common sense that Mariam Thalos, who argues against it, characterizes as the belief that "all the real action of the universe ... happens at the smallest scales – at the scale of microphysics".[9] If what-is just boils down to atoms, we have to ask how it scales up to the things we interact with in our lives and indeed boils up to people who interact with them; and also whether the boiling down stops at atoms or continues to probability waves or, as Ladyman suggests, to mathematical structures.

While the conviction that fundamental physics is the last word on what-is and that the "in-itself" of nature is sub-atomic dies hard because of the astonishing power of physics to predict, and to help us manipulate, the world according to our wishes, it is, however, important to acknowledge that that power is not a stand-alone power. The microphysics in the electronic devices that have transformed our lives and vastly extended our capacity operates only in a world of macroscopic objects. What is more, the rules that apply in everyday life are those of macroscopic items and interactions – my lifting a hammer, a bus travelling along a road, a person hearing another person – that lie beyond the weird world of quantum physics or indeed relativity. *Folk* physics is the overwhelmingly, wall-to-wall, dawn-to-dusk reality of daily life. The special powers brought to us courtesy of the application of quantum physics are applied only in macroscopic localities. What is going on in the circuitry of my mobile phone delivers my conversation with you in virtue of being active in a macroscopic phone, held in my macroscopic hand, as I am sitting in my macroscopic room, standing on a macroscopic floor, moving articulate air through my macroscopic mouth – all subject to classical or folk physics.

These considerations justify rejecting the privileging of the microphysical and the faith that the laws of science will (a) converge in those of micro-physics, and (b) in so doing approximate ever more closely to nature-in-itself. If the universe were intrinsically microphysical, the macroscopic world in which we live out our lives as embodied subjects would be entirely inexplicable. Hence the case for embracing Thalos's counter-claim quoted in the main text that "The universe is scale free ... it is active at multiple scales, potentially at every scale ... it's false that the large-scale features are simply inert, and that all of us – large and slow-moving beasts that we are – are banished from the true dance of the universe".[10]

The most significant consequence of this important argument is that it challenges the hierarchy of the sciences that grants ultimate reality to fundamental particles and while denying it to physicists or even their macroscopic apparatus and the laboratories in which they and their apparatus are housed. Equally, it challenges the assumption, common among realists, that there will be a future unification of the sciences into physics, when they will shake off the stigma of being a rather accidental collocation of disciplines that do not reflect the intrinsic nature of nature. The envisaged point of convergence, sought in order to counter the anti-realist charge that the laws are the progeny of the accidents of human interests frozen in disciplinary or institutional silos, is elusive. When nature becomes a handful of equations, it has all but disappeared.

This is not to say that fundamental physics does not capture some profound truths about the universe, including our own bodies. Descriptions at different levels capture partial truths but this only highlights how those truths are not intrinsic to nature. What is more, given that nature does not divide itself into levels, those partial truths are not to be confused with an uncontaminated statement of what is "really" out there, of the universe in itself.

FROM NATURE TO MATHEMATICS AND BACK AGAIN

Which may not be too bad a thing. There is a sense that, as the natural sciences become more fundamental, they get further from, rather than closer to, nature. The atoms in DNA do what they do only as part of that extremely complex double helix. And the double helix is what it is as a key to cellular division. And those cells play their part as small elements of the organs that are what they are as parts of organisms, with the latter being at least in part defined by their role in ecosystems.

What we get in place of nature is structure. The emphasis on structure being conserved as we move from one level to another is in part a response to the anti-realist challenges that comes from the history of science marked by revolutions. Yes, theory replaces theory, forces and stuffs are replaced by other forces and stuffs; but something remains unchanged. What is unchanged is the *structure* of theories; more specifically, given that advanced sciences are mathematical, what they reveal are mathematical structures. We can be realistic about scientific laws, but not naively so, by embracing a *structural* realism that retains mathematical relationships between parameters even when the entities and parameters proposed by theories alter fundamentally.

This radical form of structuralism is called ontic structural realism. It claims to be about the actual stuff of the universe, not just our knowledge of that stuff (epistemic structural realism). If we conflate the laws that propose mathematical structures with the objects of those laws, we can see that nature itself boils down – or evaporates – to mathematical structures. However baffling and counter-intuitive that is, it does seem to be in tune with quantum mechanics according to which the universe is not built out of atomic particles zooming all over the place and banging into each other but is a nexus of non-localized entanglements.

This interpretation of what is going on at the basic, micro-physical level makes the challenge of understanding the world of macroscopic items – mountains, trees, and people – yet more difficult. It is difficult to ascend from such depths to the surface without a severe case of diver's bends. Nevertheless, philosophers who want to attach their wagon to the ever-rising star of physics seem undaunted. The passage earlier quoted from Searle continues as follows: "Such a 'bottom up' picture of the world allows for top-down causation (our minds, for example, can affect our bodies). But top-down causation only works because the top level is already caused by and realized in the bottom levels".[11]

While not everything in the universe is, for example, living matter described by biology, everything is made of matter and in theory described by physics. The laws of physics encompass all of society but the laws of society do not encompass all of the physical world.

The trouble is that the most fundamental laws seem to be empty of content sufficiently specific to deliver what appear to be the contents of our world. The ascent from such basic elements to that which can exert top-down causation seems inexplicable. If a statesman signing a peace treaty, and the treaty itself, and his pen, are best to be understood as collections of sub-atomic elements, it is difficult to see how those sub-atomic elements spontaneously add up separately to statesmen, treaties, and pens. (Understatement of the century.) Granted, the ascent from physics to peace treaties is not an immediate jump – chemistry, biology, anthropology, sociology, history, laws, etc. intervene – but the journey has somehow to be accomplished. And Searle's claim that the top level is both caused by and realized in the bottom level seems contradictory. If the top level is identical with the bottom level (in the sense of being "realized in" it), it is difficult to see how it could be a *product* of that level and, what is more, have causal properties unknown to that level. (The reader may recall the discussion of the statue and the lump of clay in Section 4.3).

While multiplying the steps between sub-atomic physics and (say) sociology – with a multitude of "intertheoretical" bridges – may make the steps smaller, the ascent seems no less improbable. The most obviously improbable step is the passage from insentient to conscious and self-conscious entities. Appeals to "emergence" and "supervenience" do not contribute to solving the problem: they simply restate it. And the suspicion that nothing non-physical – indeed non-microphysical – is truly, really real, remains. "Emergence" is a miracle invoked to correct the self-inflicted injury of reductionism; and "supervenience" corrects the connected self-inflicted injury of an "infravenient" explanation.

Nothing could better illustrate the conflict between the wish to claim a hidden unity in the laws of science – admittedly yet to be discovered – and the need to acknowledge the irreducible heterogeneity of the world such that the laws must be (to use Nancy Cartwright's lovely phrase[12]) a patchwork in a "dappled" world. No law looks like having a universal application or being subsumable by one that does. The expected ultimate unification of the laws of all the sciences in that of fundamental physics – the historically vulnerable and heterogeneous laws being approximations to, or aspects of, a final theory – does not deliver any kind of reassurance to those of a realist persuasion.

Even at the most fundamental level, notwithstanding some elegant math-ematics and stunningly accurate predictions, things are very untidy. The fun-damental equations around the standard model draw on four separate forces – gravitational, electromagnetic, and the weak and strong nuclear forces – and there has been recent talk of a fifth. The menagerie of the fundamental objects of quantum field theory is even more untidy. There are observed particles: fermions, leptons, quarks, and bosons (which come in several varieties – photons, W-bosons, Z-bosons, Higgs bosons, and gluons). And "observed" is generous; it is more accurate to describe them as inferred from observations. Physicists have also to requisition any number of unobserved and perhaps unobservable particles, such as charginos, gluinos, and gravitinos. In addition, there are all sorts of composite items such as hadrons, baryons, and mesons. And some theories predict or requisition an additional menu of hypothetical bosons and fermions – 17 at the last count.[13]

While the growth in the number of particles admitted to the club has slowed since the standard model of the atom was (presumably temporally) finalized in the final quarter of the last century, there is no reason why new particles should not be requisitioned in order to tidy up the maths in future. Either way, this is a rather messy place for science to end up. And unsatisfactory, given that the two over-arching theoretical frameworks – quantum theory and relativity – are incompatible with one another. The hope of redeeming what seems to be an ad hoc collection of laws belonging to different eras of different disciplines by demonstrating that they will converge in a single law or compact set of laws, as a perspectival painting will converge on a vanishing point that transcends perspective, seems forlorn.

THE HIERARCHY REVISITED

Even so, the feeling that higher-level special sciences are cognitively inferior to micro-physics dies hard. This, and the sense that the special sciences are derivative, second-order, or ignorant of what lies at their heart, is not con-fined to physicists. Unadmitted "physics envy" lay behind much of the endeav-our during the "science wars" of the 1990s when many practitioners in the human sciences denied the greater objectivity of the natural sciences. This was before a U-turn at the turn of the century when some in the humanities capitulated and accepted the cognitive superiority of natural sciences. The dream of "consilience" – a marriage of humanities with the sciences on terms set by the sciences – was expressed in such monstrous hybrids as "neuro-humanities".[14]

The relative cognitive status of the disciplines of (say) physics and economics is less important than two general observations that cannot be denied. It may be helpful to reiterate what we have already said on this matter.

The first is that the particular nature and the multiplicity of laws is not dictated by nature herself. The laws of science will be shaped by direction and grain of the interests of the scientific community and those whom they serve. Observations, as has often been noted, are theory-laden and they are laden with more than theories: custom and practice shapes the direction upon which the gaze is turned and the nature of that gaze. The multiplicity of laws is an irreducible feature of the practice of science because the latter necessarily approaches nature from an outside opened by intentionality which develops historically through the joined intentionality of the community of minds as it is expressed in disciplined inquiry. That outside is the necessary condition of the processes of investigation – of observation, measurement, experimentation under controlled conditions – that reveal the laws. Investigation will always take its rise from a platform of pre-existing science – concepts, techniques, questions, areas of interest belonging to individual disciplines – that evolve over time. It is worth at this point again quoting a passage from Quine (cited in Chapter 2, note 19):

> For, in the midst of all this formless freedom for variation, our science has developed in such a way as to maintain a manageably narrow spectrum of visible alternatives among which to choose when need arises to revise a theory. It is this narrowing of sights, or tunnel vision, that has made for the continuity of science, through the vicissitudes of refutation and correction. And it is this also that has fostered the illusion of there being only one solution to the riddle of the universe.

The second undeniable fact is that, as attention moves to more fundamental levels, generality is bought at the cost of draining specific content. Ultimately, content is replaced by mathematical structure and it is not at all clear how it might be possible to recover the rich variety of the manifest world from these structures. Appeals to emergence and supervenience are something between a promissory note and handwaving. It is the problem of explaining how out of supposedly fundamentally uniform, soberly mathematical nature – uniform stuff with unvarying habits – we get "the drunkenness of things being various".[15]

For the quantum-mathematical reductionist, all riches are an embarrassment, especially those captured in the manifest image of the world in which we live our lives. The suggestion that these riches are contaminants put in by the human mind is of no help to the microphysical reductionist. Firstly, it would presuppose that consciousness is not part of the quantum world. This, I believe, happens to be true; it is, however, at odds with the physicalist standpoint. Physicalism identifies consciousness with neural activity which, being physical activity, ultimately falls within the curtilage of quantum theory. Secondly, it would give the conscious subject no reason or grounds for transforming the homogeneous world into any particular manifest image, which seems to be connected with her being identified with a particular (macroscopic) organism and its needs.[16] The manifest image of the world is made of things that quantum physics cannot even dream of – macroscopic, unentangled, self-subsistent objects such as populate physics laboratories. And that is before we have got to even more awkward entities such as colours, poems, and peace treaties. The correct response is not to call them out as ontologically dubious or worse (for example illusions) but to acknowledge the limited scope of quantum physics and, indeed, the supposed fundamental sciences.

REAL PATTERNS

It is useful at this juncture to examine a particularly heroic attempt to rescue realism about the laws of science: the endeavour to identify laws with so-called *real* patterns, a term introduced by Daniel Dennett.[17] The idea was developed by Ladyman *et al.* and is central to their understanding of the laws of science: "discovering laws is, in the end, just a matter of correctly describing real patterns".[18] The mathematical structures revealed by fundamental laws are correctly described real patterns, which are the most general regularities in nature.

There are obvious surface connections between the idea of the laws (or indeed the habits) of nature and patterns. Those patterns connect parameters or variables in a mathematical way; for example, to return to our well-worn example of Boyle's law, pressure (measured in units) varies inversely with volume (also measured in units). The outcome of observations on this relationship would be a straight line. If this pattern were real, it would be possible to predict changes in volumes of an individual body of gas from changes in individual pressures (assuming no other variables are at work) and the succession of volumes discovered in response to a succession of pressures could be summarized in a law.

Describing laws as reflecting *real* patterns is to claim that they are more than merely economical and wide-ranging accounts of observations – the anti-realist account of science. What, then, counts as a real pattern as opposed to any old pattern we might extract from or read into succession of events or data-points? Ladyman follows Dennett (and many others) and appeals to the principle of economy. A real pattern is not susceptible to algorithmic compression.

As John Barrow has explained it,

> The recognition of ... a pattern allows the information content of the observed sequence of events to be replaced by a shorthand formula which possesses the same, or almost the same, information content ... Any string of symbols that can be given an abbreviated representation is ... *algorithmically compressible* ... On this view, we recognize science to be the search for algorithmic compressions ... Without the development of algorithmic compressions of data all science would be replaced by mindless stamp collecting.[19]

Ladyman *et al.* made the same point more succinctly: *real* patterns are descriptions that cannot be captured "using a smaller number of bits of information than the bit-map transcription of the data from which the pattern could be computed".[20]

For some, the implication of "real" in "real patterns" is that they are inherent in nature. They are not projected by us into what we observe, like the images we fancy we see in ink blots. Before accepting that algorithmically incompressible patterns are in that modest sense real, it is worth reminding ourselves of some of what we discussed in Chapter 2 regarding the long journey from nature and its habitual modes of unfolding to the laws of science.

The journey begins with data, typically the product of the measurement of a parameter such as pressure or volume. As for parameters, they are not stand-alone realities in the physical world, even though they are separated in the scientific account of that world. That is why it is possible to extract (at least) two patterns of behaviour from a particular specimen of gas – one relating pressure to volume (Boyle's law) and another relating volume to temperature (Charles's law). They do not seem therefore to be fundamentally real patterns. Indeed, we see rival patterns evinced in the same stuff; or two aspects of another underlying pattern.

Does the subsequent gathering up of the two laws into the higher-order laws of the kinetic theory of gases bring us nearer to real patterns; that is to say patterns inherent in nature? The obvious response is yes. But it overlooks the unnatural process of data acquisition and data processing. There is also the initial positioning that transforms experience of the physical world into a source of data. It may be less obvious, but it adds to the original distance between patterns observed and any putative "real" or "inherent" patterns in nature.

What is more, while the patterns revealed by more advanced and fundamental sciences may be the result of greater algorithmic compression, we have seen how this is bought at the cost of losing more content. The end-stage of an ultimate algorithmic compression that excludes any contamination by the interests, the mode of attunement, or the direction or scale of attention, of the scientist or science community is the replacement of nature by mathematics. It follows inescapably from progressive economization on symbols – and the extrusion of anything subject to algorithmic compression – the over-riding criterion of scientific advance. As Ladyman *et al* put it, "Fundamental physics is in the business of describing the structural properties of the whole universe".[21] And if it is structure "all the way down", it is difficult to find a place for content. The asymptotic "view from nowhere" looks dangerously like a view of nothing.

The summarizing, empty equations of the Final Theory, adding up to an abstract gaze encompassing the totality of things, present the world as a frozen grid. Patterns insofar as they are summaries of kinds of change, and kinds of kinds of change, and kinds of kinds of kinds of change, are, at best, space-like rather than unfolding in time. Such stasis is hardly an accident: the over-arching laws are intended to capture what is unchanging in a changing world. They have no dynamism; they are structures of the relationship between changes. To descend from the airless heights to our homely example, Boyle's law captures an unchanging relationship between changes in pressure and changes in volume, though other things may not be constant. The most fundamental laws are embedded in the presupposition that at bottom nothing really changes and, perhaps, that everything is the same.

The most charitable interpretation of real patterns is that they correspond to the most general habits of nature, leaving out any substrate in which those habits are expressed. In making this point about the end-point of science I have a surprising ally in Stephen Hawking. While he claims that "the ultimate triumph of human reason" would be to "know the mind of God", he goes on to say that "Even if there is only one possible unified theory, it is just a set of rules and equations. What is it that breathes fire into the equations and makes a universe for them to describe?"[22]

More than fire would be required to get from rules and equations to a universe. What is needed to get from "real patterns", the most general possibilities, to a world would be actuality. Something is needed to breathe *content* – encounterable, experiencable, localized, content – into the equations. Real patterns require something other than themselves for a world actually to exist.

We are anyway a long way from "the ultimate triumph of human reason". Even the most fundamental laws fall short of universal application, encompassing the totality of what is. It is important to see this so that we can put science in its appropriate place – elevated, of course, but not so elevated that it counts as nature speaking for itself and could occupy the space vacated by the deities. These most fundamental of equations do not amount to the material world becoming self-conscious. As a secular humanist, I would not expect them to reveal the mind of God. Nor do they reveal the mind of Man, Or, indeed, nature herself.

CONCLUDING THOUGHTS

It seems that we need an account of the nature of laws that avoids both a naïve realism and a sceptical anti-realism. Such an account would reject the claim that the progress of science is analogous to the development of an increasingly accurate mirror image of nature, free of any distortion from the (individual, collective, institutional or historical) human mind. It would also distance itself from the opposite claim of Kant that the laws of nature are the product of the synthetic activity of the mind.[23]

Nevertheless, the very idea of reality uncontaminated by the sense organs, cognitive processes, the discourses, the channels of experience and understanding, of those who judge it to be real is contradictory. We cannot conceive what-is becoming the Given without any contribution from the distinctive properties of the recipient, even though, courtesy of intentionality, the relationship between the given and the recipient is not merely one of mutual interaction and similar contamination. A complete convergence between what-is and any *account* of what-is is not possible. Laws are not simply "there", waiting to be discovered, with the scientific gaze being the progressive unpeeling of appearance from reality.

The ultimately mathematical gaze is not a revealer of supposedly intrinsic laws of nature but the most spectacular manifestation of the extent to which humanity is able to stand outside of nature in its endeavour to see how nature "works". This capacity to stand outside of nature would be no less miraculous if the laws of science were merely operationally or instrumentally true rather than an undistorted image of the most general habits of nature. In either case, they enhance our capacity to summarize, predict, and manipulate the natural world. No other part of the natural world does this.

APPENDIX B

Paying attention to attention

I have focused in the main text on macroscopic expressions of our freedom – journeys to London, plans to get fit, decisions to take an umbrella. There is much more going on in the humble interstices of our agency. Particularly striking is the most mysterious of all preparations to act: the (meta-)act of paying attention. While this is not central to my argument, I find this exquisite exercise of self-control, of promoting our own agency, fascinating. I hope readers will forgive my self-indulgence.

Attention – the active direction of the mind upon some object, event, or topic – is etymologically "reaching" ("*tendere*") towards ("*ad*"). It is intentionality in italics; in some respects, a more muscular or active mode of this relationship between consciousness and object. We may direct our attention in the literal sense of looking or ear-cocking or groping in one direction rather than another; and in the more rarefied sense of deciding at what level we should focus our interest. We may look through a window at a landscape, or examine a fly crawling over the pane, tune into a conversation, or return to the page on which we are planning next year's events. We may employ a range of mental techniques and physical kit to enhance our capacity to scale up and scale down our attention, using literal and metaphorical microscopes and telescopes.

Paying willed attention, and controlled switching of attention, are the most intimate means by which we act on ourselves, in order to gear up for action. "Keeping an eye on" something, some situation, or some ongoing process, "listening out for" a sound indicative of an important signal – these belong to the ground floor of regulated attention. We may do this unaided or with the help of others who may point things out to us, instruct us in what to look out for, or help us to "snap out of" one mode of attention in order to adopt another. Such are the delicate levers by which we can act upon ourselves to enhance and regulate our agency.

Attention is a crucial link between the intentionality of mental states and forming and fulfilling intentions. It is often overlooked. Indeed, I overlooked it myself until the nature of attention as a mental act was drawn to my, er, attention by Tom McClelland's "The Mental Affordance Hypothesis".[1]

AFFORDANCES

"Affordance" was a term introduced by psychologist J. J. Gibson over half a century ago. Gibson wanted to remind his colleagues that perception is not merely a spectator sport. It is interwoven with actual or possible action and is in part regulated by action. How we perceive the world is structured by the possibilities for interaction with it: perception is action-orientated. Affordances are perceived items that increase the disposition to certain actions and, indeed, may gird us up for them – a phenomenon described as "potentiation". Our environment is experienced as a shifting set of such affordances against a background of things that are less or not at all salient.[2] Even a neonate wriggling in a cot, pans round to see what it can see, though it has limited head control, preferentially seeks out faces, and connects its mother's carnal presence with the possibility of warmth and of the satisfaction of hunger.

Artefacts are obvious affordances: they have been manufactured to serve a certain purpose. A chair is a standing invitation to sit down. Naturally occurring objects are also experienced as opportunities for action: a tree may be "climbable" or a cave may be encountered as a potential hiding place – a "me-hideable" – or a shelter.

At any given time, however, only a few of the items that surround us are experienced explicitly as affordances because most are irrelevant to our ongoing concerns. The trees whizzing by the train window as I work on a paper for a meeting do not invite me to engage with them, though they may trigger a pang for a lost boyhood. Opportunities for action, that is to say, are preoccupation- or agenda-dependent. A book on my shelf may be promoted from mere background to an affordance when I need to consult it. The decision to climb a mountain transforms its surfaces into footholds and handholds. Affordances are not confined solely to individual material objects: they include scenarios such as deteriorating weather or the crowdedness of a room.

Affordances are the building bricks of a world of opportunity – or possibility-for-me or possibility-for-us – as when I or we see something that

I or we might make use of. Alternatively, they may be present under the guise of necessity, as when I see something such as a predator or an oncoming car that I must avoid.[3]

MENTAL AFFORDANCES

McClelland extends the notion of an affordance beyond affordances for *bodily* actions, such as gripping, walking, eating, and fleeing, to affordances for *mental* actions. Mental actions are mental events that seem to be under our own control. They include imagining, counting, and most importantly, perhaps over-archingly, attending. McClelland distinguishes, among events or scenarios that "afford attention", those on the one hand that we attend to deliberately or at least voluntarily, from others which press themselves on us, and insist on being attended to, even when our minds are, or even should be, on other things. Attention to a pain or a loud bang is involuntary: we are "hailed" (to use McClelland's term) by such events. They are distractions that may be irresistible. By contrast, focusing on something in response to one's own or another's instruction – "Pay attention!" – seems to be voluntary and may involve mental effort. The differences are of course a matter of degree.

REGULATING OUR ATTENTION

"Attention" therefore occupies a wide zone between passive or receptive awareness on the one hand and on the other active or permissive, exclusive and deliberate focusing of consciousness. These gradations of attention may be illustrated by vision, which encompasses involuntarily registering a flash, voluntary looking, watching, staring, peering, scrutinizing, interrogating, and, finally, making formal observations, including measurements whose extraordinary nature we discussed in Chapter 3. Deliberate attention, being "on the look-out" for possibilities – as when we are waiting for something to happen or someone to turn up – involves active differentiation of what count as signals from what is discarded as mere noise. Under such circumstances, we predetermine what might qualify as affordances – things worthy of our attention, justifiably soliciting action.

This is where the idea of mental affordances gets particularly interesting because it is relevant to wider issues of agency and volition. The regulation of our own attention is central to the exercise of free will and indeed a coherent life. Let us unpack this a bit.

An action seems to be most clearly voluntary, something that I *do*, when I "pay attention" to at least some of its elements, and those elements explicitly connect both the goal of the action and the present circumstances in which it is taking place. This, more than anything, distinguishes action from a mere *re*action as when I duck to avoid a missile or jump in response to a loud sound, which seems closer to a happening than a doing. Attending can itself seem like or involve an action, as well as being the condition of a successful action. I can pinch myself to keep myself alert or utilize instruments to sharpen my senses or systematically pan round, searching for something of relevance to my present concern.

Under such circumstances, perception seems like an achievement, even an action in itself. "I *make* an observation". Part of that achievement is the ability to select the scale of attention – from landscapes to fly's legs. Nature itself does not have such scales, any more than (to refer back to our discussion of the so-called laws of nature) it is an atomic physicist, a chemist, a zoologist, a microbiologist, or a geologist.

ATTENTION, INATTENTION AND ACTION

While it seems obvious that controlled, selective attention is the condition of a truly voluntary action, the closer we inspect it, the more complex appears the relation between attention and the exercise of our agency. Consider something pretty quotidian such as going to a pub to see a friend. During the journey I am aware of much that is happening. Only a small minority of the events are relevant to my walk, offering, requiring, or demanding my attention. While there will be plenty of stimuli that could force themselves upon me, I reject them as mere distractions, unless they have a unignorable significance as when a hoot warns me that I am about to step in the path of a car. I likewise ignore a lot of the stuff that is going on in my mind – thoughts and daydreams – on the way to my destination. I narrow the scope of my outer attention to that which is demanded of me by the action in which I am engaged, though I may interweave this with controlled attention to my own thoughts. If the route, the setting, or the context is familiar, so that I do not have to suss out where I am and which way I should go, my attention to my surroundings can be safely narrowed even further. I can cognitively coast.

The attentional affordances that shape, guide, or energize voluntary actions are often prescribed in advance. What makes street signs or the pub names privileged as affordances is their relevance to our goals. Behind this is a network of "becausations": my going to see you in the pub – for example to discuss a joint plan – draws on a multiplicity of sources that make sense of the action as it fits into my life insofar as it overlaps with yours. It includes your instructions as to the route, that require me to look out for the labels on the roads. This is one of many ways in which our conscious purposes shape our attention and our choice of attentional affordances keeps us on what now counts as "the straight and narrow" as we endeavour to fulfil those purposes. We must also strike a balance between focused and open attention, between inwardly regulated "concentration" and responsiveness to happenstance events, if we are to deal with the unexpected but important, such as a car heading towards us or a generous helping of dog dirt on the pavement.

There is an even more complex interdigitation of outer and inner attention when I am engaged in large-scale tasks, such as taking a train to London, mixed with other smaller scale actions such as having a coffee or carefully reading the documents relevant to the meeting for which I am headed. Once I am on the train, I can switch attention completely to the papers I am reading or making my tottering way back to my seat from the buffet with a coffee in my hand.

As we noted in Chapter 4, the action of going to London is as it were outsourced to the train service and I do not need to "do" going to London or even to continuously try to do so. While I don't have continuously to intend the journey, I should always be able, if asked, to say what I am intending to do. The journey is not a two-hour sustained physical, intentional, or attentional effort: nothing is required of me to continue journeying other than that I do not leave the train. My ride is an elective "being done to", with the exertion of volition lying in the past or the future. This interdigitation of activities does not alter the fact that the sense of what I am about – or ought to be about – must continue to direct my choice of what is salient in my environment and indeed my choice of environment; what I ought to attend to. If the train breaks down and we have to disembark, then my attention switches back to "doing" the journey and I engage with a different set of attendabilia.[4]

Voluntary attention, then, is dappled with inattention, which may range from deliberately ignoring or shutting out what is happening within or around me to being spontaneously oblivious of it. Because I do not usually need to *do* most of the elements that are involved in walking to the pub – maintaining my balance, putting one leg in front of the other – I don't have to attend to most of the perceptions associated with them, unless something goes awry. The semi-automatic generation of standardized steps is contrasted with the bespoke action of navigating myself to a particular destination, in the service of a singular goal, executed with the aid of street signs or written instructions that are consulted to support a decision to turn left or right or just carry on.

Attentional affordances will be replaced during an action as we judge what has to be done, how it is to be done, and monitor our performance in ongoing actions – whether we are "on course", and have or have not arrived at our goal.

The distribution of attentional affordances, and the balance between *doing* and *happening* in an action, will be radically different when I am learning to walk or recovering mobility as after a stroke (when I will need to concentrate on my balance) as opposed to just walking; or when I am following instructions as opposed taking a route I could follow in my sleep (when I have no need to consult street signs). Training and practice, which will enable us to do effortlessly things which initially had to be enacted consciously, painstakingly, and attentively, are only the most obvious expressions of our capacity to manipulate ourselves in order to focus on certain things and safely ignore others.

Learning how to regulate our own attention – its level, its direction (including outward versus inward) and its grain – is a particularly striking expression of our capacity to improve our ability to exercise our freedom. It reminds us of the extent to which we have a hand in creating the cognitive opportunities we take advantage of in furthering our interests. We can regulate our attention directly, or indirectly, immediately or from an interval of time. We can set traps for our attention, ambushing ourselves with reminders to look, listen, or read. We can even manipulate the very possibility of any kind of attention – namely being wide awake – by a variety of means such as pinching ourselves, taking a breath of fresh air, drinking a coffee, making sure we had a good night's sleep, setting an alarm, or asking someone else to wake us up in the morning.

This regulation of our global levels of attention – sleeping and waking, drowsiness and alertness – is particularly impressive. The harder we try to switch off wakefulness, the more sleep eludes us. Nevertheless, we can increase the likelihood of our getting the beauty sleep we deem necessary by creating conditions – outside or inside our bodies – that will favour dropping off. And clearly, while we need to be awake to act upon the intention to wake ourselves up, we can outsource the necessary means of arousal to other people or alarm clocks.

The transformation of our surroundings into a source of solicited or planted or rigged "attendabilia" – profoundly different from the world as seen through the lens of physics – is one of the keys to the difference between a life that is a mere succession of moments, and a *vita* that has a curriculum. Our inwardly manipulated attention is a striking development of our capacity to turn and *face* the world rather than being merely part of its flow. Obeying the strange inwardly-directed command "to pay attention" – is central to self- and world-control, and to the creation of an ever-increasing distance between on the one hand a mere train of reactions driven by a torrent of unsolicited experiences and on the other carefully chosen journeys undertaken in the interval between the womb and the tomb.

CONVERGENT ATTENTION

Throughout this book, I have highlighted the extent to which our unique capabilities are rooted in joining of consciousness maintained between groups of different sizes and duration. One expression of this is the extent to which our communal lives are built on past and present convergent attention. Attending to things together in order to intend together enables modes of cooperation and self-development unknown even in our nearest primate kin. Beyond this, our public spaces are crammed with "notices" that directly or indirectly solicit or demand attention addressed one and all.

A striking example is what we may call "institutionally prescribed" attention. In my professional life as a doctor, most of my waking consciousness was directed towards attentional affordances that I was obliged to seek out, respond to, and interpret. My (relatively!) expert, technologically-trained attention would extract "attendabilia" such as elements of the patient's history, signs ranging from the demeanour of the patient to subtle changes in movements that might indicate neurological disease, and the appearances of scans. My years of training and (alas) mistakes transformed aspects of the perceived world into "signs" – mental affordances that would require my response, at the very least an interpretation of what they might signify. All of this was supported by the material and human infrastructure of an institution called "a hospital", expressing a sedimentation of collective attention.

CONCLUDING REFLECTIONS

The notion of attentional affordances takes some of the sting out of the very idea of perceptual affordances, where the object seems perhaps to be calling the shots, allowing less scope for the exercise of discretion. Such a direct connection between perception and action may seem to cut out the middle person – or middle term – and threaten to narrow the distance between the agent and the world upon which she acts. This gives an image of organism–environment coupling that is not fundamentally different from that which is seen in higher, and indeed lower, animals. As Markus Schlosser points out, the "[a]ppeal to [physical] affordances may help to explain intelligent interactions that are governed by features that are present, here and now. But it clearly cannot explain temporally extended planning agency".[5] McClelland's highlighting "mental affordances" restores that distance. (We shall revisit this issue in Appendix D).

Our capacity to regulate our attention – scale, direction, intensity – is the most intimate and mysterious aspect of our freedom. The individual and shared control of attention is central to the many shared worlds in which we achieve things far beyond the scope of other living creatures. It is a crucial link between intentionality and intention. In any discussion of agency and free will, it deserves our meta-attention.

APPENDIX C

Beastly freedom? Animals as agents

Some readers may feel that there is a serious omission in this volume: a discussion of whether or not animals are true agents and the extent of any freedom they may have. There are several reasons for not engaging with this controversial topic. The first is that my central purpose has been to defend the possibility of human freedom. The second is that many of the arguments around animal freedom are empirical and draw on contested interpretations of their behaviour. The third is that the topic of animal versus human consciousness and behaviour is one I have discussed elsewhere at some length. In a range of books, I have highlighted what I believe to be a huge gap between ourselves and other living creatures, even our nearest primate kin.[1] While I believe it is clear that other animals do not seem to be free to the extent, or in the manner, that we are, a few words on the question of whether they have *any* freedom of the kind that we have discussed seem justified.

In this book have argued that human freedom is rooted in the following characteristics of our human being:

1. A consciousness marked by full-blown and shared intentionality;
2. The intentions, beliefs, desires, hopes, reasons, and envisaged goals that lie at the heart of actions;
3. The ability to entertain and share explicit possibilities;
4. Tensed time, with a developed sense of the future informed by an explicit past;
5. And, growing out of this, an ability – whose most sophisticated expression is the discovery and exploitation of the laws of nature – to

approach the material world from an ever-expanding outside offset from what-is.

It might seem to follow from this that genuine agency is unique to human beings. While it seems likely that the consciousness of higher animals has some intentionality, it is not developed in the way it is in humans, not the least because of the absence of the kind of communication that fills our human days. We do not have direct evidence on this issue, but it seems reasonable to suppose that, for example, beliefs, knowledge, and thoughts, the holistic spaces created out of them, that are central to agency, are not present in animals, or not to anything like the degree they are present in humans.

Although beasts are sentient, and hence capable of suffering, and consequently deserving of protection from gratuitous ill-treatment, their behaviour does not seem to be freely chosen in the light of a planned or envisaged future drawing on an explicit past. The life of an animal is nothing like what is described in the biography of a human being. Beasts seem to pinball through their lives. The behaviour that serves the fundamental Darwinian purpose of survival and reproduction can be plausibly boiled down to conditioned and unconditioned reflexes, instincts, and tropisms, tuned by passive associative learning to the contingencies of a particular environment, rather than being the product of deliberation, intentions, reasons, knowledge, and so on that direct it towards envisaged possibilities. The beast, as an organism destined to follow out a biological prescription, is consequently more like a conduit through which the flow of nature passes, deflected only by properties expressed in propensities it has not itself chosen.

Of course, freedom is not a yes or no phenomenon: it is graded. Some individuals in some circumstances are freer than others in other circumstances. If freedom is graded, why should it not be present, though to a lesser degree, in non-human animals? After all, the human body and brain was generated by the same Darwinian processes that gave rise to other organisms. There does not seem to be any basis for a metaphysical difference between *Homo sapiens* and other organisms, let alone her nearest primate kin.

There is a vast literature arguing for the belief that the difference between humans and (other) animals is a matter of degree rather than kind and some have argued that this applies to the capacity for freedom. Helen Steward has presented a particularly clear case for "agency ... as a power, or set of powers that can be safely ascribed to a wide variety of animals".[2] Animals are capable of genuine actions that are sufficient to challenge universal determinism, which Steward defines as "the thesis that whatever happens anywhere in the universe ... is necessitated by prior events and circumstances combined with the laws of nature".[3]

Steward's argument for animals as agents is anchored on their being "self-moving". Beasts choose at least some of their movements. As a result, their future is open: there is more than one physically possible future. Importantly, she defines "self-moving" carefully to distinguish it from the self-propulsion of, say, a single-celled creature or a robot. Genuinely self-moving organisms are sufficiently complex and integrated to "own" their bodies: they possess "a capacity for a kind of top-down determination of what will occur with respect to the movement of their own bodies, in such a way that their contribution *does* amount to something over and above the contribution of the processes inside them which eventuate in the resulting bodily movements".[4]

In short, they are beings that make their bodies move and have an element of discretion in the choice of those movements and can consequently adjust their behaviour to the changing demands of a changing environment. Crucially, they are genuine *originators* of certain chains of events. This takes Steward to a bold conclusion which embraces what she describes as "part of our everyday commonsense metaphysics" – namely "that the universe is, as it were, loose at those places in it where animals act – that they are free, within limits, at those junctures, to make it unfold as they will".[5]

Someone might even argue that there are respects in which humans are *less* free than some other animals. Cultural constraints and "mind forg'd manacles" do not seem to be especially developed in animals – though some beasts are assigned roles or places in the pecking order that are biologically prescribed: omega males and drones accept their place in the social order, not the least because they are not explicitly aware of it. And if our freedom has been vastly enhanced by our fellow humans past and present, our extended interdependency adds to the power we have to limit, indeed to destroy, each other's freedom. While the social order is the cornerstone of personal freedom, it can also be the basis for lifelong oppression.

Steward's argument for animal agency may seem to have something going for it. Anyone who claims that human beings are true agents, can deny agency to all other living creatures, she says, only "on pain of postulating an absurd and inexplicable discontinuity in the natural order".[6] Human exceptionalism seems a pre-Darwinian stance, even a theological hangover. For a secular humanist such as myself who is persuaded of Darwin's account of the origin of the species, including *H. sapiens*, this is a worrying thought.

And yet there is manifestly a vast gulf between human agency and that of other animals, even when the animals in question are our nearest primate kin. By identifying agency with self-movement, Steward sets a rather low bar, given that in many instances what counts as the "self" that is moved is hardly the kind of conscious being that we associate with agency that knows its own why, what, and wherefore and is situated in a many-layered, many-stranded, temporally deep, self that is realizing, or trying to realize, a multitude of goals that make sense in relation to some larger life plan.

There is little evidence in non-human animals for the elements that we have invoked in relation to human agency – full-blown and joined intentionality,[7] the explicit entertainment and articulation of possibilities, the elaboration and sharing of plans drawing on a shared and extended past and future, higher-order reflection, reasoning, and other modes of connectedness of the self-as-agent with all her apparatus of taking responsibility. Of course, non-human animals may anticipate what is going to happen and may be wrong. Nevertheless, those unfulfilled possibilities are not free-floating general ideas, entertained in the way that people entertain them. Their scope is limited. Unlike the possibilities that make sense of my unfolding activity, they are typically anchored to events within a sensory horizon. My agenda is frequently disconnected from what is before me in my sensory field and my realization of intentions is quite unlike an animal bouncing from stimulus to stimulus, just as researching is a far cry from an animal following a trail of cues. The future to which I am self-directed is largely invisible except insofar as it is entertained and often located in post-tensed time – as when I try to finish something by next Wednesday or commit myself to an appointment a couple of weeks hence. This fundamental difference is captured in Wittgenstein's penetrating observation that "We say a dog is afraid his master may beat him; but not, he is afraid his master will beat him tomorrow".[8]

We need to distinguish adaptive behavioural mechanisms from voluntary behaviour directed by an explicit purpose with a bespoke goal. If we fail to make that distinction, there is a danger of extending the agency to all living organisms; to, for example, the mechanisms that secure the passage from the seed to the full-grown tree or those that guide the behaviour of even relatively simple animals. The danger is real: Steward instances the Portia jumping spider as an agent. It certainly meets her criteria for agency.

Animals, unlike humans, seem to live in the moment. Mental time travel has been ascribed to a few animals – for example scrub jays. It is, however, expressed only in a specific set of behaviours. It is not generalized, and is not apparently shared.[9] Moreover, there is nothing corresponding to the sedimentation of tensed consciousness into calendrical and historical time that is so central to our individual, and even more to our shared, agency.[10] Such time is necessary for the kinds of contractual obligations that fill our human lives. Even less do animals enhance their powers by exploiting the habits of nature that they have made explicit. They do not even seem to mobilize a pre-scientific appreciation of general principles, the sense of how things work, in problem-solving.[11]

While thinking of animals as agents may help to organize the thoughts of bioscientists, the use of the term outside of human contexts should be seen as metaphorical. Biological mechanisms – including the countless macroscopic and microscopic processes that constitute the functioning of my body – are mindless, though they serve a purpose which is visible to biologists and other intelligent observers. Such mechanisms are no less implacable than the wider habits of nature, except insofar as they can be derailed by external forces. They do not fall under their own control.[12]

These differences seem to justify our identifying a fundamental difference – one of kind rather than of degree – between what prompts and guides animal behaviour and the actions of human agents. This leaves some important unfinished business; namely, addressing the question of how human beings, and their agency, got to be so different. This, however, is a topic for another book. Indeed, it has been such a topic.[13]

APPENDIX D
Agency, enactivism and embodied cognition

"The longer Levin went on mowing, the oftener he felt moments of oblivion, in which his arms did not seem to move the scythe, but the scythe itself, his whole body, so conscious of itself, so full of life, and as if by magic, regularly and definitely without a thought being given to it, the work did itself of its own accord".

Leo Tolstoy, *Anna Karenina*

THE ENACTIVIST CORRECTIVE: ABSORBED COPING

Much of this book has been a corrective to those who see us as natural objects wired into nature. An unintended consequence may have been to suggest that we are somehow entirely cut off from nature and live at a spectatorial distance from the material world. For many contemporary philosophers, this kind of thinking is the last trace of a departing Cartesian ghost. The idea that actions are in some sense driven by, informed by, or even prompted by, propositional attitudes – such as desires, less full-blooded ones such as beliefs, even more anaemic ones such as intentions, and entirely bloodless ones such as reasons – is untrue, they argue, to the reality of voluntary behaviour. We are not mere spectators who, every now and then, choose to dirty ourselves by engaging with the material world.

This is not the view that is advanced in this book; nor is it one with which I am in agreement. Yes, and crucially, we are able to operate on a material world with and in the service of our material bodies from an outside opened up by intentionality and greatly expanded by the joining of intentionality within ourselves (notably through memory) and with that of others to create the vast realm of knowledge and expertise supplemented by technology. But we are not metaphysical flâneurs, engaging with that world as and when and how we like. What we do is part of an ongoing life. We are swimming in a sea into which we are often thrown by events. Our daily existence, that is to say, is not as reflective and elective as the emphasis on the central role of propositional attitudes in our behaviour may suggest to some.

We have already examined what has been characterized as the over-intellectualization of behaviour in Section 4.1, acknowledging the role of automaticity in much of what we do, and addressing concerns about "the unbearable automaticity of being" by invoking Markus Schlosser's concept of a derivative intention.[1] This is not radical enough for some philosophers. There has been a movement in philosophical psychology, going under a variety of names – "enactivism" and "embodied cognition" being particularly prominent – that has subjected the notion of behaviour driven by mental states such as propositional attitudes to a more radical critique.

Several concerns motivate this turn in the philosophy of action. Foremost is a laudable wish to correct a narrow, exclusive focus on the brain and quasi-computational information processing performed in discrete intracranial modules as the basis of action. It acknowledges that the body is a constraint on cognitive function, distributes cognitive processing, and regulates cognitive activity over space and time, ensuring the coordination of action and cognition.

Reinstating the body at the heart of action is hardly something that one would want to quarrel with. The other drivers of enactivism – the desire to marginalize the role of consciousness and mental items such as propositional attitudes – are more problematic. These concerns go beyond acknowledging what can be reasonably accepted: that many elements of complex actions and well-practised routines do not seem to depend on a formulated intention and/ or a representation targeting a goal.

Consider what psychologists call the "time-gap experience" in which an agent engaged in a sustained action can realize that time has passed without her having been aware of it. It typically arises in relation to a complex series of well-practised routines, as when you are driving a car in quiet traffic conditions or along a motorway. The actions have become habitual, and if they have relatively unchanging demands, they do not require conscious attention. The apparent gap in time is a gap in alertness or conscious attention. The effort of driving seems to have been outsourced to an automatic pilot. The sense that "I am doing this" seems to weaken to the point where it is almost a case of "it is happening".

The time-gap experience highlights what Heidegger referred to as the forgetful "absorbed coping" that characterizes much voluntary activity. Hubert Dreyfus, in particular, built on the Heideggerian account of human beings as "thrown" beings-in-the-world dealing with ongoing situations rather than rational agents calculating their way through the world and their lives. Highlighting absorbed (or skilled) coping marginalizes the intelligence mobilized in planning and performing actions as if agency were "fundamentally calculative, computational, or rule- based involving explicit and codifiable thought, the paradigm of which is inferential thinking".[2] Moreover, as Kristina Gehrman and John Schwenkler express it, Dreyfus emphasized that "rather than being *individual, agential* and *rational*, human beings are *embedded, absorbed, and embodied*".[3] This notion of agents as "embodied" also drew on Merleau-Ponty for whom humans are, as in this volume, "embodied subjects".

Dreyfus's argument went beyond merely reinserting the body at the heart of the regulation of action. He asserted "the sovereignty of practical over all other forms of intelligence". This led him "to forsake the contested terminology of practical reason, action, and intention altogether, and he couched his positive views instead in terms of practical skill, practical expertise, phronesis, and skilled, absorbed, or embodied coping".[4] In a wide variety of situations "human beings relate to the world in an organized purposive manner without the constant accompaniment of a representational state which specifies what the action is aimed at accomplishing".[5]

REPRESENTATIONALISM AND ANTI-REPRESENTATIONALISM

Why should this seem to be relevant to our present inquiry? Because many proponents of "enactivism" and "embodied cognition" – certainly the extreme or radical wing – set out their stall in opposition to what is called "representationalism". Representationalism is the belief that understanding human cognition and (more importantly for us) agency require the ascription of mental representations to the agent. Enactivism more broadly "rejects the idea that biological systems operate on the basis of internal representations and information processing mechanisms".[6] As Markus Schlosser expresses it, "A mental representation is presumed to be an agent-internal 'stand-in': an internal state or process that is about something and that has the potential to initiate and guide the agent's interactions with the world".[7] The idea of "an internal state or process that is about something" is close to that of a propositional attitude, that has been so central to our understanding of agency. The radical enactivist approach sees cognition as the bodily activity of the whole organism which can be explained without invoking discrete mental states.

Insofar as it challenges the idea that action is driven by "mental representations" – for example of future states of affairs – enactivism contains some truth. The vision of our multi-tasking moments – where short- and medium- and long-term goals are pursued side-by-side, and the "in order to" connection operates at different levels and granularity – being sustained by simultaneous mental representations clearly has little to recommend it. The conception of our daily life as being strung together out of a sequence of discrete intentions that are the proximate causes of our actions also seems untrue to the busy, distracted, reality, we have described in Chapter 4. As Schlosser expresses the anti-representational argument "the explanation of skilled coping in terms of mental representations would be both costly and clumsy".[8]

The need for a corrective to the idea of an agent as being guided by a series of clear-cut, discrete mental states, is understandable – indeed, welcome. In particular, I would be sorry if it were concluded from the arguments in this book that our actions are driven by *representations* – understood as mental images of the future states that are their goals or some kind of computationally coded versions of such images. Nevertheless, there are brands of enactivism that go too far – removing or marginalizing the intermediary propositional attitudes that are central to action. There is a need for correction to the correction.

Schlosser points out that the anti-representationalists have traditionally had difficulty with actions whose goals are absent or abstract – actions characterized as "representation-hungry" by Andy Clarke and Josefa Toribio.[9] Schlosser extends the scope of "representation-hungry" agency to encompass "temporally extended agency". This is a vast extension. It is larger, perhaps, than he appreciates because, as we discussed in the main text, much of agency is temporally extended – both in the sense of having goals located in the future and being envisaged as occupying extensive stretches of said future.

The need for a corrective to the enactivist corrective is highlighted by the fear that it proposes too close a coupling between the agent and her environment. This threatens to reduce behaviour to a mere response to a mere stimulus. While the stimulus in question may be better understood as a situation than a collection of physical states and events, radical enactivism still threatens to exclude something central to agency: the capacity literally and metaphorically to stand back, and to reflect, and plan. While we are not spectators, engaging with what is outside of us at our leisure, nor are we totally immersed in the flow of events. Action is not reducible to reaction. More, therefore, is needed than the "absorbed coping" that we also see in our animal kin. Without that "more", absorbed coping would absorb the coper.

These fears about enactivism are fulfilled in radical schools of enactivist thought that focus on the "sensorimotor coupling" between organism and environment common to all organisms (even single-celled ones) and human agents. Such versions of enactivism undermine the assumption that we generally know what we are doing and that that knowledge is essential to our being able to do it; more particularly that acquired skills or know-how require a significant background of "knowing-that" in order to be exercised at the appropriate time, in the appropriate way, towards a specific, chosen goal. Even moderate versions of enactivism threaten to narrow the gap between actors and the natural world and to squeeze the distance that creates the outside-of-nature from which genuine actions are performed. They lie at the top of a slope which may be more slippery than many moderate enactivists appreciate. If, to requote Gehrman and Schwenkler, "rather than being *individual, agential* and *rational*, human beings are *embedded, absorbed, and embodied*", there is not much space for true agency.

I have argued elsewhere that the human agent is an "uncoupled animal".[10] Any account of our agency must hinge on the distance that separates active subjects from the world upon which, or within which, they act out their intentions. This distance marks the difference between on the one hand the rational, deliberate activity – or even the relatively absent-minded performance of learned skills (which are themselves the reward for much rational, deliberate activity) – seen in human agents and, on the other, the instincts, imprinted responses, tropisms, drives, conditioned and unconditioned reflexes, that prompt animal behaviour. The distance is particularly evident in the period in which we are transitioning to the effortlessness of practised performance; when we are learning to acquire a variety of skills, "to find our way round" in a multitude of senses of this phrase. This period is, in fact, lifelong: it is not as if there is an apprenticeship which ends with adulthood. We are always practising something. At any given time of our life, "the deft and sure activity of the expert and the humbling behavior of the novice"[11] are side by side.

What is more, when we do employ automatic skills this is often, indeed usually, part of something bigger that is not automated. As Schlosser puts it, "most instances of skilled coping are in the service of higher intentions and plans. They are usually sub-actions or sub-routines that we perform in order to achieve higher ends or long-term goals".[12] Our standardized, absent-minded perambulation serves novel, bespoke, ends that we have in mind.

The more radical versions of embodied cognition and enactivism therefore threaten to collapse something central to the understanding of agency – and indeed the very possibility of genuine agency in a seemingly law-governed universe; namely, the distance between agent and world that enables the former to act upon the latter from a virtual outside opened up by intentionality. Taken to the limit, enactivism squeezes out the cognition that coldly animates, or "amimates" the body of a person explicitly weaving a strand of her life's course.

Just how complete this collapse may be is flagged up by the literature on radical enactivism sympathetically reviewed by Tobias Schlicht.[13] He explores the endeavour to naturalize not only intentionality but also the states of mind with which it is associated. He cites Thomas Metzinger's bold claim that "it is an *obvious fact* that biological nervous systems are able to generate representations of the world and its causal matrix by forming internal states which then function as internal representations of this causal matrix" (italics mine).[14] That this is far from an "obvious fact" to this writer will be evident from the Overture to this book. Assuming that the impact of the "causal matrix" on the nervous system is sufficient to "cause" an internal representation of itself bypasses the mystery of the intentionality of conscious events. Indeed, it overlooks it or, at least, the distinctive contribution it makes to our human being.

The consequences of this are jaw-dropping – if not entirely unexpected. Citing the neurophysiologist Antonio Damasio, Schlicht concludes it is "only a question of scale to accept a single cell as the bearer of intentionality, since the cell shares the same basic organization as a complex organism such as a human being".[15]

There is worse to come. Schlicht cites (though he does not support) Metzinger's position that if we ascribe intentionality to single cells, we must also grant that they have representational capacities. Schlicht resists this final step by defending the distinction between intentional and representational states. Intentionality, he argues, is a feature of a whole embodied agent while representation is a feature of mental states. By separating intentionality from representation in this way, he believes he opens the path for a radical enactivism, in which sub-human creatures right down to single-cell organisms, have a "directedness" towards certain features of the environment.

An unsympathetic commentator such as the present writer might conclude from this that separating intentionality from an aboutness that has content opens the way to such a *reductio ad absurdum*. This, however, is the predictable consequence of trying to tame intentionality; that is to say to see it as a physical property absorbed in the law-governed causal network of the natural or physical world. What is clear is that radical enactivism, taken to the limit, mislays that which is distinctive about human agency – or indeed the very idea of agency. We lose the distinguishing feature of actions, of events which are *done* as opposed to that which merely *happens*.

JUSTIFIED ANTI-REPRESENTATIONALISM

The plausibility of radical enactivism owes much to a popular caricature of the mental elements involved in actions as being "representations" of their goal. The representational theory of mind has been justly described as a hangover from a long tradition in Western philosophy whose peaks are Plato and Descartes and which was made newly respectable in the late twentieth century through the idea of the mind, or even the conscious subject, as a computer. The "cognitivism" to which enactivism offers itself as a corrective sees the mind as a kind of mirror in which that which is present is re-presented as an image.

The images in question are not necessarily literal images, like that of a cloud in a lake or of my face in a mirror. Indeed, for those who embrace the once madly fashionable computational theories of the mind – according to which cognition is information processing as in digital computers – the images are neurally "encoded" in activity that is not a literal portrait of the item in question. For example, it has no modality-specific features – the image does not look, sound, or smell like its object – but shares certain formal properties.

Nevertheless, this more sophisticated version of the representational theory of mind runs into all sorts of difficulties. The most serious is that of explaining the intentionality of neural or computational activity – such that it is *about* what is out there and indeed counts as a representation of it. What cannot be replicated or encoded – or not without the assistance of a conscious subject, the very entity representation is invoked to explain – is the "out thereness" of what is supposed to be represented. Messages in Morse code come to represent language and hence to be "about" the world, rather than just a succession of dots and dashes, only courtesy of a conscious recipient who interprets those messages. It is difficult to find anything corresponding to such a self-interpreter built into the brain, even less into the neural structures of more primitive organisms. The "translation" of one lot of neural activity into another is merely a passage from one code to another. There is no-one to turn encoded representations into decoded representations. Or – and this is central – into *presentations*.

To regard mental states as "representations" is to put the cart before the horse. Representations are *re*-presentations. As such they must presuppose presentations. Without presentations to form the content of perceptual fields there are no representations. Within the perceptual field, there are things that are presented and second- or higher-order representations. They are both, however, objects of conscious perception, as are the cloud and its image in the puddle or the cloud and its image in a painting. The representational theory of mind fails because the idea of mental contents such as perceptions as "representations" places them at a level above themselves. The representational theory of mind is a meta-mental theory of mentality.

Most directly relevant to the arguments of this book, is the fact that representationalism also fails as an account of what the mind is or does because it does not capture those mental contents such as propositional attitudes – intentions, desires, hopes, beliefs – that are central to action. These are hardly mirror images of anything, not the least because their intentional objects are (general) possibilities. My general intention, desire, hope, to go to the gym some time tomorrow is hardly something to which an image could correspond. Any images I do have – for example, the front of the building, the member of the gym staff who was very helpful the other day, someone I bumped into when I was last there, or a treadmill – hardly does justice to the action of going to the gym in 24 hours' time with the intention of improving my cardiovascular fitness. These random items are not directly connected with agency; they are in a sense mental litter, however rich they may be.

The difference in the way the representational theory of mind fails for perceptions and even more dismally for propositional attitudes highlights another flaw: that it homogenizes fundamentally different mental states. Conflating "sapient" items such as reasons and beliefs that lack any distinctive feels with desires and urges and wants that seem to have such feels (though this is not their whole story) conceals the layers of complexity in what lies behind, and shapes, actions.

SEEING AGENCY ARIGHT

We could discuss representational theories of mind at much greater length. The philosophical and psychological literature directly or indirectly associated with them is vast. It is more useful to look at what motivates the arguments about the extent to which agency is or is not "representation-hungry", and remind ourselves of two features of deliberate, planned, action that have seemed (incorrectly) to some to justify the appeal to representations as a necessary mediator that enactivists oppose: possibility and tensed time.

Agency is directed towards possibility – to the realization of that which agents think might, could, or ought to be the case. Possibilities exist only insofar as they are envisaged by a conscious subject. By definition, they are not part of (physical) nature: the latter is confined to the actual, to what-is. The possibility of possibility is, as we have discussed in Section 4.2, rooted in the intentional consciousness of a subject who conceives (for example) objects as items that have intrinsic properties that transcend what is perceived of them. Even at the level of fairly basic perception, the actual is thus bathed in a halo or nimbus of possibilities. Those possibilities are vastly expanded when the intentional object of consciousness is delivered through knowledge: when we encounter it through being told about it.

Possibilities have two additional characteristics that are central to agency. Firstly, they are of a general nature: there are many ways of realizing them. Secondly, they are tensed: they are rooted in a future that is informed by a past. "Temporally extended agency" – which is said to be particularly representation-hungry – therefore, is not a sub-type of human agency. Human agency is always temporally extended. That in which it is extended is tensed time, or post-tensed time, not the tenseless time of the material world as reflected in physical science. Physics tells us that tensed time is absent from the physical world – including that part of the physical world that is the flesh of which we are made. While our agency is typically expressed through our body in material interaction with the material world, the tensed time that pervades every aspect of agency suggests that we should be talking not so much about "embodied cognition" as a more intimate "*am*bodied cognition", rooting it in the first-person being of the ambodied human subject.[16] Schlosser's focus on temporally extended agency as if this were a special, higher level kind of agency is therefore misplaced.

Every action worth its name requires some kind of intermediary. This intermediary is not, however, a representation (for reasons already given) but an explicit intention, reason, plan, directed towards an explicit goal. Granted, it would be burdensome for such an intermediary to be sustained throughout the period between the intention to do something and completing the business of doing it. (In this we are at one with enactivist thought.) The relevant propositional attitude may be dormant but it will be refreshed at intervals, amid the multitude of sub-personal activities necessary to keep the journey to the goal on track. My anti-representationalist account of the contents of mind that are relevant to action does not deny that such contents – items such as beliefs, thoughts, wishes, hopes, and so on – are essential. Fully naturalized accounts of action marginalize these items and/or conflate intentionality with a causal relationship, reducing intentional connections to something causally wired.

Radical enactivism is an (over-)corrective to hyper-intellectualized cognitivism.[17] We need a correction to that corrective, to uphold to the distance from which true agency acts upon, and indeed investigates, nature.[18] Without such a distance there is no difference between a human action and the response of an organism to a stimulus; between something that merely happens in an organism caused by something that happens to it and things that agents do. That difference is fundamental and real. While living is not a spectator sport, everyday life – including absorbed coping – requires a spectatorial distance if agents are to deliver on their plans.

Notes

PREFACE

1. Ismael, "Fate's scales, quivering".
2. James Boswell quoting Dr Johnson, 16 October 1769.
3. This divide is no longer as clear-cut as it used to be. It was largely based on a mutual misunderstanding. See, for example, Tallis, "Philosophy of consciousness and philosophies of the concept" in *Enemies of Hope*, 327–54. The ending of this divide is most conspicuously signaled in the central place now occupied by the concept of "intentionality" in philosophical discourse both sides of the divide.
4. For general readers wishing to test the arguments in this book against the views prevalent in the wider discipline, the online *Stanford Encyclopaedia of Philosophy* is an extraordinarily rich, user-friendly, scholarly, and reliable resource.

OVERTURE: INTENTION AND INTENTIONALITY

1. This characterization of intentionality and the arguments around it is lucidly discussed by Tim Crane in "Intentionality as the mark of the mental". Crane usefully deals with two objections to the idea that intentionality is the mark of the mental: first, that there are mental states that do not have intentional objects – something that I will touch on in Section 4.3; and, secondly, that there are *non*-mental phenomena that, it is claimed, exhibit intentionality, such as the disposition of plants towards a source of light, something that I shall examine briefly in Appendix D. For the present, I find it difficult to disagree with Sartre (quoted in Crane, 230) that "It is of the very nature of consciousness to be intentional and a consciousness that ceases to be a consciousness of something would *ipso facto* cease to exist".

   Crane also rejects the complaint made by many philosophers that "mind" or "the mental" is a rather heterogeneous collection of items. He quotes the philosopher

Kathy Wilkes to the effect that "it is improbable that something bunching together pains, and thoughts about mathematics, is going to be a reliable pointer towards a legitimate natural kind" (250). These entities may not add up to a natural kind but it is sufficient for our present purposes that they have an important common characteristic: intentionality. Such items also seem to be necessarily conscious. The notion of "unconscious mental states" is deeply problematic, notwithstanding its prominence in Freudian and allied quackeries. At any rate, they have little role to play in agency, although cultivating automaticities through training and practice does, as we shall discuss in Chapter 4 and Appendix D.

2. Jacob, "Intentionality".

3. Dennett, *Consciousness Explained*, 33. There are philosophers who, while agreeing that intentionality is the distinctive mark of the mental, maintain that, since mental events are physical events (e.g. in the brain), it is possible to reconcile physicalism with accepting the reality of intentionality. The arguments in this Overture and elsewhere I hope persuade the reader of the impossibility of identifying the mental with the physical – certainly if we use the term in the way that Dennett uses it in the passage quoted.

   Among the various attempts to naturalize intentionality the most prominent over the last 30 years have been various forms of "teleosemantics", particularly associated with Ruth Millikan and many philosophers who have been influenced by her writing. Teleosemantics claims to explain the truth-conditions of perceptions, beliefs and other propositional attitudes by their biological functions, hence collapsing the distance between the conscious subject and the material world. I have criticized teleosemantics in "Deflating the mystery: *Logos* as bio-logos" in *Logos: The Mystery of How We Make Sense of the World*, 77–114. The fundamental assumption of much teleosemantic thought is that consciousness is representational. Representation of what is supposed to cause it does not, however, succeed in naturalizing intentionality, given that nothing else in nature causes a representation of itself or has an effect that is *about* its cause. There are other reasons for rejecting the representational theory of consciousness (see Appendix D).

   Even less is contributed by those naturalisers who separate intentionality from representation. One version identifies intentionality as a feature of any entities that are self-organizing. Intentionality is "a basic feature of an organism's embodied interactions with the environment, not as mental states" (Schlicht, "Does separating intentionality from mental representation imply radical enactivism?", 8). Consequently, it can be ascribed to, for example, marine bacteria that have intentionality inasmuch as their locomotion is directed towards oxygen-free waters. Given that bacteria are not conscious of themselves or of oxygen as an object of consciousness, it would appear that intentionality is *not* the mark of the mental. An alternative conclusion – which seems more plausible – is that bacteria's directedness has nothing to do with intentionality. I don't think the reader will have much difficulty in deciding which alternative to choose (some of these arguments are further discussed in Appendices C and D).

4. It has been suggested that the problem of intentional reach – ensuring that the aboutness of mental phenomena should alight at the right place – can be dealt with by appealing to biology. Vision, so the argument goes, would be useless if it fell short and

supplied reports of what was going on in the retina or overshot and revealed a stretch of the path of the light from the sun. It would clearly be a good idea to alight on a predator as the intentional object of the gaze than either activity in the retina or light rays before they reach the predator. That it is indeed a good idea does not, however, explain it.

5. The causal theory of perception is also at odds with a (post-Humean) understanding that causal necessity is a *product* of perceiving minds. The appearance that the thunder is necessitated by the lightning, so the argument goes, is to be ascribed to our propensity to translate constant conjunction between types of events into a necessary connection between them (see Chapter 3). The point is that, if causation were a mind-dependent connection, mind could not be "explained" as a necessary effect of external, material causes.

6. The qualification "full-blown" might be used to highlight a distinction between sensations such as tingles or flashes on the one hand and on the other perceptions of objects "out there". As we discuss in note 1 above, it has been argued that intentionality cannot be a universal mark of the mental since sensations such as "pains" and "itches" are not *about* anything other than themselves. I would still maintain that sensations have intentionality but the intentionality is full-blown when there is a definite object of consciousness that is located outside of the subject.

As Sartre pointed out (see note 1 above) contents of consciousness are obliged to have intentionality. And we could argue that sensations are about, for example, the places where they are experienced: the pain in my ankle is about a state of my ankle or indeed my ankle. And, being located in my ankle, and something I can point to, the pain is in a sense "outside" of me. I might also experience these sensations as having the aboutness of *signs*, given that they are signs of something going wrong with my ankle or that I have been stung by a wasp.

Which mental contents count or do not count as having intentionality is less important than the "outside" that is delivered by full-blown intentionality, where the object of perception is clearly separate from me and is (correctly) intuited as having properties that are more than those which I am experiencing at present – properties, what is more, that will be discoverable by others.

7. A detailed and scientifically informed treatment of shared, joined or collective intentionality understood as unique features of human consciousness is Michael Tomasello's *A Natural History of Human Thinking*. Tomasello traces the journey from second-person shared intentionality – "you and I" – to third person (and seemingly no-person) "objective-reflective-normative thinking" and its connection to uniquely human cooperation.

8. Declarative pointing, which is unique to humans and a human universal, is an early manifestation of shared intentionality in infants. Its significance is discussed in Tallis, *Michelangelo's Finger: An Exploration of Everyday Transcendence*. It is of course soon overtaken by language as the predominant means of sharing experience.

9. I am here touching very fleetingly on a nexus of issues that Edmund Husserl examined over many decades.

10. Recently, philosophers who embrace "embodied cognition" and "enactivism" have endeavoured to slim down the space opened by intentionality, arguing that in everyday engagement with the world ("absorbed coping") intentionality has directedness

but not aboutness or "representational content". I am not persuaded either that it is possible to have intentionality without aboutness nor on the other hand that aboutness implies representational content. Some mental contents do seem to be representations, as when I consciously summon up a mental image of something that I have seen in the past. But such images are secondary to the primary experience that is perception (this issue is addressed in more detail in Appendix D). The important point remains: that intentionality opens up and maintains a space between a subject and her world.

11. Discussed in detail in Tallis, *The Explicit Animal: A Defence of Human Consciousness*.

12. For more on the ascent from ordinary perception to science, see Tallis, *Logos*.

13. Brentano, *Psychology From an Empirical Standpoint*, 180–81.

14. Two things may strike some readers about this brief introduction to intentionality as the basis of the possibility of free action. They are connected. Firstly, by focusing on vision, I may seem to suggest that perception is a spectator sport and to imply that ordinary consciousness is not caught up in the hurly-burly of action. Secondly, I have bypassed the part played by intentionality in the writings of philosophers of freedom such as Martin Heidegger and Maurice Merleau-Ponty for whom action was "absorbed coping" (to use Heidegger's phrase). Both of these concerns have been reflected in a relatively recent development in the philosophy of action in the analytic tradition – so-called "enactivism" with the emphasis on "embodied cognition" – already alluded to in note 7 above.

Regarding the second point, I have also made no reference to Sartre's use of "Nothingness" as the term for an outside (of Being) that made free actions possible. I have always had trouble with Ness monsters and one attached to Nothing is particularly troublesome. The curdling of Nothing by Ness seems to give it some kind of muscle, although how its metaphysical muscles are attached to a particular place in space and time is not at all clear. I shall, however, touch on Sartre in Chapter 6 because his standpoint on freedom overlaps in many places with the one developed in this volume.

CHAPTER 1 THE IMPOSSIBILITY OF FREE WILL

1. van Inwagen, *An Essay on Free Will*, v.

2. Kane, *The Significance of Free Will*, 4.

3. Not all philosophers believe that the possibility of doing otherwise is an essential feature of free will. I am, however, happy to make it harder for compatibilism by including choice between genuine alternatives as an aspect of free will. If I was not free to behave in any other way, then behaving in the way I did could not have been free.

4. Nagel, *The View From Nowhere*, 110. What is overlooked in this passage is the *viewpoint* which is presupposed in passing judgement on the nature of actions. If one takes "viewpoint" for granted, one overlooks where freedom is to be found. The view from somewhere, and the scientific view from nowhere which is built on it, both sustain the possibility of freedom. Strictly, of course, the view from (absolutely) nowhere is mythical. Even a view liberated from individual subjects is still rooted in a cognitive

community, although the human presence may be concealed by the mediation of the gaze through instruments, techniques, units and mathematics.

5. Exceptionless, that is, *if other things are equal*. Behind this so-called *ceteris paribus* qualification lies a big story which we shall explore in Section 2.2.

6. Some have looked to indeterminism – the play of chance – as a source of freedom. We shall discuss this in Chapter 2.

7. I have discussed "neuromania" – the view that to be a person is to be a brain in some kind of working order – in *Aping Mankind: Neuromania, Darwinitis and the Misrepresentation of Humanity* and, more recently, in *Seeing Ourselves: Reclaiming Humanity from God and Science*. Not everyone who identifies persons with their brains concludes from this that we are not free. Some thinkers have argued that, although everything in the brain is dictated by the laws of nature, we are free because our actions and the decisions behind them are determined by what is in the brain and not by external factors. This reassurance doesn't work because the brain, subject to the laws of nature, is wired into the external world; indeed, there are no grounds for the idea of the brain as being "internal", as constituting the "within" of "the I". What is more, there is no obvious basis for the metaphysical difference between the brain and the body or, indeed, the brain and the spinal cord.

8. A leading philosophical determinist Derk Pereboom argues in *Living without Free Will* that "given our best scientific theories, factors beyond our control ultimately produce all our actions and we are therefore not morally responsible for them" (quoted in Dennett, *Freedom Evolves*, 226). The idea that we are prisoners of our brains overlooks not only (but most obviously) where the "our" comes from but also the investigative, scientific processes by which we arrive at the conclusion that we are prisoners of our brains. I shall return to the unnatural nature of the science of nature in the next chapter.

9. Libet, "Unconscious cerebral initiative and the role of the conscious will in voluntary action".

10. See Soon *et al.* "Unconscious determinants of free decisions in the human brain".

11. There is no surefire diagnostic sign of the operation of free will. We shall certainly not find it in the local evidence sought by neuroscientists; rather we need to discover it in the wider context of human life. It is analogous in this respect to the challenge of demonstrating that an organism is not a zombie – an unconscious being functionally identical to human beings. The possibility of zombies should, however, not worry us because it would be impossible for the concept of a zombie to arise in a universe where all apparently conscious beings were in fact zombies. Zombies could not entertain the (necessarily conscious) illusion of being conscious beings. As for the possibility that all human beings other than myself are zombies, it is difficult to see how the language in which I argue this could arise in the absence of true interlocutors (see Tallis, "Arguing with a solipsist").

12. Some of the evidence that experiments such as those of Libet and Haynes do *not* show that our brains are calling the shots is helpfully summarized in Shields, "Neuroscience and conscious causation".

13. This is clearly demonstrated in a series of experiments reported in Miller, Shepherdson and Trevena, "Effects of clock monitoring on electroencephalographic activity".

14. As Shields has expressed it, "Naïve participants have extreme difficulty generating truly random sequences, and deciding to press one button or another in succession creates sequence dependencies and response biases" ("Neuroscience and conscious causation", 572). The experimental design cannot pick this up, even less correct for it.
15. Making and keeping appointments is so commonplace that its extraordinary nature is overlooked. Supposing I agree, after an email exchange with Professor Libet, to attend the laboratory at 12 noon next Wednesday. This agreement is built on the sense of a future – a future that is mine and also shared with others. As we shall see in Chapter 4 tensed time is central to agency, as is the collectivization of tensed time that creates the "post-tensed time" of the clock, calendar and the diary.
16. Philosophers contrast free will with "the liberty of indifference", a choice where there is nothing at stake. It is discussed by Kane in *The Significance of Free Will*, 109. Markus Schlosser beautifully sets out how the experiments of Libet and Haynes "fail to capture ... free will *proper* – the freedom to make choices on the basis of reasons" ("The neuroscientific study of free will", 262).
17. Some have denied the possibility of free will on the grounds that the future is already *logically* pre-determined. The classical – in both senses of the word – statement of this argument is Aristotle's "sea battle" example. Supposing I say that there will be a sea battle tomorrow. This must be either true or false – and it must be true or false now, when I assert it. If it is true or false today then the sea battle or the lack of it is pre-determined. Attempts to head it off or to influence its outcome are therefore doomed. The case against logical determinism is complex and interested readers may wish to consult "The pre-determined future: logical fatalism" in Tallis, *Of Time and Lamentation: Reflections on Transience*, 375–400.
18. Some free-will deniers account for the "illusion" that we have free will by claiming that it is of adaptive value. The thought that I can change things is, as it were, motivating. This claim raises three questions. First, how did there arise in a cluster of mechanisms – even organic ones – the idea of something that goes beyond mechanism? Second, if free will really is an illusion, that is to say a false idea, how does it help us to deal with the challenges presented to survival? Finally, if free will is an illusion, what is the basis for the apparent distinction between actions that an agent performs and events that merely happen in and around her?

CHAPTER 2 BRINGING THE LAWS ON SIDE

1. Laplace, *A Philosophical Essay on Probabilities*, 4.
2. Van Inwagen, *An Essay on Free Will*, 3. And, of course, there is also only one possible past. Even this, seemingly common sense, determinism should not, however, go unchallenged. First, the notion of a universe-wide temporal instant t does not survive relativity theory. Secondly, and central to the argument of this book, there is in the natural world not even one future. We shall discuss this in Section 4.2.
3. The ownership of brains by persons is difficult to accommodate if persons *are* brains. I could not own my house if I were that house.
4. Mill, "Nature", 152.

5. Kane (*Significance of Free Will*, 130) has suggested that chaotic processes in the brain, arising "in neural networks that are globally sensitive to quantum indeterminacies at the neuronal level" may create opportunities for the exercise of free will. It is not clear to me – or indeed to many other philosophers – that a neuronal network surfing a wave of indeterminacy would correspond to anything recognizable as free will, even less the expression of free will in making a choice between one course of action and another – particularly when we consider the sustained, complex nature of even ordinary actions such as planning a day out.

6. In avoiding this task, I have an illustrious predecessor in David Hume: "I begin with observing that the terms of *efficacy, agency, power, force, energy, necessity connexion,* and *productive quality* are all early synonyms; and therefore 'tis an absurdity to employ any of them in defining the rest" (*A Treatise of Human Nature*, 157). It is interesting to note that Francis Bacon was even more sceptical, making Hume seem gullible by comparison: "There is no soundness in our notions whether logical or physical. Substance, Quality, Action, Passion, Essence itself, are not sound notions; much less are Heavy, Light, Dense, Rare, Moist, Dry, Generation, Corruption, Attraction, Repulsion, Element, Matter, Form, and the like; but all are fantastical and ill-defined" (*The New Organon and Related Writings*, Bk 1: 5). I am grateful to David Scott for drawing these passages to my attention.

7. The idea of laws as constraints on the direction of the unfolding of things presupposes that there is any number of ways they could evolve. This must imply that there is a primordial randomness or chaos that needs to be called to order – a rather unlikely scenario. It also assumes that the unfolding of the universe is guaranteed from the get-go; that it inertially free-wheels after the Big Bang; its dynamism is a kind of passive continuation.

   The contrast between laws as horses or horse-riders was exploited (unsuccessfully) by Descartes to explain how the mind could have a causal effect on the body: it did not drive the body's "animal spirits", he said, only changed their direction, so that the total quantity of motion was conserved. Of course, as Leibniz pointed out, what has to be conserved is not motion but momentum, which latter would be altered by a change in direction of motion.

   Stephen Mumford has argued that there is no job for laws additional to that which is already delivered by properties (see note 10 below). Properties, he says, could not have causal roles other than their actual ones, so no laws are required for them to exercise or express those properties. Without their playing some role, Mumford concludes, it is doubtful that there are real laws in nature. Moreover, the concept of a law of nature "suggests that the world's properties are governed externally" ("Laws and lawlessness", 409) – something to which we shall come presently.

8. Beebee, "The non-governing conception of the laws of nature", 585. Simon Blackburn suggests that the desire for a causal connection (to be discussed in Chapter 3) is that for "a straitjacket on a possible course of nature" ("Hume and thick connexions", 241). The notion of "thick connexions" encompasses both what (in Chapter 3) we shall call "oomph" and what we shall call "glue" or "cement".

9. Beebee, *Ibid.*, 3.

10. The regularity of the universe is something we take for granted, although it is accepted that the most metaphysical of the laws of science – the second law of thermodynamics – is predicated on the fact that there are more ways for a system to be disordered than ordered, so that the former is overwhelmingly more probable. Indeed, we could characterize the second law of thermodynamics as the law of lawlessness.

   Some philosophers, notably C. S. Peirce – who also spoke of the "habits" of nature – have argued that the laws of the universe evolve, from which it would follow that the universe is *not* regular over astronomical time. That the laws may be mutable is a view shared by some contemporary physicists. Notable among them is Lee Smolin. However, he has argued for the possibility of a meta-law that "governs the change of the laws and other regularities in nature" (Unger & Smolin, *The Singular Universe and the Reality of Time*, 9).

11. A more radical dissent from the regularity assumption notes that successive states of the universe, as opposed to certain aspects of it, are unique. No overall instantaneous state of the universe is like that any of its predecessors or its successors in all respects.

12. The contrast between stasis and dynamism, however, is problematic when applied to the totality of things and laws of unrestricted scope. We have learned from relativity theory that mechanical states at rest and in motion are not absolute; they are relative to frames of reference. There is, by definition, no external frame of reference enclosing the totality, available to establish the difference between change and stasis. That may be why, as James Ladyman *et al.* have argued, the most fundamental laws describe real patterns or structures but are not causal (*Every Thing Must Go: Metaphysics Naturalized*, 283). We shall return to this in Appendix A.

13. What we might call the "taste" of explanation, experienced when we move from a single event to a covering law, does not last when we pause on that law. Likewise, when we move from a lower-order to a higher-order law. Illumination, necessity, reason seem doomed to evaporate and reveal brute contingency: "This is just how things are".

   The contingency of the most fundamental laws of nature – strikingly illustrated by the arbitrariness of the fundamental constants, such as the charge or mass of basic particles – appears to reflect this. While, as noted, there seems to be an arrow of necessity tracking the arrow of explanation – as when we move from an individual event to a covering law or see a lower-order law as a manifestation of a higher-level law – even this attenuated sense of necessity terminates in contingency. The laws are simply the most general, economical descriptions of the regularities in how things happen to be. They gather up unchanging, intrinsic patterns of unfolding that have an unbroken, indeed unbreakable, regularity. At the very least, they describe the structural characteristics of that unfolding.

14. I have spoken of "the habits *of* nature" as if to separate the one from the other and to suggest there is a definite number of them. It may be more precise to talk of the habitual behaviour of nature.

15. Putnam, "Philosophy and our mental life", 73. Scholars quarrel over this assertion. There are anti-realist accounts of the laws of nature – such as the constructive empiricism of Bas van Fraassen – which, it is claimed, do not make the success of science a miracle. The arguments are set out in Monton, "Constructive empiricism".

16. I have skated past a vast and fascinating literature on the nature of laws. Within that literature is a school of thought that holds that there are no laws (though I have already referred to Mumford's excellent "Laws and lawlessness"). Certainly, the idea that laws are items that exist in their own right is difficult to sustain. One has only to ask what sort of things they are – and how they would act upon nature from outside of nature's stuff – to lose any appetite for thinking of laws in this way. Any powers the laws may have are redistributed by many philosophers to dispositions, capacities, properties, etc., evident in the world and attached to objects, events, or states of affairs. What are thought of as laws, they argue, are simply ways of gathering up these items – their distribution, attachments and interactions – into generalizations.

   Unfortunately, the identification of powers with properties, as Mumford does, is simply to place one ill-defined blob on to another. And it does not distinguish between what we may call passive properties such as fragility or solubility – that rely on other items to be expressed – from active properties such as being hot or radiant. Alexander Bird's proposal that the laws of nature are merely *grounded* in properties, rescues laws from sinking into properties but does not entirely eradicate the suspicion that properties do all the work, making the laws redundant (*Nature's Metaphysics: Laws and Properties*). David Armstrong and others have argued that "laws of nature are relations between universals": the laws link properties with things and things with things. There is a necessity – specifically a material necessity not a logical one – "linking the relation between universals and the uniformity it produces" (*What Is a Law of Nature?*, 85–6.) Although this view has attracted a huge literature, it is not at all clear to this reader at least what it means.

   The term I have fallen back on – "the habits of nature" – encircles, even if it does not capture, the nuances of – laws, properties, capacities, powers, universals, etc.

17. The title of this section echoes Lewis Wolpert's brilliant *The Unnatural Nature of Science: Why Science Does Not Make (Common) Sense*. Having said this, I ought to point out that Wolpert himself was committed to a more naturalistic account of the world, including science, than is advanced in this book.

18. Einstein, Letter from Prague to Erwin Freundlich, 1 September 1911, *Collected Papers of Albert Einstein*, Volume 5, 202.

19. This observation by W. V. Quine is worth reflecting on: "For, in the midst of all this formless freedom for variation, our science has developed in such a way as to maintain a manageably narrow spectrum of visible alternatives among which to choose when need arises to revise a theory. It is this narrowing of sights, or tunnel vision, that has made for the continuity of science, through the vicissitudes of refutation and correction. And it is this also that has fostered the illusion of there being only one solution to the riddle of the universe" ("The nature of natural knowledge", 81).

20. G. W. Leibniz spoke of "the art of inquiry into nature itself and of putting it on the rack – the art of experiment which Lord Bacon began" (quoted in Pesic, "Nature on the rack").

21. It also makes a change from the obsession of philosophers (including for a time this one) with fundamental physics that seems (erroneously I believe) to be the royal road to metaphysics. Besides, we all understand Boyle's law and only pretend we understand quantum mechanics.

22. *Ceteris paribus* seems to apply throughout science though, at the most fundamental level, where laws with unbounded scope give way to mathematical structures, there will be no outside *ceteris* to be kept *paribus*. We may assume that a putative Theory of Everything would have no Terms and Conditions; for Everything would also encompass anything that could contribute Terms and impose or breach Conditions.

23. Our capacity to discover laws of nature is an appropriate source of wonder reflected in Einstein's observation that "the eternal mystery of the world is its comprehensibility". By comprehensibility he meant capturability in quantitative physical science. But an equal mystery, perhaps, is the way the order of the world is hidden from the gaze that guides us through daily life. If the order is universal, how could it be hidden and, if hidden, uncovered or partly hidden and partly uncovered? What comprises – and regulates – the surfaces that conceal the depths? The most obvious answer to the question is that the distance between the disordered surface and the ordered depths is provided by the parochial viewpoint of the subject. That answer, however, only transfers the mystery from the known world to the knower – both her limitations and her ability to overcome them. And it does not help us to understand how any putative single over-riding law (captured in a Theory of Everything) could break up into multiple local laws and thence into individual experiences that then conceal it.

24. Discussed in Sargant, "Robert Boyle's Baconian inheritance: a response to Laudan's Cartesian thesis".

25. It is salutary to recall that while Boyle was extracting the relationship between two variables out of many more – indeed as many as distinct local laws might highlight – his body was in the grip of all the changing variables merged in its organic unfolding. The particular law he was revealing, exploited in his respiratory cycle, with the inspiratory fall in intrathoracic pressure driving air into his lungs, was connected with a multitude of other laws, such as governed the biochemical processes active in all the cells of his body. All of these processes, largely unknown to Boyle, were appropriated in the service of his intentions to serve his activity of uncovering the relationship between pressure and volume of gases.

26. This may not be evident at the quantum level but we have to remember that physicists perform their experiments in a macroscopic world using macroscopic equipment handled directly or indirectly by their macroscopic bodies.

27. This arrest is replicated at a higher-order level when repeated, discrete observations of the same phenomenon are reduced to a single observation by averaging; or when a series of measurements made on the successive phases of an unfolding process are set out in a graph or otherwise tabulated and thus placed side-by-side such that their temporal succession is translated into a line or a spatial array whose parts are co-present.

28. Mach, *Knowledge and Error: Sketches of the Psychology of Inquiry*, 171.

29. As Goethe, responding to Bacon, put it with surpassing eloquence, "Nature falls silent upon the rack" (quoted in Pesic, "Nature on the rack", 197). The world as mathematics is not only speechless but colourless and unchanging. The mathematical laws assert that, at a certain level, nothing changes: that is the force of the notion of the conservation of mass-energy. That is why this writer at least feels ambivalent about Newton's famous claim that "Truth is ever to be found in simplicity, and not in the multiplicity

and confusion of things" (*Fragments of a Treatise of Revelation*). Simplification may clarify, making the world mind-portable, but it also impoverishes.

30. Born, *Einstein's Theory of Relativity*, 5–6.

31. Einstein, "Autobiographical notes", 59. I have quoted this passage in other works but I do not apologize for repeating myself in this way because it is revelatory. It certainly puts into question Hilary Putnam's assertion that "Measurements are a subclass of physical interactions – no more and no less than that … Measurement can never be an *undefined* term in a satisfactory physical theory, and measurement can never obey any 'ultimate' laws that the laws 'ultimately' obeyed by *all* physical interactions" ("A philosopher looks at quantum mechanics (again)", 618). While it is true that measurements are no less than physical interactions, they are – as the present chapter has been devoted to demonstrating – much more than such interactions. Measurement is nothing without a vast hinterland – purpose, units, know-how, skill, equipment. It is not merely an interaction between material bodies but an action by an embodied, knowing subject.

32. For a more detailed discussion, see Tallis, *Seeing Ourselves*, 118–33. Clocks, etc., also belong to the *post-tensed* time discussed in Section 4.2.

33. Thalos, *Without Hierarchy: The Scale Freedom of the Universe*, 1. If everything in nature really were emergent from an initial atomic level, there would be an interesting question about the apparent ability of instances of one emerged type of being – human beings – to drill down to the atomic level and to other lower levels from which they are supposed to emerge.

34. As Thalos has put it, "The boundaries between sciences are being constantly negotiated" (*Without Hierarchy*, 152).

35. It has been suggested that quantum mechanics and general relativity are not, after all in conflict: they simply capture different aspects of the same thing. Leaving aside what could be meant by "the same thing" – given that the scope of both is the totality of physical things – this simply moves the question on: we have to say what we mean by "aspects" – which don't sound like part of nature but products of views on it – and what physics has to offer regarding how these aspects are separated.

36. James Ladyman pointed out that according to A. J. Ayer "it is our cognitive attitudes that determine which regularities we raise to the status of laws" (Ladyman, "The history of philosophy of science", 208).

37. James Ladyman and his colleagues have called this principle, or article of faith, the "Primacy of Physics Constraint" and characterized it as follows: "There is a methodological rule observed in the history of recent science that practitioners of special sciences at any time are discouraged from suggesting generalizations of causal relationships that violate the broad consensus in physics at any time, while physicists need not worry reciprocally about coherence with the state of special sciences" (*Every Thing Must Go*, 38). While sociology must be constrained by physics, physics need not be constrained by sociology. This is an inevitable consequence of the priority given in science to "primary qualities" – shape, size, number, distance – and laws that connect them. Primary qualities are not, of course, qualities at all. Even shape, and the contrast between the curved and the straight, which may seem closest to being qualities, can be reduced without remainder to mathematical expressions.

38. In my discussion I have not separately addressed entities, forces and laws. This would be a serious omission were I endeavouring to make a contribution to comprehensive philosophy of science. My aim, however, is the more modest one of highlighting the distance between the habits of nature insofar as they are captured in the laws of science and the processes by which those laws are arrived at insofar as they are relevant to the question of free will.

39. The consequence of this is that "every thing must go", an outcome that is welcomed by the authors of the book with that title (James Ladyman and colleagues). It is most illuminatingly expressed in so-called "ontic structural realism" according to which there are no such things as things – only mathematical structures: "This will yield an interpretation of fundamental physics that has nothing to do with putative tiny objects or their collisions … fundamental physics for us denotes a set of mathematically specified structures without self-individuating objects" (*Every Thing Must Go*, 44).

    This does not address the problem that the homogenizing gaze of mathematical physics, if taken to be revealing the most fundamental truth about what there is, presents of how to reconstitute the heterogeneous world of actual things – of pebbles, trees, chimpanzees, tables, and hurtful comments. How, from the most fundamental laws can we derive the particular laws that connect properties or parameters such as heat and volume and even more particular laws that connect, for example, supply and demand of consumer goods?

    In the background is a question, explored for example by Owen Barfield in *Saving the Appearances: A Study in Idolatry*, of what kind of world there is prior to conscious subjects. This in turn connects with this question: By what means did the preconscious world give rise to consciousness and, more specifically, what kind of reality could give rise to the unreality that is our ordinary, pre-scientific vision of that reality?

40. The argument is spelled out in more detail in Tallis "Against the neural philosophy of mind".

41. The journey is examined in Tallis, *Logos*.

42. Discussed in Suddendorf, *The Gap: The Science of What Separates Us from Other Animals* and in Tallis, *Seeing Ourselves*.

43. Quine, "The nature of natural knowledge", 72.

44. Popper, *Conjectures and Refutations: The Growth of Scientific Knowledge*, 192.

45. I apologize for the italics if they seem to imply a lack of trust in the reader. The typeface is addressed only to determinists who are determined to exercise their free will by denying its existence.

46. Crucial aspects of these habits are not, so far as we know, replicated in non-human animals.

47. Mill, "Nature", 152.

48. The multiplicity of laws applicable to a single situation, process, or event is an inevitable consequence of the fact that the laws are general. Hence, they do not reach down to token events which are singular, and touch only on general aspects of them. The process by which events are individuated by subjects as being unique – things that are happening here and now – ultimately places them outside of the reach of general laws.

This is reflected in Donald Davidson's view that while causation is a relationship between events, events are discovered to instantiate laws only under some particular description (Davidson, "Mental events"). Unfortunately, he seems to take the existence of descriptions for granted, as if they, too, are physical events that are somehow also mental events. This dual nature requires further explanation and no such explanation is forthcoming.

49. Or no more metaphysically privileged than all the spaces conscious subjects open up in the material world. The manipulation of affairs inside a laboratory is an elevated example of the way we manipulate things (including ourselves) in the wider space that is called the human world.

50. The same applies to the search for general causes. The search is active and may involve manipulations of conditions to establish causal relations. In order to decide whether the relationship between two kinds of events A and B is or is not causal, I may manipulate an example of A to see what happens to an example of B. If more of A results in more of B, I may conclude that A has a causal relationship to B. Such manipulations can take place virtually, as when I analyse data. If, for example, I found that the incidence of lung cancer (amount of B) rose in proportion to the number of cigarettes smoked (amount of A), I would feel justified in ascribing a causal role to smoking. I could test this belief in the causal role – and check that the association is not just a statistical freak or a mere correlation – by looking at another set of data or by (morally and scientifically dubious) experiments in which animals are exposed to cigarette smoke. The important point, however, is that manipulation lies at the heart of the process by which we arrive at both laws and causes.

51. The fact that the manipulations that enable us to discover the habits of nature as the laws of science are the same as those that enable us to exploit the laws of science in creating empowering technologies is reflected in our tendency to read back into nature the technologies that we have built on the basis of our knowledge of it. Hence the universe is seen as a great clock, the brain as a computer, and nature as a collection of large and small machines.

52. It is important not to exaggerate the role of experimental science in technological advance. Seeing how things work, or might be made to work, or improved is often more direct. Anyone doubting this should read the life of Henry Maudslay who was a major figure in the industrial revolution that made mass production possible. He looked at the problem and *saw* the answer. His invention of the cup leather washer for hydraulic presses was but one such example. Nevertheless, the outside from which he saw, diagnosed, and solved the problem of leaky pistons – which transformed productivity – mobilized the same generalizing, principled gaze as is at work in experimental science. (For the full story read the lovely Wikipedia article on this extraordinary man).

53. Quine, "The nature of natural knowledge", 67. The correct conclusion from this is that, contrary to Quine, there is nothing natural about scientific knowledge. After all, our belief in the existence of objects that transcend our experiences is rather extraordinary. This was beautifully captured by David Hume: "We readily suppose an object may continue individually the same, though several times absent from and present to the senses; and ascribe to it an identity, notwithstanding the interruption

of the perception, whenever we conclude, that if we had kept our eye and hand constantly upon it, it would have conveyed an invariable and uninterrupted perception" (*A Treatise of Human Nature*, 67).

54. Ismael, *How Physics Makes Us Free*, 111.

55. For a lengthy, but alas inconclusive, discussion of this the reader might like to consult my *Seeing Ourselves*, 326–37. I fail to decide between, or even to reconcile, two views: that we fit into the history of the universe; and that the universe fits into our history.

56. I am grateful to an anonymous reader of the manuscript of this book for the misunderstanding that prompted this clarification.

CHAPTER 3 UNPICKING CAUSATION

1. Carl Hoefer argues for speaking of "causal determinism" as "determinism", acknowledging that it is not easy to disentangle arguments about determinism from the notion of causation (Hoefer, "Causal determinism"). As we shall discuss later, causation is often invoked to refer to the connection between individual events, notwithstanding that those connections are thought to be law-governed and (as we have noted) may be expressions of more than one law. Hence the uncertainty as to whether laws *and* causation count as one obstacle or two to free will.

2. Hume, *Enquiries Concerning Human Understanding and Concerning the Principles of Morals*, 76.

3. Hume, *A Treatise of Human Nature*, 152. Incidentally, some philosophers argue that constancy, contiguity, and temporal order cannot be directly perceived – or not at least in the way that, say, individual events can be perceived. I am, however, happy to accept the traditional starting place for the richest discussions of causation in anglophone philosophy.

   Galen Strawson has controversially argued that Hume was not sceptical of the idea of "natural necessity". In *The Secret Connexion: Causation, Realism, and David Hume*, he claims that Hume's position was that, while things behave in the way they do because they have a certain nature, it is not possible to form a positive, empirically legitimate conception of what this nature is. In other words, while there is more to causation than the mere regularity of the succession of events, that "more" is not accessible to empirical experience. This seems a surprising position to ascribe to a passionate empiricist such as Hume. I don't think this re-reading of Hume, even if true, would undermine any of the conclusions in this section.

4. Lichtenberg's dismissal of causation as an "occult force" is cited in Berlin's *The Age of Enlightenment*.

5. Hume, *Treatise*, 152.

6. *Ibid.*, 156.

7. And whether events are classified with other events depends on the acuity (or rather the blurredness) of attention. In reality all events are unique and all co-classification is approximation.

8. Quoted in Berlin, *Age of Enlightenment*, 276.

9. Kant, *The Critique of Pure Reason*, 44 et passim.

10. This is discussed in Maxwell, "Can there be necessary conditions between successive events?" Maxwell argues that we can never know for certain that logically necessary connections can exist between successive events. Others, notably J. J. Smart, have argued that any necessary connection between individual events is a reflection of a necessary connection between universals – the universal properties of individual events. Not surprisingly, this ad hoc endeavour to overcome Hume-iliation has not won many adherents. In *I Am: A Philosophical Inquiry into First-Person Being*, I discuss a form of *de re* necessity in the first-person necessity of the existential intuition that 'I am this'.

11. "Mechanisms" provide stitching between the elements of a continuous process that, because they have been observed separately – the inhalation of smoke over years and the coughing of blood – seem to be discrete events between which a link has to be found.

12. Adam Rostowski (personal communication) has suggested that this is not an oversight on Hume's part but consistent with his intention to give an anti-realist, empiricist interpretation of causation. "Of the Causes of Belief" represents an example of an empirical psychology. This distinction and its implication for Hume's thought is discussed in Millican, "Hume, causal realism, and causal science".

13. "No-one can doubt but causation has the same influence as the other two relations of resemblance and contiguity" (Hume, *Treatise*, 92).

14. Hume, *Treatise*, 69.

15. Adam Rostowski (personal communication) reads this passage as arguing for the necessary contiguity of our attributions of cause and effect – of discrete successive events we pick out – rather than a seamless process ontology intrinsic to the universe. Nevertheless, it is clear that any discontinuities causation is supposed to bridge are hidden.

16. The arresting title of an influential book on causation by J. L. Mackie: *The Cement of the Universe: A Study of Causation*.

17. The seamlessness is maintained where the link is a force field (such as gravitational or electromagnetic fields) permitting "action at a distance", with various ideas being entertained in the history of science as to what fills or reaches across that distance.

18. It is a reaction to the unpalatable notion of the universe as being composed of "loose and separate" existences. See Hume, *Enquiries Concerning Human Understanding*, 74.

19. To return to our earlier separation of the lightning from the thunder, the formation of the thunder–lightning pair may seem justified not only because the partners have a fixed period at which they are perceptible but also because they are addressed to different senses: the thunder can be heard over such-and-such time and could not be seen; and the lightning was seen for another such period of time and could not be heard. But this merely reinforces the point just made. The distinction between the heard and the no-longer-heard and the seen and the no-longer-seen is clearly subject-dependent. In the absence of a conscious subject the lightning is colourless and the thunder soundless. Nothing therefore would pick them out as discrete entities requiring to be stitched together. Behind this is a broader issue; namely the different status of "events", "processes" and "objects". For a further discussion, see Tallis, *Of Time and Lamentation*, 306–16.

At the sub-atomic level, we are assured, the universe is a continuum, with everything dissolving into a single wave function. I haven't invoked this earlier in support of the present argument because one shouldn't accept gifts without understanding their origin or being able to vouch for their validity and I am one of those who believe themselves to have the Socratic wisdom of not understanding quantum mechanics. More importantly, one should not privilege the microphysical level over other levels – as we discussed in Section 2.2. The (relatively) macroscopic level of feet and inches and miles is privileged in our lives because we are macroscopic beings. That privilege is lost in the viewpointless realm of nature-in-itself.

20. As for the number of events that are involved in the collision, it is dependent on description – and grain-of-attention. It could be described as: a single event – "the collision"; two events – A strikes B and then B and A move off in different directions; more events – A strikes B, there is compression of B followed by expansion and a push against A, etc., etc.

21. Quoted in Woodward, "Causation and manipulability", 15.

22. "All events seem entirely loose and separate. One event follows another; but we can never observe any tie between them. They seem *conjoined* but never *connected*" (Hume, *Enquiry Concerning Human Understanding*, 74). Hume is echoed by a twentieth-century philosopher David Lewis, according to whom "the world is vast mosaic of local matters of particular fact, just one little thing, and then another" (*Philosophical Papers*, volume 2, ix). Where the unifying idea of "the world" comes from, heaven knows. Or where the "local matters of particular fact" add up to a "mosaic", which conveys the impression of something tight-fitting. Equally unexplained is the decision that the contents of the universe are "little" (as opposed to "big"). To say that worlds are simply totalities of states of affairs that can co-exist (or, to use his term, are "compossible") leaves unexplained what it is that brings these items together. For a lucid and entertaining examination of the role of causation as glue, Helen Beebee's "Does anything hold the universe together?" is strongly recommended.

23. See Kutach, "The asymmetry of influence".

24. See Price, *Time's Arrow and Archimedes Point* (especially Chapter 6).

25. Price, *Time's Arrow*, 155.

26. *Ibid.*, 157.

27. *Ibid.*, 160.

28. Ascribing the asymmetry of causal influence to our experience as agents seems to address a puzzle arising out of two seemingly incompatible facts: first, that causation is regarded as law-governed but asymmetrical; and, secondly, that overwhelmingly the laws of science are time symmetrical. Regarding the latter, we can see the time symmetry of the laws of motion at the microphysical level where atoms are free to jig up and down and indeed to move in any direction. It is equally evident in scientific equations which can be read from left to right as from right to left. Although there are conventions of representation, what is represented in equations does not contain beginnings and ends: $mc^2=E$ is just as true as $E=mc^2$. Nothing in them decrees that the universe should move from State A at time t_1 to State B at time t_2 but not vice versa. Once the initial conditions are set, then the direction of travel is fixed. But what counts as initial conditions have, as it were, to be put in by hand by an interested subject.

There is of course one law that is time-asymmetrical: the second law of thermodynamics, according to which available energy tends to decrease with time, and entropy (or disorder) increases. This law is not relevant to the present discussion because its time irreversibility is a statistical consequence of a vast population of random microphysical events that are individually time-reversible: molecules can jig up and down or jig down and up. For further discussion, see Tallis, *Of Time and Lamentation*, 59–81, especially, 62–9.

29. Quoted in Isaacson, *Einstein: His Life and Universe*, 540.

30. The idea of backward causation is deeply problematic. For an excellent, but inconclusive, discussion see Faye, "Backward causation". Pending a conclusion to this discussion, the contrast between time-symmetric laws and time-asymmetric causation seems to be upheld.

31. The place of such projection in allocating the roles of "cause" and "effect" is particularly clear when we think of sustained processes such as chemical reactions or the formation of a solution (out of a solvent and a solute) or the reverse such as crystallization out of a supersaturated solution. Where the process begins and which element counts as the cause and which the effect depends on where we begin in our observation of the process. Where we begin is subject – and even agent – dependent. In the case of a solute dissolving in a solvent, we think of the cause as, perhaps, the act of dropping the former into the latter.

It is not clear, therefore, in the case of overlapping processes – and most causally connected processes are overlapping – how we should allocate the roles of cause and effect once the overlap is in place. It is traditional to think of a crystal dissolving in a solvent as being passive and the latter as active but this does not hold up at the microphysical level. The monologue of a sustained cause telling an effect what to be is replaced by a dialogue where the effect-as-process feeds back to the cause-as-process.

32. Indeed, given that any presence the past has is in our memory, there is a sense that we have more control over it than we have over the present. I am not, of course, referring to "done and dusted" previous states of the material world which lie beyond our control. I cannot alter the teenager I was or the world around me then. I have (some) control only over what I recall of them and what may feed into shaping my future – as, for example, in the way that I have used the story of my teenage fear of determinism to justify this book.

33. Thomas Reid conceived of matter as "a substance altogether inert, and merely passive" (quoted in Alvarez & Hyman, "Philosophy of action 1945–2015"). This seems to contradict our experience that matter is also active and dynamic. It is perhaps more accurate to say that it cannot sustain these distinctions: it cannot be ascribed one side of a contrast – for example passivity – without the other side – for example activity. Just as we are not entitled to think of a pebble as asleep because we cannot imagine it as awake. Besides, in physics post-Einstein, there is no absolute difference between motion and a state of rest: it is relative to a frame of reference which the material world does not generate of or within itself. The asymmetry between an event as cause and an event as effect with the former being the benefactor of oomph and the latter a beneficiary but each occupying both roles in turn is even more dubious when we see

that the passivity of the effect is seen as an external relation that is conferred by the (external) cause while the activity of the cause is supposedly intrinsic.

34. It is the character of bringing something new to the party rather than merely transmitting what they receive that distinguishes agents from causes. The failure to notice this difference leads to rather startling claims. Take, for example, this passage from Markus Schlosser, "In a very broad sense, agency is virtually everywhere. Whenever entities enter into causal relationships, they can be said to act on each other and interact act with each other ... In this very broad sense, it is possible to see agents and agency, and patients and patiency, virtually everywhere" (Schlosser, "Agency"). It is hard to think of a falling stone breaking a windowpane as an agent in any way comparable to the person who threw it.

35. The causal theory of knowledge is particularly associated in recent philosophy with the Australian philosopher David Armstrong. For Armstrong, the conditions for knowledge are met when you have a belief that is justified by being caused by some process in the external world. Just how literally this is meant is revealed by his example of a thermometer the truth of whose readings is guaranteed by the fact that they reflect the temperature of the environment. As we have discussed in the Overture, energy exchanges between the conscious subject and the environment do not generate perceptions, never mind other more sophisticated propositional attitudes such as "knowing that" and beliefs that such-and-such is the case. Thermometers do not know how hot it is. Any truths generated by a thermometer depend on us to translate its states into statements about temperature.

36. Ladyman *et al.*, *Every Thing Must Go*, 289. A classic paper linking causation with information is Collier, "Causation is the transfer of information".

37. Interested readers may consult the very tetchy entry on "Information (Knowledge)" in Tallis, *Why the Mind is Not a Computer: A Pocket Lexicon of Neuromythology*.

38. The counterfactual theory of causation is particularly associated with the American philosopher David Lewis but it is implicit in the italicized sentence in this passage from David Hume, we cited earlier, "We may define a cause to be an object followed by another, and where all the objects, similar to the first, are followed by objects similar to the second. *Or, in other words, where, if the first object had not been, the second had never existed*" (cited in Note 3 above).

39. John Stuart Mill quoted in Schaffer, "Metaphysics of causation", 31.

40. The same applies to a further development of counterfactual theory: the notion of causation as being in some cases the pre-emption of events. Supposing there are two possible future happenings that are mutually exclusive, so that if one occurs the other cannot occur. There will be circumstances in which an event, in virtue of "bringing about" one of the possibilities, will prevent the other (see Thalos, *Without Hierarchy*, 132–3).

In a classic example favoured by philosophers, two assassins plot to kill a political figure. The plan is for Assassin 1 to fire at the intended target, killing him – event E_1. If Assassin 1 fails, then Assassin 2 will kill the intended target – event E_2. If Assassin 1 is successful, E_2 will no longer be possible, because the life of the politician will no longer be available to be taken. The cause of event E_1 consequently has two effects – the death of the politician and the prevention of the death of the politician occurring at the hands of Assassin 2.

Fortunately, we do not have to entertain blood-boltered scenarios to remind our-selves how the occurrence of one event precludes the occurrence of another. Suppose a tile falls off the roof of my house at time t_1 and is smashed into pieces. It cannot fall off the roof at time t_2 and knock me out. And other events are prevented. For example, a bird cannot walk over it on the roof, it cannot stop the rain leaking into the loft, and the roof cannot give me pleasure by looking smart. Any path taken by objects (and of course people) through the world will pre-empt another path being taken at the same time by the same object (or person) or the same path by another object (or person). Every event will prevent alternatives occupying the same stretch of space-time. Events will also have consequences that may not be reversible so that it is not possible to retrace the sequence of events to the node at the origin of the fork in the road. Pre-emption is permanent. Repairing and replacing the tile will not leave things as they were before it fell off: consequences will have rippled through the world and the things that were pre-empted before replacement will remain forever pre-empted. None of this is, I believe, at all controversial. Its relevance to our under-standing of the seeming obstacle presented to agency by causation is that it further undermines the notion of a cause as a distinct natural power or, more broadly, a necessity, to bring about, or prevent, some happening.

41. There are no forks – either/or at time t_1 – in the road of nature; as we shall see, they are imported into the order of things by conscious subjects envisaging, by agents planning, futures. That is why Peter van Inwagen's assertion, quoted earlier, that at any given time there is only one future is incorrect: there is not even one future. Consequently, there is no range of possible futures. What happens happens outside of agency and it does not happen as the realization of a prior possibility.

42. Quantum mechanics that has replaced definite states of the universe with probabil-ity waves has made this kind of thinking respectable. This, however, is of uncertain relevance when we are thinking of the macroscopic objects that populate the macro-scopic lives of macroscopic humans exercising their macroscopic agency.

43. The example of a see-saw is also worth our attention. We can see its displacements either as single movements or as paired movements: end A goes up and end B goes down; and *vice versa*. An asymmetry is introduced by the choice of end to which to apply pressure. If I press end A, then the movement at A looks like a cause and the movement at B looks like an effect. If I press B, the reverse applies.

44. Quoted in Beebee, "Does anything hold the universe together?", 510.

45. J. J. Smart cited in Beebee, *Ibid.*, 509.

46. Quoted in Menzies, "Counterfactual theories of causation", 20.

47. Arguments for replacing the very idea of causation are set out by Mumford in "Powers and capacities". Mumford, as we have seen, also argued that a metaphysics of powers and capacities renders laws redundant. His starting point is the rejection of Hume's vision of the world as being a sum of "loose and separate" distinct existences.

A striking re-think of the very idea of causation is captured in this passage from Thalos: "the cement of the universe is its ever-evolving set of filters. At one time, the universe held no more than a set of elements … But, with time, new and more organ-ized things came to be. And with their existence new possibilities for new forms of organisation came to exist. With each new order or organization, new avenues for further organization reached the horizon of possibility" (*Without Hierarchy*, 153).

48. Is it perhaps too fanciful to think of the ideas of "oomph" and "glue" being united in the idea of a "force field"? (Incidentally, forces that are attractive and repulsive are equally in the business of securing continuity though connectedness.)

49. As Thalos puts it, "there is a fundamental reason for being sceptical that causal language can be the ecumenical language of science" (*Without Hierarchy*, 153).

50. Wittgenstein, *Tractatus Logico-Philosophicus*, para. 6.36. Earlier, he asserted that "belief in the causal nexus is *superstition*" (para 5.1361.)

51. The smithereening is formalized, frozen, and standardized when the universe is viewed collectively and then individually through the lens of discourse.

52. Although many think they do have an explanation. Religious believers ascribe the emergence of conscious subjects to a separate act of God – the culminating moment in the act of creation. Materialist philosophers look to Darwin and the supposed survival advantage conferred by consciousness. This latter does not work. As Thomas Nagel pointed out, "[Evolution] may explain why creatures with vision or reason will survive, but it does not explain how vision or reasoning are possible. [...]. The possibility of minds forming progressively more objective conceptions of reality is not something the theory of natural selection can attempt to explain ... since it does not explain possibilities at all, but only selection among them" (*View from Nowhere*, 78–9). The benefits, if any, of consciousness could be made available through evolution only if consciousness were on the table in the first place.

53. Thalos, *Without Hierarchy*, 127.

54. *Ibid.*, 146. An interesting light on this is cast by Jaegwon Kim's principle of causal individuation of kinds: "Kinds in science are individuated on the basis of causal powers; that is, objects and events fall under a kind, or share in a property, insofar as they have similar causal powers" (Kim, "Multiple realizations and the metaphysics of reduction", 17; quoted in Rostowski, "Special Interests: The Methodological Unity of the Sciences"). It is not entirely clear from this whether or not we consequently have direct knowledge of causal powers.

55. There are fewer handles in reality than we tend to imagine, as cargo cultists discovered when, observing B following A, they imagined that bringing about A would automatically bring about B.

CHAPTER 4 ACTIONS

1. Some of the distinctive features of human actions discussed in this and the following sections have been highlighted by Michael Bratman. He identifies "our reflectiveness, our planfulness, and our conception of agency as temporally extended" as core features of agency (see Bratman, "Reflection, planning, and temporally extended agency"). He does not, however, share my view of the implications of these characteristics and asserts that "we are fully embedded in an event causal order".

2. Anscombe's *Intention* and Davidson's "Actions, reasons, and causes" are classics. Some commentators question whether Anscombe denied that actions had causes (see, for example, Gjelsvik, "Freedom to act").

3. Davidson, "Actions, reasons, and causes", 11.

4. See, for example, "I am and it is: persons and organisms" in *Seeing Ourselves*, 75–114.

5. This is a phrase particularly associated with Davidson, for whom the community of minds is "the basis of all knowledge and provides the measure of all things" (see Avramides, "Knowledge of other minds in Davidson's philosophy").

6. This topic is a central theme in recent decades in the philosophy of action. I have therefore explored it further in Appendix D devoted to enactivism and embodied cognition.

7. Reviewed and developed by Markus Schlosser in "The dual-system theory and the role of consciousness in intentional action". The discussion that follows is heavily indebted to Schlosser's excellent article.

8. *Ibid.*, 39–40.

9. *Ibid.*, 42.

10. *Ibid.*, 52.

11. Quoted in Schlosser, *ibid.*, 40.

12. Harry Shearer on BBC Radio 4, "Saturday Live", 19 September 2020.

13. If reasons were causes, we would be entitled to ask whether sustained actions would require them to act in a sustained way or simply act as triggers that set things going following which they are no longer required. A sustained reason – like a sustained force – is hardly comprehensible, and it would have to be switched on and off as we move between one task and another. The idea of a reason as a trigger – as when something that is knocked off a cliff continues falling until it reaches the ground – is likewise odd.

14. Quoted in Dennett, *Freedom Evolves*, 170.

15. This is one of the many reasons for rejecting the increasingly common claim that the brain is a Bayesian machine and its fundamental activity is to make predictions. It is (to use the words of one of the most articulate advocates of this view) a "probabilistic prediction engine" (Clarke, "Surfing uncertainty"). Prediction and probability, like possibility, are tensed activities and for this reason tenseless material events (neural discharges) in tenseless material objects (neural pathways) do not seem to provide an appropriate substrate.

16. Quoted in Rosar, "The dimensionality of visual space", 555–6.

17. My relationship to my own body is, of course, more complex, as befits its status as the primary or primordial agent of my agency. I have here touched on a huge topic. It is discussed in Tallis, *The Hand: A Philosophical Inquiry into Human Being* and more recently in *Seeing Ourselves*, especially Chapter 3.

18. For a fascinating exploration of visual space (and hence, by extension, conscious space), see Rosar, "The dimensionality of visual space". Rosar's conclusions – that (1) visual space is a "real" space *sui generis*, and (2) that it is not homeomorphic with the structure and activity of the brain – bear directly on the central arguments of this section and what is subsequently built on them.

19. We could put this technically by saying that there is no modality in the natural world.

20. Van Inwagen, *An Essay on Free Will*, 3.

21. For more on this story, see Tallis, *Of Time and Lamentation*, especially 291–300.

22. In Chapter 3 it was suggested that causation may be a secondary quality of material events, like colour, rather than an inherent property of them. We can develop this idea

further by connecting the causal status of events with tensed time. Consider three successive events E1, E2, and E3 that are apparently causally connected. If we adopt the standpoint of E1, such that it is "now", it is a cause; and E2, which lies in its future, is its effect. If we adopt the standpoint of E2 as happening now, E1 is located in the past and counts as its cause; and E3 is its effect. In short, the asymmetry of causal influences can be translated into a temporal asymmetry captured in tensed time. To make this asymmetry the child of tensed time is to tame causes even further.

23. See Wittgenstein, *Philosophical Investigations*, para. 350, 111e.

24. This observation is connected with the fact, acknowledged by Einstein, that clocks are not natural objects, as discussed in Section 2.2.

25. Time markers such as "last Wednesday" and "the day after next" occupy a space between purely tensed time, indexically defined with respect to the present (e.g., "tomorrow"), and post-tensed time (e.g., 12 May 2020). Its residual tensed nature is reflected in the fact that, unlike "It will rain on 12 May 2020", "It will rain next Wednesday" or "It will rain in a week's time" have truth values dependent on when they are uttered.

    The erroneous naturalization of tensed time is assisted by the erroneous naturalization of post-tensed time. We know that material events do not pass from the future to the present to the past. An event does not have a contradictory, pre-natal existence (in the future before it has happened), an actual existence (in the present) and a contradictory, posthumous existence (in the past after it has happened).

    We may be deceived into naturalizing tensed time if we attach an event to a scaffolding of post-tensed time. We are tempted to say of an event that took place on 12 May that on 11 May it was "in the future" and on 13 May it was "in the past". Of course, it was neither past or future or indeed outside of the time when it happened. It is we who, by locating it in a place in the calendar, attach it to the entire calendar and give it tensed temporal relations that it could not possibly have, given that it does not have "not-yet-existence" or "no-longer-existence". This temptation to confer pre-natal and posthumous lives on events is also increased by the fact the calendar is set out in space, with successive times existing side-by-side (for a further discussion, see "Time as the fourth dimension" in *Of Time and Lamentation*, 29–97).

26. The passage from tensed time to post-tensed time may be captured by what is called "deindexicalization". The reference of terms such as "now" and "tomorrow" depends on the time at which they are used. If I say "now" at 12 noon on 12 May, "now" means 12 noon on 12 May. And if I say "tomorrow" on that day, it means 13 May.

27. It is not for nothing that Nietzsche called man "the promising animal".

28. A leading champion of so-called eliminative materialism is Patricia Churchland for whom propositional attitudes are relics of a folk psychology that will be cast aside as neuroscience advances. For a short critique of these ideas, including their extension to the moral dimension of propositional attitudes, see Tallis, "Wired to care".

29. It has frequently been suggested to me that possibilities exist in (non-human) nature in the form of the probability amplitudes that capture the relationship between wave functions and the results of observations (or more precisely measurements) of that system. The interpretation of the value of a wave function as a probability amplitude is central to the Copenhagen interpretation of quantum mechanics (QM). There are

several reasons why this is irrelevant to the claim that possibilities entertained by subjects are unique to human agency and the key to the distance between actions and happenings. First, QM applies to a sub-microscopic level. Secondly, the Copenhagen interpretation is only one interpretation of QM and is increasingly contested. Thirdly, the probability amplitude is revealed only through measurements made by conscious human subjects. And, finally, and most importantly, it is not *entertained* as a range of possible (macroscopic) outcomes from which one is preferred and chosen. The probability amplitude does not entertain the values that are encompassed by it.

30. The paucity of references to Sartre and in particular *Being and Nothingness* in this book may seem an especially serious omission in this section. It is. But repairing this omission – and in particular tracing the connection between intentionality, possibility and genuine agency in Sartre – would be a major task. I suspect that a discussion of the places where I am in agreement with, and disagree with, Sartre – a compare and contrast job – would be of limited interest to the reader. It is perhaps worth noting that the account of freedom offered here is less ontologically expensive than Sartre's system which makes the in-itself and the for-itself – not to speak of Nothingness – do a lot of work.

  Heidegger is another apparently Missing Person. As with Sartre, his is a pervasive implicit presence. My *Being and Time: A Conversation with Martin Heidegger* gives my take on Heidegger. Like Sartre, he will make a brief appearance in Chapter 6. In particular, I shall there take on board the emphasis in existentialist philosophy on the fact that "the human form of existence and engagement with the world is basically active and practical, rather than cognitive and theoretical" (Alvarez & Hyman, "Philosophy of action 1945–2015", 2) – something that is explored in Appendix D. The fundamental concern of the present book is with the intentional relationship, that holds open the distance, and creates the outside which makes active and practical, as well as cognitive and theoretical, engagement possible.

31. Davidson, "Actions, reasons, and causes", 3. Andrei Buckareff remarks that it is "now almost universally taken to be the standard story of action and its explanation" (Buckareff, "Reasons and causes"). I mention this because an anonymous referee of this manuscript wondered why I should pay so much attention on a 57-year-old paper. For all its faults, it remains a classic, and belongs to that part of philosophy that is "news that stays news".

32. Davidson, "Introduction", *Essays on Actions and Events*, xi. It will be evident from this that Davidson does not clearly distinguish the claim that actions are the result of causes and a (more ambitious) causal theory of action (see Gjelsvik, "Freedom to act"). Both claims, however, are rejected here.

33. Davidson, "Actions, reasons, and causes", 11.

34. Davidson, "Introduction", xii.

35. It has also prompted much metaphysical wriggling by philosophers who believe in free will. Most notable among the wrigglers is Davidson himself who promulgated the doctrine of anomalous monism (see Davidson, "Mental events"). Anomalous monism has three principles: (1) mental events interact causally with physical ones; (2) events related as cause and effect fall under strict deterministic laws; and (3) there are no

strict deterministic laws on the basis of which mental events can be predicted and explained. If this seems inconsistent, it is because it is inconsistent.

The inconsistency is embraced by Davidson even more tightly when he asserts that mental events are identical with physical events. Nevertheless, he argues, they are different under different descriptions, which is why they are not connected by psycho-physical laws. Against this, it is to be noted, that while an entity may have two descriptions, those descriptions are not intrinsic to it. And an entity does not acquire two kinds of properties by being looked at through the lens of two different descriptions. We shall discuss this presently in relation to the idea of a mental phenomenon being "realized" in a physical event.

36. I have discussed this distinction and the nature of "thatter" – and the "thatosphere" – in various places. Recent treatments are in *Logos* (chapter 6) and *Seeing Ourselves* (chapter 4).

37. It is even more difficult to apply the notion of durations to implicit beliefs. For example, I have lived in my present house for over 30 years and I believe that if I go downstairs, I will find a lounge with a bookshelf. The belief will be seen to exist only if it is made explicit by being proved to be wrong – I go downstairs to get a book and there is no bookshelf – or it is challenged by someone who denies that there is a bookshelf in the lounge. Otherwise, this belief hardly seems to figure in my mental contents. It is, however, more than a stretch to suggest a causal relationship between the implicit belief – that certain books are downstairs – and an effect, namely, the reason I go downstairs when I intend to fetch that book – and thence to a further effect – I walk downstairs.

38. The openness of beliefs is still evident even when they are mediated by direct experience and when their object is seemingly something definite. Consider my belief, triggered by my hearing a meowing sound, that there is a cat in the next room. The possibility flagged up by the belief can be realized in a range of states of affairs: there is (to steal the engineering term) a wide tolerance built into the specification. They encompass your cat and my cat, black or brown cats, cats sitting or prowling, the cat near the door or away from it, cats in different internal states, and so on.

The open nature of expectations is a consequence of the sense of possibility built into ordinary experience. Possibilities are not individuals but types that may be realized by a range of token events; many "thisnesses" can instantiate a "whatness". This is acknowledged by Davidson when he says, of wanting to turn on a light, that "It makes no sense to demand that my want be directed to an action performed at any one moment or done in some unique manner. Any one of an indefinitely large number of actions would satisfy the want and can be considered equally eligible as its object" ("Actions, reasons, and causes", 6).

39. Which is why so many philosophers of a materialist persuasion, notably neurophilosophers, have persuaded themselves that propositional attitudes are unreal (see note 28 above).

40. Davidson, "Actions, reasons, and causes", 3.

41. We may accept that propositional attitudes are not events causing other events but still argue that they are properties or dispositions of a subject just as brittleness is a property of glass, raising the probability of a particular line of action. This, however,

won't help to narrow the gap between causes as they are usually understood in the physicalist world picture and propositional attitudes such as beliefs. Brittleness is not, in itself, directed towards a particular range of futures, although a human agent might direct it thus, as when I move a glass out of harm's way if a toddler is at large. While the brittleness of glass will influence its possible futures, the glass does not own, even less anticipate or try to control, those futures; and, even less still subject those futures to comparative evaluation. In contrast, my decision *re* the glass is connected with evaluated futures. I may be aware that, if I move the glass pre-emptively out of harm's way, I may annoy or offend the toddler's parent for being fussy or twitchy. Even so, I may prefer this outcome to the alternative of the glass being broken with the unattractive consequences that may result.

42. See Davidson, "Mental events", 217.

43. Block, "Holism, mental and semantic", 360.

44. This double duty is clearer in the case of, say, desires than in the case of reasons. "I did this because I wanted to" sounds like a more full-blooded explanation than "I did this for the following reason".

45. There is a vast literature on this. The *locus classicus* is Harry Frankfurt's "The freedom of the will and the concept of a person", which is a reminder of the distinction between (for example) first-order desires and second-order desires – desires we desire to have, that we approve of, and wish that we should act upon. The issue is interestingly teased out in Bratman, "Reflection, planning, and temporally extended agency".

46. Indeed, there is a double dissociation between intentions (and other propositional attitudes) and states of affairs that fulfil them: a wide range of physical states may realize a propositional attitude; and a particular physical state of affairs or event may realize a range of intentions. As an example of the latter, I may raise my hand in order to vote, catch someone's attention, to command silence, annoy someone, or to cast a shadow. And, of course, we can often control, or choose, the description under which an action falls.

47. Sellars, "Empiricism and the philosophy of mind", 298–9. The "space of reasons" refers to the network of propositional discourse that enables people to navigate the world in an intelligent fashion and – closer to the main thrust of the previous section – is connected with the fact that reasons, etc. cannot be mapped on to a causally connected physical reality.

48. Behind the fact that goals – or what qualifies as their realization – are not defined by a set of physical events or states located in space and time is something else of great significance. Consider the voting – the raising of hands – that delivers the aim of my trip to London. It is a set of physical events but it counts as a goal only insofar as there is a convention that translates the hand movements into votes and a background of agreements and shared presuppositions that connect those votes with a rather complex goal: the promotion of a campaign to improve national stroke services. The goal in other words is delivered by means of symbols. These, like the vast majority of symbols, are "arbitrary", in the technical sense used by linguists, that they do not look like, or replicate, any characteristic of that for which they stand. This is yet another reason why achieved goals cannot be defined in terms of a set of physical events with certain physical characteristics.

The omnipresence of arbitrary signs in the lives of agents is another marker of the divergence between on the one hand something that counts as the achievement of a goal and on the other the effect of a physical cause understood as an event occupying a determinate stretch of space over a definite period of time.

49. This echoes a point made by Gilbert Ryle, concerning volitions, in a famous passage from his classic *The Concept of Mind*: "By what sort of predicates should they be described? Can they be sudden or gradual, strong or weak, difficult or easy ...? Can they be accelerated, decelerated, interrupted, or suspended ...? Can I do seven of them simultaneously?" (63).

50. Davidson, "Mental events", 209.

51. The case for denying type identity between neural activity and mental entities is supported by the facts that: (1) widely different patterns of neural discharges may be correlated with similar mental experiences or functions; and (2) the similar patterns of neural discharges may be associated with profoundly different experiences or functions. Irrespective of whether this is fatal for type identity theories, it does not alter the fact that token identity as Davidson understands it reinserts mental activity into the causally closed physical nexus and thus rules out genuine freedom of action.

52. Davidson adopts a rather vague hand-waving approach, suggesting that "some physical description applies to each mental event" (quoted in Yalovitz, "Anomalous monism", 19).

53. This is very helpfully discussed in Arnadottir & Crane, "There is no exclusion problem". While what follows does not agree with all the conclusions of this paper, it has drawn heavily on the way it presents the problem of mental causation.

54. Arnadottir & Crane, "There is no exclusion problem", 248.

55. Some philosophers conflate these quite different relationships. For example, John Searle states that "Conscious states are entirely caused by neuronal processes, *and* are realized in the brain" (italics mine). It is difficult to see how they could be both. Pieces of clay could no more cause statues than statues could cause pieces of clay. Nevertheless, this is the justification for reducing the problem of consciousness to a neurobiological question "How exactly does the brain cause conscious experiences, and how are those experiences realized in the brain?" (Searle, *Freedom and Neurobiology: Reflections on Free Will, Language and Political Power*, 6).

56. This remains true even if we agree with Huw Price that the asymmetry of causal influence is viewpoint-dependent, as we discussed in Chapter 3.

57. This is an important connection between agency and the imputation of causal beginnings and subsequent effects to the unfolding of the natural world.

58. Rogers Albritton quoted in Watson, *Free Will*, 20. We cannot be entirely responsible for the consequences of our actions because those consequences never stop, though, typically, as we move causally downstream from the action, they become less relevant and our contribution is attenuated. We may, of course, be responsible for the significant, foreseeable, consequences of our actions, even though they may be unintended.

There is a further problem in separating the processes of the action and the outcome – determining when the process ends and outcome begins. It is particularly acute in the case of complex, temporally extended, actions that have many steps, stages and interwoven routines. Ambitions without clear end-points – such as "being the best I can be" – do not have defined goals. It is up to me to decide when I have arrived; and to define the distinctions between arrival, settling for a certain end-point, and giving up.

59. This is evident even in the case of the seemingly literal trajectory from A to B. Think of the movements involved in consulting a map, or dialing up such a map on an i-phone or reading the instructions printed out in advance. Or choosing a route that, although longer, will avoid crowds, or reduce the possibility of running into someone to whom one owes money.

CHAPTER 5 THE HUMAN AGENT

1. Indeed, there is a sense in which causes-as-handles are "developed" in the way in which a photographic plate is developed, although in the case of causes-as-handles, the developing medium is the idea of a future. It is this that unifies a present state of affairs as an *opportunity* or a source of *obligations*. As bridges between a current situation and a desirable future possible one, causes are of course remote from the kinds of causes identified in natural science. The role played by causes-as-handles, while constrained by the laws of nature, is not defined by them. The assassin's bullet breaks no physical laws but what it actually brings about – and why – is not captured by those laws in the way that a landslide that killed the person the assassin wanted to kill is captured by those laws.

   The situation that provides the rationale for a particular action and specifies its broad characteristics and the general outline of its goal will not be defined by a defined set of physical characteristics, not the least because the situation will go beyond anything that could be actual and present. The relevant past and an imagined future create the agenda which shapes the gaze we direct on the present and transform states of affairs into opportunities or platforms for possible action realized through causes-as-handles. More precisely, there will be more than one relevant past and imagined future because actors are, at any given time, engaged in a multiplicity of connected and parallel actions, some short-lived with immediate goals, and others with medium-term and distant goals.

2. I owe this definition – and much else besides – to Ann Whittle's "A defence of substance causation". My indebtedness is undiminished by my dissent from her defence of the idea that substances are causes. I also use "objects" rather than "substances" in this discussion because "substance" is a term that has acquired a heavy load of often conflicting connotations with its successive appearances during the history of philosophy. As David Wiggins has pointed out: "The notion of a substance – of a persisting and somehow basic object of reference that there is to be discovered in perception and thought, an object *whose claim to be recognized as a real entity* is a claim on our aspirations to understand the world – has been host at various times to countless internecine battles, not all of them very well understood by the protagonists of the warring doctrinal persuasions" (Wiggins, "Substance", 214). I am grateful to David Scott for drawing my attention to this passage.

3. Admittedly, whether or not an entity counts as a single item, or as part of a larger item or as a collection of smaller items may depend on the scale or grain of attention or description. For example, a portion of sand may be one sandcastle, a multitude of sand grains, or a small detail of a beach. And a grain of sand may be a vast number of discrete atoms. Even the temporal boundaries of events as perceived items are not self-imposed. For example, as we noted, how long a clap of thunder lasts depends on the presence of ears to hear – their distribution and acuity. Only persons are self-unifying or self-defining – at a time and over time.

   Those who concede to fundamental physics the last word on ontology may argue that there are no bounded objects in the real world (see, for example, Ladyman *et al.*, *Every Thing Must Go*). If, however, we are talking about causation, we may confine ourselves to the macroscopic world. Even philosophers who believe in the reality of causal necessity accept that there is no causation in the entangled, indeterminate reality of sub-atomic physics. As regards everyday experience, discrete objects are real.

4. Quine, *From Stimulus to Science*, 85.
5. For a more detailed discussion, see Tallis, *Of Time and Lamentation*, 309–13.
6. Russell, "The ultimate constituents of matter", 124. The phrase in this passage "each lasting for a very brief period, though probably not for a mere mathematical instant" is telling. An object that lasted only for a certain finite number of (durationless) mathematical instants would have no duration at all. It is difficult, however, to see what would deliver more-than-instantaneous time slices, if it were not a conscious observer. That observer in turn might develop the idea of an object existing in itself beyond the time it is being observed in virtue of her experience of herself as an embodied subject. See Tallis, *Seeing Ourselves*, 103–14. We shall return to this later in the present chapter.
7. And it would be difficult to find the temporal asymmetry of cause and effect if the partners were objects extended over time. Billiard ball A – the apparent assailant nudging billiard ball B into motion – would bring all of its history to the collision so would billiard ball B. Some (later) time-slices of A would be earlier than some (earlier) time-slices of B.
8. Shoemaker, "Causality and properties", 212.
9. Mumford, "Causal powers and capacities", 266.
10. *Ibid.*, 275.
11. *Ibid.*, 266.
12. Which would have a privileged standing in the world, being a "basic ontological category" acceptance of which, it is claimed, enables philosophers to "produce plausible theories of properties, laws of nature, modality, and causation" (Mumford, "Causal powers and capacities", 266).
13. Beebee, *Free Will: An Introduction*, 120.
14. Taylor, *Metaphysics*, 51–2. I am grateful to David Scott for drawing my attention to this passage.
15. O'Connor, *Persons and Causes: The Metaphysics of Free Will*, 43. O'Connor expressed a similar view more recently: "[M]etaphysical freedom consists in being the ultimate, reasons-guided *causal* source of an intention to act in the face of alternative possibilities for action" (italics mine) (O'Connor, "Free will and metaphysics", 27).

16. Nearly four hundred years of arguments since Descartes have not thinned the cloud of suspicion that hangs over mental causes.

17. Broad, "Determinism, indeterminism, libertarianism", 215.

18. For a discussion of the nature of human beings as embodied subjects see "I Am and it is: persons and organisms" in *Seeing Ourselves*, 77–114. There I argue that it is incorrect to see an object such as a cup as a "logical construction" out of experiences. It is an existential construct: we *live the endurance* of the objects in our niche and our belief in their endurance and independent existence is justified in our daily life.

19. Underlying this is something yet more fundamental: the very idea of an object as something that exists in itself and transcends any experience of it, as being rooted in our experience of our own body. This is discussed in *Seeing Ourselves* (addendum to Chapter 3, "Ambodiment: The I and the It"). It is, of course, central to full-blown agency. The lived unity and temporal extendedness of my body underwrites the continuity of the objects by which I am surrounded, and justifies belief in this continuity as something that survives the discontinuity of my experiences of them.

20. For more on the self, see Tallis, *Seeing Ourselves*, chapter 5.

21. This thesis is elaborated in Wegner, *The Illusion of the Conscious Will*.

22. The most notable advocates of this view have been Sartre and Heidegger, though it is widespread in what in analytical circles used to be called "Continental Philosophy".

23. I am not alone in arguing that agents should not be regarded as causes. Most notably, Carl Ginet has argued over many decades that free actions are – and must be – uncaused (a relatively recent iteration of this position is Ginet, "A defence of a non-causal account of reasons explanations"). His argument is particularly directed against Davidson's assertion – discussed in Section 4.3 – that if reasons are not causes, they do not do any explanatory work. Ginet responds by saying that reasons are connected to actions by means of intentions. This is of course true. Unfortunately, Davidsonians would argue that intentions, too, are causes, since they are token events identical with brain activity. Invoking intention consequently simply inserts another link in the causal chain. For this reason, a more radical critique of the very idea of causation is necessary entirely to exorcise the ghost of causation from voluntary action. Hence the discussion in Chapter 3 and in the present section.

24. There is, however one context in which it is legitimate to use the idea of an agent as a cause: where blame and liability are being assigned either in everyday life or in the more formal context of the law courts. Consider the situation where a trial comes to the conclusion that the driver was the cause of a fatal accident. The sense in which cause is used here is remote from that which it is used, or was used, in science. The reason the driver is picked out as the "cause" of the fatality is that, had his behaviour been different – for example, he had not been driving so fast – the road death would not have occurred or was less likely to do so. Or he would not have let it happen. There are of course many other circumstances that have made the accident possible: the location of the car, the location of another car, their respective velocities, the wetness of the road. What picks out the driver's action as *the* cause is that it is blameworthy. The example is a reminder of the way in which cause is associated with agency.

   What qualifies careless driving as the cause of the accident has less to do with its   physical properties and more to do with our normative expectations of people;

namely that they should behave responsibly. Carelessness or "not taking due care and attention" are not properties of material events. It is the legal status of a certain event rather than its physical properties, or other events which are equally important for the outcome, that makes an agent seem like a cause in a narrow sense. This does not fit into a causal chain originating from the Big Bang. The stick that is transformed into a murder weapon retains its innocence.

25. This is a central insight in Heidegger's key work, *Being and Time*.
26. Our sustained projects, the context in which we realize them, the places we construct for them, the interaction with others and the mutual recognition which they create and foster, amount to a kind of cladding or exoskeleton for the self and its agency. See Tallis, *Seeing Ourselves*, chapter 5, "The elusive, inescapable self".
27. Dennett, *Consciousness Explained*, 33.
28. Heidegger's account of The Open as "a clearing" is discussed in *Being and Time*. There is a lucid discussion of the place of this concept in Heidegger's thought in Schatzki, "Early Heidegger on Being, the clearing, and realism", from which this definition is taken.
29. The irreducible gap between X and "that X is the case" is discussed in, for example, *Logos*, chapter 6.
30. And the hand is the primordial tool or, as Aristotle described it, "the tool of tools". For extensive discussion of the role of our hands with their unique properties in imbuing us with a sense of agency, see Tallis, *The Hand*.
31. Discussed in *Seeing Ourselves*, chapter 5.

CHAPTER 6 THE LIMITS OF FREEDOM

1. Huxley, "Fifth Philosopher's Song", from *Leda*.
2. Larkin, "The Old Fools", from *High Windows*.
3. Quoted in Alvarez & Hyman, "Philosophy of action 1945–2015".
4. Daniel Wegner spent much of his career trying to prove that our conscious will was an illusion. His findings were summarized in *The Illusion of Conscious Will*.
5. G. Strawson, "The impossibility of moral responsibility".
6. Sartre, *Being and Nothingness*, 489.
7. *Ibid.*, 477. This is close to regarding the world as a nexus of affordances, see Appendix B.
8. René Descartes quoted in Albritton, "Freedom of will and freedom of action", 408.
9. Albritton, "Freedom of will and freedom of action", 412.
10. Jean-Paul Sartre quoted in Wiggins, "Towards a reasonable libertarianism", 114.
11. Sartre even suggested that "in a certain sense I choose to be born" (quoted in Carman, "Sartre and Merleau-Ponty on freedom", 372.) There is, perhaps, a kind of truth even in this seemingly absurd claim. We implicitly choose our birth retrospectively by embracing ourselves. Although the temptation here to echo Thomas Carlyle's famous response to transcendentalist Margaret Fuller's cry "I accept the universe!" – "Gad, she'd better" – is irresistible.

12. For a brief account, see *Seeing Ourselves*, 351–8. For a longer account, see Tallis & Spalding, *Summers of Discontent: The Purpose of the Arts Today*.

13. A thesis that is present throughout Sartre's later work but especially in *What is Literature?*

CODA

1. Spinoza, *Ethics*, 30.

2. H. D. Lewis, *Persons and Life After Death*, 41.

3. Taylor, *Metaphysics*, 53. I am grateful to David Scott for drawing my attention to this passage.

4. Some physicists have suggested a means by which the universe could come from "nothing". What they offer is less a Creation story than an exercise in creative accounting. For a discussion, see Tallis, *Of Time and Lamentation*, 450–55.

5. For those who are fond of their Latin, the original quote is "*Initium ergo ut esset creatus est homo, ante quem nullius fuit*" (Augustine, *City of God*, Bk XII, Ch. 27, final sentence).

6. Bradley, *Appearance and Reality*, 2. Bradley, however, continues as follows "but to find these reasons is no less an instinct".

APPENDIX A FROM THE HABITS OF NATURE TO THE LAWS OF SCIENCE

1. Putnam, *Mathematics, Matter, and Method*. The division between realist and antirealist interpretations of the laws of science may be an over-simplification. Mauro Dorato has highlighted other ways of classifying interpretations: "[R]oughly ontological realists about laws claim that statements expressing laws of nature refer to mind-independent properties and relations between obtaining between natural systems, while semantic realists claim that law statements are approximately true, or at least are susceptible of receiving a definite truth-value. Ontological antirealists about laws deny them any referential character, while semantic antirealists regards law-statements as merely useful but do not grant them the property of being true or false" (Dorato, "Why are (most) laws of nature mathematical?", 55). For the present discussion, however, the simpler, perhaps simplifying, dichotomy will probably suffice.

2. Putnam, *Ibid.*, 73.

3. Richard Rorty quoted in Freidman, "Postmodernism vs postlibertarianism", 155.

4. Steven Weinberg quoted in Kauffman, "Breaking the Galilean spell", 1.

5. Fodor, "Special sciences (or: The disunity of science as a working hypothesis)", 97. I am grateful to Adam Rostowski for drawing my attention to this characteristically perceptive observation by Fodor.

6. Ladyman *et al.*, *Every Thing Must Go*, 44.

7. *Ibid.*

8. Searle, *Minds, Brains, and Science*, 94.

9. Thalos, *Without Hierarchy*, 1.
10. *Ibid.*, 31. This is at odds with what Ladyman *et al.* refer to as "scale-relative ontology" according to which "what (really, mind-independently) exists should be relativized to (real, mind-independent) scales at which nature is measurable" (200). For Thalos (and for this writer) the mind-independent universe is scale-less. Thalos points out the oddness of privileging the microphysical scale and assuming "that the universe is active only at scales smaller than those we can inspect with the naked eye, in spite of its vast size, estimated at nearly 100 billion light years, or 10^{27} metres" (*Without Hierarchy*, 6).
11. Searle, *Minds, Brains, and Science*, 94.
12. Cartwright, *The Dappled World*.
13. Philosopher of science John Dupré has likewise pointed out that the project of uniting all sciences – and the phenomena they observe – to physics doesn't even get off first base, given that so-called elementary particles are heterogeneous and some of them actually "fail to be elementary by being composed of simpler entities, quarks. The sense of 'composed', however, is obscure, as quarks are generally said not to exist other than in such 'compositions'" (Dupré, *The Disorder of Things: Metaphysical Foundations of the Disunity of Science*, 103). I am grateful to Adam Rostowski for drawing this passage to my attention.
14. See, for example, Tallis, "A suicidal tendency in the humanities".
15. Louis MacNeice, "Snow", from *Selected Poems*.
16. If the world were homogeneous stuff unfolding according to universal laws it would also be difficult to understand the possibility of a threshold that marks the difference between detected and undetectable change. We need something outside of the changing physical state of the universe to register its changes.
17. Dennett, "Real patterns".
18. Ladyman *et al.*, *Every Thing Must Go*, 288.
19. Barrow, *Theories of Everything: The Quest for Ultimate Explanation*, 11–12.
20. Ladyman *et al.*, *Every Thing Must Go*, 202.
21. *Ibid.*, 286.
22. Hawking, *A Brief History of Time: From the Big Bang to Black Holes*, 174.
23. "Thus the understanding is something more than a power of formulating rules through comparison of appearances; it is itself the lawgiver of nature" (Kant, *Critique of Pure Reason*, 148 (A126)).

APPENDIX B PAYING ATTENTION TO ATTENTION

1. McClelland, "The mental affordance hypothesis".
2. This entirely reasonable thesis is taken to unreasonable places in radical forms of enactivism and embodied cognition as we shall discuss in Appendix D.
3. Our capacity to select the targets of our attention is another reason why the causal theory of perception does not hold up. If perception were a mere effect of the external world impinging on the organism, it would not seem to be amenable to active regulation by the perceiving subject. Effects do not requisition or regulate causes that bring

them about. That is why attention, far from solving the "distality problem" associated with the causal theory of perception – how it is that we are aware of an object through events occurring in it but not of the causal ancestors or descendants of those events – exacerbates it. And a good thing, too.

4. This capacity seems more extraordinary the more you think about it. I find myself suddenly recalling an event that took place a couple of years ago. Why on earth is this on my mind now I wonder? I retrace the train of thought to its beginning from a present, seemingly irrelevant, event that triggered it off. Retracing our thoughts is a manifestation of the ability to rack our brains to remember something and to fight off distractions while we do so. In short to exercise a mode of attention we are justifiably inclined to characterize as "inwardly directed". Thinking our way back to whatever it was that triggered off a train of thought is like navigating upstream in a craft made of water.

5. Schlosser, "Embodied cognition and temporally extended agency", 2100.

APPENDIX C BEASTLY FREEDOM? ANIMALS AS AGENTS

1. The most recent iteration is *Seeing Ourselves*; see especially Chapter 2 "Against naturalism".
2. Steward, *A Metaphysics for Freedom*, 1.
3. *Ibid.*, 9.
4. *Ibid.*, 16–17.
5. *Ibid.*, 21.
6. *Ibid.*, 21.
7. See Tomasello, *A Natural History of Human Thinking.*
8. Wittgenstein, *Philosophical Investigations*, para. 650, 116e.
9. For a detailed discussion see Tallis, *Seeing Ourselves*, 115–44. One striking difference is the absence of declarative (experience-sharing) pointing as opposed to impera-tive ("gimme!") pointing in non-human primates. For an authoritative summary of the evidence on this question, see Brink, "On the evolutionary origin of declarative pointing".
10. It might be argued that distant goals pursued and realized over long periods of time are observed in non-human animals. However, their goals do not have to be envisaged to be realized. It seems reasonable to assume that migrating or nest-building birds or hive-building bees complete these tasks without imagining them.
11. See Suddendorf, *The Gap*, especially 133–56.
12. There is a useful and illuminating discussion of the fundamental difference between animals and humans in McDowell, *Mind and World*. McDowell develops Hans Gadamer's distinction between the animal's mode of life in an environment struc-tured by immediate biological imperatives to which animals are enslaved and human's being in a world. For humans, the environment "is more than a succession of prob-lems; it is a bit of objective reality" (p.116) and as Gadamer puts it they can "rise above the pressures of what impinges on us from the world". It is this, of course, that frees us to *intervene* in nature to the extent that we do.

13. More precisely four other books: *The Hand, I Am, The Knowing Animal* and *Aping Mankind*.

APPENDIX D ENACTIVISM AND EMBODIED COGNITION

1. Schlosser, "The dual-system theory and the role of consciousness in intentional action".
2. Gehrman & Schwenkler, "Hubert Dreyfus on practical and embodied intelligence", 123.
3. *Ibid.*, 123
4. *Ibid.*, 124.
5. Mark Wrathall quoted in Gehrman & Schwenkler, "Hubert Dreyfus on practical and embodied intelligence", 126.
6. Villalobos, "Enactive cognitive science: revisionism or revolution?", 160.
7. Schlosser, "Embodied cognition and temporally extended agency". The exposition that follows is heavily dependent on this excellent paper.
8. *Ibid.*, 2091.
9. Clark & Toribio, "Doing without representing?".
10. See Tallis, "The uncoupled animal" in *The Knowing Animal*, 197–216.
11. A contrast frequently employed by Dreyfus, quoted in Gehrman & Schwenkler, "Hubert Dreyfus on practical and embodied intelligence", 130.
12. Schlosser, "Embodied cognition and temporally extended agency", 2108.
13. Schlicht, "Does separating intentionality from mental representation imply radical enactivism?"
14. Thomas Metzinger quoted in Schlicht, "Does separating intentionality from mental representation imply radical enactivism?", 2.
15. Schlicht, "Does separating intentionality from mental representation imply radical enactivism?", 8.
16. For a discussion of ambodiment, see "I am and it is: persons and organisms" in *Seeing Ourselves*. The ascription of tensed time to conscious subjects is less radical than the Kantian claim that all time belongs to the conscious subject, as a "form of sensible intuition".
17. Embodied cognitivists admit that there is more to absorbed coping than a relatively mindless interaction between bodies, represented as body schemata, and physical environments in which they are embedded. As Schlosser puts it: "This embodied interaction is often 'scaffolded' by the use of external 'props' and through participation in conventional and social practices" ("Embodied cognition and temporally extended agency", 2091).
18. Adam Rostowski has suggested that I have perhaps focused rather too heavily on radical versions of enactivism. He adds that the concept of autonomy – central to enactivist accounts of cognitivist systems – is missing from my treatment. I would argue that, insofar as enactivism is a radical departure from the account of action in this book, it underplays the unique form that autonomy takes in the human agency. There is, of course, a wider sense of autonomy that encompasses, for example, insects and robots, which is remote from agency.

References

Albritton, R. "Freedom of will and freedom of action". *Proceedings and Addresses of the American Philosophical Association* 59:2 (1985), 239–51.

Alvarez, M. & J. Hyman. "Philosophy of action 1945–2015". In B. Kelly & I. Thomson (eds), *The Cambridge History of Philosophy, 1945–2015*. Cambridge: Cambridge University Press, 2019.

Anscombe, E. *Intention*. Oxford: Blackwell, 1959.

Armstrong, D. *What Is a Law of Nature?* Cambridge: Cambridge University Press, 1983.

Arnadottir, S. T. & T. Crane. "There is no exclusion problem". In S. C. Gibb, E. J. Lowe & R. D. Ingthorsson (eds), *Mental Causation and Ontology*. Oxford: Oxford University Press, 2013.

Augustine. *City of God*. Trans. M. Dods. New York: Modern Library, 1950.

Avramides, A. "Knowledge of other minds in Davidson's philosophy". In E. Lepore & K. Ludwig (eds), *A Companion to Donald Davidson*. Oxford: Wiley-Blackwell, 2013.

Bacon, F. *The New Organon and Related Writings*. Indianapolis: Bobbs Merrill, 1960.

Bargh, J. & T. Chartrand. "The unbearable automaticity of being". *American Psychologist* 54 (1999), 462–79.

Barrow, J. *Theories of Everything: The Quest for Ultimate Explanation*. Oxford: Clarendon Press, 1991.

Becker, K. (ed.). *The Cambridge History of Philosophy 1945–2015*. Cambridge: Cambridge University Press, 2019.

Beebee, H. "The non-governing conception of the laws of nature". *Philosophy and Phenomenological Research* 61:3 (2000), 571–94.

Beebee, H. "Does anything hold the universe together?" *Synthese* 149 (2006), 509–33.

Beebee, H. *Free Will: An Introduction*. London: Palgrave Macmillan, 2013.

Berlin, I. *Age of Enlightenment*. New York: The Mentor Philosophers, 1956.

Bird. A. *Nature's Metaphysics: Laws and Properties*. Oxford: Oxford University Press, 2007.

Blackburn, S. "Hume and thick connexions". In R. Read & K. Richman (eds), *The New Hume Debate*. London: Routledge, 2000.

Block, N. "Holism, mental and semantic". *Routledge Concise Encyclopaedia of Philosophy.* London: Routledge, 2000.

Born, M. *Einstein's Theory of Relativity.* Revised edition prepared with the collaboration of G. Leibfried & W. Bien. New York: Dover Publications, 1962.

Bradley, F. H. *Appearance and Reality.* Second edition. Oxford: Oxford University Press, 1893.

Bratman, M. "Reflection, planning, and temporally extended agency". *Philosophical Review* 109:1 (2000), 35–61.

Brentano, F. *Psychology from an Empirical Standpoint.* London: Routledge & Kegan Paul, 1973.

Brink, I. "On the evolutionary origin of declarative pointing". University of Lund Workshop on Mirror Neurons, Mind-Reading, and Emergence of Language, 2004.

Broad, C. D. "Determinism, indeterminism, libertarianism". In *Ethics and the History of Philosophy.* London: Routledge & Kegan Paul, 1952.

Buckareff, A. "Reasons and causes". *Notre Dame Philosophical Reviews* 2014.02.37; https://ndpr.nd.edu/reviews/reasons-and-causes/.

Carman, T. "Sartre and Merleau-Ponty on freedom". In K. Becker & I. Thomson (eds), *Cambridge History of Philosophy 1945–2015.* Cambridge: Cambridge University Press, 2019.

Cartwright, N. *The Dappled World.* Cambridge: Cambridge University Press, 1999.

Clark, A. & J. Toribio. "Doing without representing?" *Synthese* 101 (1994), 401–31.

Clarke, A. "Surfing uncertainty" (letter). *Times Literary Supplement,* 11 November 2016.

Crane, T. "Intentionality as the mark of the mental". In A. O'Hear (ed.), *Contemporary Issues in the Philosophy of Mind.* Cambridge: Cambridge University Press, 1998.

Davidson, D. *Essays on Action and Events.* Oxford: Oxford University Press, 1980.

Davidson, D. "Mental events". In *Essays on Actions and Events,* 207–27. Oxford: Oxford University Press, 1980.

Davidson, D. "Actions, reasons, and causes". In *Essays on Actions and Events.* Oxford: Oxford University Press, 1980.

Dennett, D. *Consciousness Explained.* London: Penguin, 1991.

Dennett, D. "Real patterns". *Journal of Philosophy* 88:1 (1991), 27–51.

Dennett, D. *Freedom Evolves.* London: Penguin, 2003.

Dorato, M. "Why are (most) laws of nature mathematical?" In J. Faye, P. Needham, U. Scheffler & M. Urchs (eds), *Nature's Principles,* 55–75. Amsterdam: Springer, 2005.

Dupré, J. *The Disorder of Things: Metaphysical Foundations of the Disunity of Science.* Cambridge, MA: Harvard University Press, 1993.

Einstein, A. "Autobiographical notes". In P. A. Schilpp (ed.) *Einstein: Philosopher-Scientist* Volume 1. LaSalle, IL: Open Court, 1949.

Einstein, A. "Letter from Prague to Erwin Freundlich, 1 September 1911". *The Collected Papers of Albert Einstein* Volume 5. Princeton, NJ: Princeton University Press, 1993.

Faye, J. "Backward causation". *The Stanford Encyclopedia of Philosophy* (Summer 2018 Edition), E. N. Zalta (ed.); https://plato.stanford.edu/archives/sum2018/entries/causation-backwards/.

Fodor, J. "Special sciences (or the disunity of science as a working hypothesis)". *Synthese* 28:2 (1974), 97–115.

Frankfurt, H. "The freedom of the will and the concept of a person". *Journal of Philosophy* 68:1 (1971), 5–20.

Freidman, J. "Postmodernism v postlibertarianism". *Critical Review* 5:2 (Spring 1991), 145–58.

Gehrman, K. & J. Schwenkler. "Hubert Dreyfus on practical and embodied intelligence". In E. Fridland & C. Pavese (eds), *Routledge Handbook of Philosophy of Skill and Expertise*. Abingdon: Routledge, 2020.

Ginet, C. "A defence of a non-causal account of reasons explanations". *Journal of Ethics* (2008), 229–37.

Gjelsvik, O. "Freedom to act". In E. Lepore & K. Ludwig (eds), *A Companion to Donald Davidson*, 63–74. Oxford: Wiley-Blackwell, 2013.

Hawking, S. *A Brief History of Time: From the Big Bang to Black Holes*. London: Bantam, 1988.

Heidegger, M. *Being and Time*. Trans. J. Stambaugh. New York: SUNY Press, 1996.

Hoefer, C. "Causal determinism". *The Stanford Encyclopedia of Philosophy* (Spring 2016 Edition), E. N. Zalta (ed.); https://plato.stanford.edu/archives/spr2016/entries/determinism-causal/.

Hume, D. *Enquiries Concerning Human Understanding and Concerning the Principles of Morals*. Third edition. Edited by L. A. Selby-Bigge & P. H. Nidditch. Oxford: Clarendon Press, 1975.

Hume, D. *A Treatise of Human Nature*. New York: Doubleday, 1961.

Huxley, A. *Leda*. London: Chatto & Windus, 1920.

Ismael, J. *How Physics Makes Us Free*. Oxford: Oxford University Press, 2016.

Ismael, J. "Fate's scales, quivering: why the problem of free will is not going to go away". *Times Literary Supplement*, 9 August 2019.

Isaacson, W. *Einstein: His Life and Universe*. New York: Simon & Schuster, 2007.

Jacob, P. "Intentionality". *The Stanford Encyclopedia of Philosophy* (Winter 2019 Edition), E. N. Zalta (ed.); https://plato.stanford.edu/archives/win2019/entries/intentionality/.

Kane, R. *The Significance of Free Will*. Oxford: Oxford University Press, 1998.

Kant, I. *The Critique of Pure Reason*. Trans. N. Kemp Smith. London: Macmillan, 1964.

Kauffman, S. *Reinventing the Sacred: A New View of Science, Reason, and Religion*. New York: Basic Books, 2008.

Kim, J. "Multiple realizations and the metaphysics of reduction". *Philosophy and Phenomenological Research* 52:1 (1992), 1–26.

Kuhn, T. *The Structure of Scientific Revolutions*. Chicago, IL: University of Chicago Press, 1972.

Kutach, D. "The asymmetry of influence". In C. Callender (ed.), *The Oxford Handbook of the Philosophy of Time*, 247–75. Oxford: Oxford University Press, 2011.

Ladyman, J. & D. Ross (with D. Spurrett & J. Collier). *Every Thing Must Go: Metaphysics Naturalized*. Oxford: Oxford University Press, 2007.

Ladyman, J. "The history of philosophy of science". In K. Becker (ed.), *The Cambridge History of Philosophy 1945–2015*. Cambridge: Cambridge University Press, 2019.

Laplace, P. S. *A Philosophical Essay on Probabilities*. Trans. F. W. Truscott & F. L. Emory. New York: Dover Publications, 1951.

Larkin, P. "The Old Fools". *High Windows*. London: Faber, 1973.

Lewis, D. *Philosophical Papers.* Volume 2. Oxford: Oxford University Press, 1986.

Lewis, H. D. *Persons and Life After Death.* London: Macmillan, 1978.

Libet, B. "Unconscious cerebral initiative and the role of the conscious will in voluntary action". *Behavioral and Brain Sciences* 8 (1985), 519–66.

Mach, E. *Knowledge and Error: Sketches of the Psychology of Inquiry.* Trans. T. J. McCormack & P. Fouldes. Dordrecht: Reidel, 1976.

Mackie, J. L. *The Cement of the Universe: A Study of Causation.* Oxford: Clarendon Press, 1980.

MacNeice, L. "Snow". *Selected Poems.* London: Faber & Faber, 1940.

Maxwell, N. "Can there be necessary conditions between successive events?" *British Journal of the Philosophy of Science* 19 (1967), 1–25.

McClelland, T. "The mental affordance hypothesis". *Mind* 129:514 (2020), 401–27.

McDowell, J. *Mind and World.* Second edition. Cambridge, MA: Harvard University Press, 1996.

Menzies, P. & H. Beebee. "Counterfactual theories of causation". *The Stanford Encyclopedia of Philosophy* (Winter 2020 Edition), E. N. Zalta (ed.); https://plato.stanford.edu/archives/win2020/entries/causation-counterfactual/.

Mill, J. S. "Nature". In H. D. Allen (ed.) *The Age of Ideology: The Nineteenth Century Philosophers,* 149–60. New York: Mentor, 1956.

Miller, J., P. Shepherdson & J. Trevena. "Effects of clock monitoring on electroencephalographic activity: is unconscious movement initiation an artifact of the clock?" *Psychological Science* 22:1 (2011), 103–09.

Millican, P. "Hume, causal realism, and causal science". *Mind* 119 (July 2009), 647–712.

Monton, B. & C. Mohler. "Constructive empiricism". *The Stanford Encyclopedia of Philosophy* (Summer 2017 Edition), E. N. Zalta (ed.); https://plato.stanford.edu/archives/sum2017/entries/constructive-empiricism/.

Mumford, S. "Laws and lawlessness". *Synthese* 114 (2005), 397–413.

Mumford, S. "Causal powers and capacities". In H. Beebee, C. Hitchcock & P. Menzies (eds), *Oxford Handbook of Causation,* 266–81. Oxford: Oxford University Press, 2009.

Nagel, T. *The View from Nowhere.* Oxford: Oxford University Press, 1986.

Nietzsche, F. *On the Genealogy of Morals* and *Ecce Homo.* Trans. W. Kauffman & R. J. Hollingdale. New York: Vintage, 1972.

O'Connor, T. *Persons and Causes: The Metaphysics of Free Will.* Oxford: Oxford University Press, 2000.

O'Connor, T. "Free will and metaphysics". In D. Palmer (ed.), *Libertarian Free Will: Contemporary Debates.* Oxford: Oxford University Press, 2014.

Pereboom, D. *Living Without Free Will.* Cambridge: Cambridge University Press, 2001.

Pesic, P. "Nature on the rack: Leibniz's attitude towards judicial torture and the 'torture' of nature". *Studia Leibnitiana* 29:2 (1997), 189–97.

Popper, K. *Conjectures and Refutations: The Growth of Scientific Knowledge.* New York: Basic Books, 1962.

Price, H. *Time's Arrow and Archimedes Point.* Cambridge: Cambridge University Press, 1996.

Putnam, H. "Philosophy and our mental life". In *Mind, Language and Reality.* Cambridge: Cambridge University Press, 1975.

Putnam, H. *Mathematics, Matter, and Method.* Cambridge: Cambridge University Press, 1975.

Quine, W. V. O. "The nature of natural knowledge". In S. Guttenplan (ed.), *Mind & Language: Wolfson College Lectures 1974.* Oxford: Clarendon Press, 1975.

Quine, W. V. O. *From Stimulus to Science.* Cambridge, MA: Harvard University Press, 1995.

Rosar, W. "The dimensionality of visual space". *Topoi* 35 (2016), 531–70.

Rostowski, A. "Special Interests: The Methodological Unity of the Sciences". Unpublished manuscript.

Russell, B. "The ultimate constituents of matter". In *Mysticism and Logic.* London: Pelican, 1953.

Ryle, G. *The Concept of Mind.* London: Peregrine, 1963.

Sargant, R.-M. "Robert Boyle's Baconian inheritance: a response to Laudan's Cartesian thesis". *Studies in the History and Philosophy of Science* 17:4 (1986), 469–86.

Sartre, J.-P. *What is Literature?* Trans. B. Frechtman. London: Methuen, 1950.

Sartre, J.-P. *Being and Nothingness: An Essay on Phenomenological Ontology.* Trans. H. Barnes. London: Methuen, 1957.

Schaffer, J. "The metaphysics of causation". *The Stanford Encyclopedia of Philosophy* (Fall 2016 Edition), E. N. Zalta (ed.); https://plato.stanford.edu/archives/fall2016/entries/causation-metaphysics/.

Schatzki, T. R. "Early Heidegger on Being, the Clearing, and realism". *Revue Internationale de Philosophie* 43:168(1) (1989), 80–102.

Schlicht, T. "Does separating intentionality from mental representation imply radical enactivism?" *Frontiers in Psychology*, 28 August 2018. https/doi.org/10 3389/fpsyg. 2018.91497.

Schlosser, M. "The neuroscientific study of free will: a diagnosis of the controversy". *Synthese* 191:2 (2017), 245–62.

Schlosser, M. "Embodied cognition and temporally extended agency". *Synthese* 195:5 (2018), 2089-112.

Schlosser, M. "Agency". *The Stanford Encyclopedia of Philosophy* (Winter 2019 Edition), E. N. Zalta (ed.); https://plato.stanford.edu/archives/win2019/entries/agency/.

Schlosser, M. "The dual-system theory and the role of consciousness in intentional action". In B. Feltz, M. Missal & A. Sims (eds), *Free Will, Causality, and Neuroscience*, 35–57. Leiden: Brill, 2020.

Searle, J. *Minds, Brains, and Science.* Cambridge, MA: Harvard University Press, 1984.

Searle, J. *Freedom and Neurobiology: Reflections on Free Will, Language and Political Power.* New York: Columbia University Press, 2007.

Sellars, W. "Empiricism and the philosophy of mind". In H. Feigl & M. Scriven (eds), *Minnesota Studies in the Philosophy of Mind* Volume 1, 298–99. Minneapolis, MN: University of Minnesota Press, 1956.

Shearer, H. "Saturday Live", BBC Radio 4, 19 September 2020.

Shields, G. "Neuroscience and conscious causation: has neuroscience shown that we cannot control our own actions?" *Reviews of Philosophy and Psychology* 5:4 (2014), 565–82.

Shoemaker, S. "Causality and properties". In *Identity, Cause, and Mind: Philosophical Essays.* Cambridge: Cambridge University Press, 1980.

Soon, C., M. Brass, H.-J. Heinze & J.-D. Haynes. "Unconscious determinants of free decisions in the human brain". *Nature Neuroscience* 11:5 (May 2008), 543–5.

Spinoza, B. *Ethics*. Translated by G. Santayana. London: Everyman Classics, 1910.

Steward, H. *A Metaphysics for Freedom*. Oxford: Oxford University Press, 2012.

Strawson, G. "The impossibility of moral responsibility". *Philosophical Studies* 75:1/2 (1994), 5–24.

Strawson, G. *The Secret Connexion: Causation, Realism, and David Hume*. Revised edition. Oxford: Oxford University Press, 2014.

Suddendorf, T. *The Gap: The Science of What Separates Us From Other Animals*. New York: Basic Books, 2013.

Tallis, R. *Enemies of Hope: A Critique of Contemporary Pessimism*. London: Macmillan, 1999.

Tallis, R. *A Conversation with Martin Heidegger*. London: Palgrave Macmillan, 2002.

Tallis, R. *The Hand: A Philosophical Inquiry into Human Being*. Edinburgh: Edinburgh University Press, 2003.

Tallis, R. *I Am: A Philosophical Inquiry into First-Person Being*. Edinburgh: Edinburgh University Press, 2004.

Tallis, R. *The Knowing Animal: A Philosophical Inquiry into Knowledge and Truth*. Edinburgh: Edinburgh University Press, 2005.

Tallis, R. *Michelangelo's Finger. An Exploration of Everyday Transcendence*. London: Atlantic, 2010.

Tallis, R. *Aping Mankind: Neuromania, Darwinitis and the Misrepresentation of Humanity*. Durham: Acumen, 2011; Abingdon: Routledge, 2016.

Tallis, R. "A suicidal tendency in the humanities". In *On the Human*. National Humanities Centre, 2012.

Tallis, R. *The Mystery of Being Human: God, Freedom and the NHS*. London: Notting Hill Editions, 2016.

Tallis, R. *Of Time and Lamentation: Reflections on Transience*. Newcastle upon Tyne: Agenda, 2017.

Tallis, R. *Logos: The Mystery of How We Make Sense of the World*. Newcastle upon Tyne: Agenda, 2018.

Tallis, R. *Seeing Ourselves: Reclaiming Humanity from God and Science*. Newcastle upon Tyne: Agenda, 2020.

Tallis, R. "Against the neural philosophy of mind". *Philosophy Now*, April/May 2020.

Tallis, R. "Wired to care". Review of *Conscience* by Patricia Churchland. *Times Literary Supplement*, 26 June 2020.

Tallis, R. "Arguing with a solipsist". *Philosophy Now*, December 2020/January 2021.

Tallis, R. & J. Spalding. *Summers of Discontent: The Purpose of the Arts Today*. London: Wilmington Square Books, 2014.

Taylor, R. *Metaphysics*. Fourth edition. Englewood Cliffs, NJ: Prentice Hall, 1991.

Thalos, M. *Without Hierarchy: The Scale Freedom of the Universe*. Oxford: Oxford University Press, 2013.

Tomasello, M. *A Natural History of Human Thinking*. Cambridge, MA: Harvard University Press, 2014.

Unger, R. M. & L. Smolin, *The Singular Universe and the Reality of Time*. Cambridge: Cambridge University Press, 2015.

van Inwagen, P. *An Essay on Free Will*. Oxford: Oxford University Press, 1983.

Villalobos, M. "Enactive cognitive science: revisionism or revolution". *Adaptive Behaviour* 21:3 (2013), 159–67.

Watson, G. (ed.) *Free Will*. Second edition. Oxford: Oxford University Press, 2003.

Wegner, D. *The Illusion of the Conscious Will*. Cambridge, MA: MIT Press, 2002.

Whittle, A. "A defence of substance causation". *Journal of the American Philosophical Association* (2016), 1–20.

Wiggins, D. "Substance". In A. C. Grayling (ed.), *Philosophy: A Guide Through the Subject*. Oxford: Oxford University Press, 1995.

Wiggins, D. "Towards a reasonable libertarianism". In G. Watson (ed.) *Free Will*. Second edition. Oxford: Oxford University Press, 2003.

Wittgenstein, L. *Philosophical Investigations*. Trans. G. E. M. Anscombe. Oxford: Blackwell, 1963.

Wolpert, L. *The Unnatural Nature of the Science: Why Science Does Not Make (Common) Sense*. London: Faber, 1992.

Woodward, J. "Causation and manipulability". *The Stanford Encyclopedia of Philosophy* (Winter 2016 Edition), E. N. Zalta (ed.); https://plato.stanford.edu/archives/win2016/entries/causation-mani/.

Yalowitz, S. "Anomalous monism". *The Stanford Encyclopedia of Philosophy* (Winter 2019 Edition), E. N. Zalta (ed.); https://plato.stanford.edu/archives/win2019/entries/anomalous-monism/.

Index

action. *See also:* agency; intentionality; purpose
 asymmetry with outside world 99
 automatic 92–3
 and causation 91, 130, 135, 143, 153
 conditions for 160
 and embodied subjects 147–9
 and embodiment 204
 facing the world 170
 and happenings 59–60, 91, 95, 105–6, 126, 128–9, 132, 141, 162, 212
 initiation 129–31, 135
 and intentionality 88, 92, 106, 132, 204, 211, 216n14
 and knowledge 91, 94
 and material causation 90, 134, 137, 239n1
 means/end 135
 and others 90
 and outcomes 238n58
 and perception 190, 195
 philosophy of 88, 92, 106, 135, 204, 216n14, 233n6
 and physical events 115, 168
 platform for 8, 56, 98, 134, 145, 163, 167, 170, 184
 and possibility 96, 105, 129, 132–3, 153, 168
 prioritization 91
 and propositional attitudes 107, 115–22, 211
 and purpose 90, 95, 133, 238n58
 reason-based 93, 106, 120, 145, 233n13, 239n1
 and the representational theory of mind 210
 and representations 206, 209
 and temporality 89, 93–4, 102–3, 130–31, 170
 virtual outside 99, 154, 157
affordances. *See:* attention:affordances
agency. *See also:* agent theory of causation; intentionality; perception; possibility; self
 and absorbed coping 205
 and action 87, 106, 212
 agent/cause distinction 230n34
 and attention 191–2
 and causation 13, 70, 108, 122, 150, 241n24
 characteristics of 197
 and choices 18–19, 86

and consciousness   170
and decisions   112
definition   11
embodied agent/subject   14–15, 20, 28, 53, 83, 139, 141–9, 155, 160, 205. *See also:* self
and enactivism   205–11
impossibility of   14, 22, 56, 60, 67, 72, 79, 82, 95, 153, 167–9, 218n18
and initiation   155
and intentionality   10, 87, 157, 169
and interests   157
limited   9, 12, 159, 161–2
metaphysical freedom   164–5, 240n15
metaphysical scandal   169
and morality   165
and natural laws/determinism   14, 21–4, 29, 33, 64
and neuroscience   2–25, 51–7, 67–92, 96–106, 138–54, 167–73, 180–86, 205–13
platform for   8, 56, 98, 134, 145, 163, 167, 170, 184
and possibility   7, 72–3, 100, 102, 104, 210
possibility of   9, 88, 163
and purpose   168
quasi-agency   25, 70, 72, 150
and recreation   165
and representationalism   205–6
and responsibility   165
and shared knowledge   8, 73, 98, 160
and subjects   9
tensed temporality   71, 93, 99, 102, 141, 155, 211, 234n25-26
and time asymmetry   71–2, 145, 148
virtual distance from the world   8–9, 12, 24, 47, 52, 58, 97–9, 155–7, 160, 211
virtual space, permitting   5
volition, field of   85, 145
agents. *See:* self
agent theory of causation   82, 84, 149–50. *See also:* agency

and action   143–4
and causation   143–5
definition   142
and dispositions   143
and intentionality   144
and possibility   143
and propositional attitudes   142
Albritton, Rogers   131, 238n58, 242n8-9
ambodiment   152, 155, 211, 241n19, 246n16
ancestry, causal. *See:* causation:ancestry, causal
animals   197
and agency   198–201
and determinism   198
and intentionality   198
and propositional attitudes   198
and temporality   200
anomalous monism   127, 235n35. *See also:* determinism:neurodeterminism
Anscombe, Elizabeth   88, 232n2
anti-realism   28–9, 33, 36, 173, 176, 180–81, 185, 188, 220n15, 227n12. *See also:* realism
and laws of science   243n1
(anti-)representationalism   209–10
and action   206
and agency   205–6
and intentionality   208
and mental representations   205–6, 214n3, 246n13-15
and propositional attitudes   205
Armstrong, David   221n16, 230n35
Arnadottir, S. T.   238n53-54
attention
and action   192–4
active and passive   191
affordances   97, 190–96
and agency   191, 194, 196
convergent   195
and distance from the world   194
facing the world   194
inattention   193, 245n4

and intentionality 189–90, 196
and self-action 189–90, 194
Augustine 170, 243n5
Avramides, A. 233n5
Ayer, A. J. 223n36

Bacon, Francis 40, 219n6, 221n20,
    222n29
Barfield, Owen 224n39
Barrow, John 186, 244n19
becausation. *See:* causation:becausation
Beebee, Helen 25–6, 30, 141, 219n8-9,
    228n22, 231n44-45, 240n13
Besso, Michele 71
Big Bang 22, 68, 78–9, 82, 130, 155,
    219n7, 242n24, 244n22
Big Crunch 79, 130
Bird, Alexander 221n16
Blackburn, S. 219n8
Block, Ned 116, 237n43
Boyle, Robert 26, 30–32, 34–42, 50,
    53, 55, 57, 176, 185–7, 221n21,
    222n24-25
brain / neuroscience. *See also:*
    neurodeterminism
    and aboutness 4. *See also:*
        intentionality:aboutness
    and agency 15, 22. *See also:* agency
    and the causal theory of perception
        3
    and the community of minds 90
    experiments 14–20
    and the mind 2
    and neurodeterminism 14, 48
    and perception 4. *See also:* perception
    and the person 14. *See also:* self
    and predictions 233n15
    and presence 3. *See also:* presence
    and propositional attitudes 105,
        126–8
Bradley, F. H. 243n6
Bratman, Michael 232n1
Brentano, Franz 1, 7, 9, 216n13
Broad, C. D. 145, 147, 241n17
Buckareff, Andrei 235n31

Cartwright, Nancy 80, 182, 244n12
causal ancestry. *See:* causation:ancestry,
    causal
causal closure. *See:* causation:closure,
    causal
causal matrix. *See:* intentionality:causal
    matrix
causal necessity. *See:* causation:necessity,
    causal
causation
    absence 74–5
    and agency 67, 70, 79, 84
    agent theory of. *See:* agency:agent
        theory of causation
    agent-theory of 70
    ancestry, causal 13–14, 60, 77, 80, 130
    asymmetry 71–2, 228n28, 229n33,
        233n22, 234n22, 238n56, 240n7
    backward 229n30
    becausation 82, 94, 106, 113–14,
        118–19, 126, 129, 141, 152, 154,
        168
    and blame 76
    closure, causal 12–13, 70, 80, 102,
        126, 150, 238n51
    and conditions. *See:* necessity
    and consciousness 84
    and contiguity 65, 227n15
    and contingency 78
    and correlation/conjunction 61–4,
        67, 77, 84
    counterfactual theory of 61–5, 68,
        74–5, 119, 230n38,40
    definition 76
    events as causes 78–80, 84, 170
    fifth force 143, 148, 183
    and the gaze 66
    as glue 60, 64–7, 69–70, 75, 77–9, 81,
        129, 136. *See also:* oomph
    human dependent 67–70, 83, 129,
        132–3, 168, 227n19
    Hume-iliation 76, 79, 108, 140, 155
    and induction 63
    and intentionality 59
    interventionist 64

intrinsic in nature. *See:* necessity
knowledge, causal theory of   230n35
laws and causes   22, 60, 67, 72, 82, 95,
    153, 167
manipulative theory of   35–6, 53, 64,
    70, 80, 84, 149, 176, 225n49-50.
    See also: means/end
means/end   50, 53, 70, 84, 96, 135,
    148, 151, 155, 162. *See also:*
    manipulative theory of
and mechanism   63, 227n11
necessary but not sufficient. *See:*
    necessity
and necessity   61–2, 72, 79, 84, 106,
    119, 128
necessity, causal   22, 58, 61–2, 64, 67,
    128, 140, 215n5, 240n3
necessity, causal, and action   22, 60
necessity, causal, and the mind   61–2,
    67
and objects   136–9, 239n2
as occult force   60–61, 66, 107, 226n4
as oomph   60, 64, 66–7, 69, 72–5, 77,
    79, 81–2, 95, 107, 119, 129, 136.
    See also: glue
and perception   61
and possibility   77–8, 80
as powers   66, 80, 82–3, 108, 120,
    128–9, 139–40, 144, 231n47,
    232n54, 240n12
projected   26, 45, 61, 67, 70, 82, 128,
    146, 186, 229n31
and properties of objects   139–40,
    221n16
and realism   66
reasons as causes   106, 120, 233n13
statistical account of   77–8
and sub-atomic physics   240n3
and successions of events   65–6, 72,
    227n19. *See also:* necessity
untidy   80–81
viewpoint dependent   68–71, 74, 136,
    229n31, 238n56
ceteris paribus, other things equal   36–7,
    39, 49, 56, 61, 178, 217n5

chaotic indeterminacy. *See:*
    indeterminacy:chaotic
Churchland, Patricia   234n28
Clarke, Andy   206, 233n15
closure, causal. *See:* causation:closure,
    causal
cognitivism   209
community of minds   45, 56,
    100, 184, 233n5. *See also:*
    intentionality:intersubjective /
    joined
    distanced from natural world   90
compatibilism   12, 51, 216n3
consciousness. *See also:* intentionality
    and agency   170
    and the brain   4, 14, 20, 238n55
    and causation   5, 84
    as effect of causes   84
    emergence of   83, 182, 232n52
    and enactivism   204
    and intentionality   5, 51, 73, 96, 156,
        165, 170, 210
    multiple viewpoints   128
    and the natural world   5, 51, 58
    outside of nature   6, 24, 73, 145, 156.
        See also: perception:and the
        outside world
    and representation   214n3
    and supervenience   182, 184
    and time   103, 240n6
coping, absorbed/skilled   205–7, 212,
    215n10, 216n14, 246n17
counterfactual theory of causation. *See:*
    causation:counterfactual theory of
Crane, Tim   213n1, 238n53-54

Damasio, Antonio   208
Davidson, Donald   4, 88, 106–7, 113,
    116, 122, 126–7, 143, 150, 225n48,
    232n2-3, 233n5, 235n31-35,
    236n35,38,40, 237n42, 238n50-52,
    241n23
Dennett, Daniel   2, 4, 9, 153, 185–6,
    214n3, 217n8, 233n14, 242n27,
    244n17

Descartes, René   164, 209, 219n7, 241n16, 242n8
determinism   12, 29, 51, 57, 60, 170, 198, 218n2,17, 226n1, 229n32. *See also:* brain; determinsim
and agency   14
exclusion problem   127, 238n53-54
neurodeterminism   14–20, 47, 85, 117, 126–9
Dorato, Mauro   243n1
Dreyfus, Hubert   205, 246n2,5,11
Dupré, John   244n13

Einstein, Albert   29, 44, 57, 71, 101–2, 221n18, 222n23, 223n30-31, 229n29,33, 234n24
embodied cognition   157, 203–5, 207, 211, 215n10, 216n14, 233n6, 244n2, 245n5, 246n7,12,17. *See also:* enactivism
enactivism   157, 203, 214n3, 216n14, 233n6, 244n2, 246n13-15. *See also:* embodied cognition
and agency   205–11
and autonomy   246n18
and cognition   207
and consciousness   204
and intentionality   215n10
and knowledge   207
and propositional attitudes   204 5
virtual distance from the world   206–7
endurantism   138, 146
exclusion problem. *See:* determinism; propositional attitudes
experience. *See:* perception
experiments, neuroscience. *See:* brain:experiments

fifth force. *See:* causation:fifth force
Fodor, Jerry   177, 243n5
Fraassen, Bas van   220n15
Frankfurt, Harry   237n45
free will. *See:* agency

gaze
casual   37, 49, 81
and causation   65–6
mathematical   188, 224n39
metaphysical   107
and neural activity   2
objective   12
of perception   2–3, 73
scientific   46, 167, 188
Gehrman, Kristina   205, 207, 246n2,5,11
Ginet, Carl   241n23
Gjelsvik, O.   232n2, 235n32
goal. *See:* purpose
Gregory, Richard   97

habits of nature. *See also:* laws of nature; laws of science
and agency   29, 33–4
as constraints   25–6, 57, 155, 219n7
distinct from laws of science   29–31, 33–4, 39, 41, 45, 48–9, 72, 173
and statistical theory of causation   77
Hawking, Stephen   187, 244n22
Haynes, John-Dylan   16–19, 48, 86, 95, 217n12, 218n16
Heidegger, Martin   154, 205, 216n14, 235n30, 241n22, 242n25,28
Hoefer, C.   226n1
human being   13, 128, 152, 160, 197–8, 208. *See also:* self
Hume, David   26, 60–65, 67, 70, 76, 79, 83–4, 108, 140, 150, 152, 155, 219n6,8, 225n53, 226n2-3,5, 227n10,12-14,18, 228n22, 230n38, 231n47
Hume-iliation and causation. *See:* causation:Hume-iliation
Husserl, Edmund   7–8, 215n9
Huxley, Aldous   159, 242n1

inattention. *See:* attention:inattention
indeterminacy
chaotic   23–4
quantum   23

indeterminism   23, 217n6, 241n17
information   9, 73, 117, 186, 204–5, 209
instrumentalism, scientific   173–4. *See also:* anti-realism
intentionality. *See also:* action; agency; consciousness; perception
   aboutness   2, 4, 111, 127, 208–9, 214n3-4
   and action   88
   and agency   10, 91, 169
   and agent-theory of causation   144
   and attention   189–90, 196
   and the "causal matrix"   208
   and causes   88
   and consciousness   5, 51, 73, 156, 165, 170, 210
   definition   1
   derivative   92, 204
   and embodied subjects   146
   emergent property   4–5
   and enactivism   203–11
   facing the world   2, 8, 41, 51, 55–6, 73, 98–9, 140. *See also:* perception:facing the world
   intersubjective / joined   7, 41, 44, 53, 55–6, 73, 90, 97, 100, 103, 184, 197, 200, 204, 215n7-8
   laws of science   50
   mark of the mental   1, 213n1, 214n3, 215n6
   and material causation   3–5, 7, 13, 22, 88, 208, 211
   and neural activity   105, 208–9
   and outcomes   237n46
   and perception   3–4, 8, 49, 55
   and possibility   96, 98–9, 105
   and propositional attitudes   120
   purpose   54, 87–8
   and representation   208, 214n3
   subject/object distinction   7, 55–6, 66, 69, 81, 97–8, 215n6
   teleosemantics   214n3
Inwagen, Peter van   11, 21, 79, 100, 216n1, 218n2, 231n41, 233n20
Ismael, Jennan   57, 213n1, 226n54

Kahneman, Daniel   92
Kane, Robert   11, 216n2, 218n16, 219n5
Kant, Immanuel   62, 188, 226n9, 244n23
Kim, Jaegwon   232n54
Kuhn, Thomas   175
Kundera, Milan   93

laboratory. *See also:* laws of science
   and agency   48
   agent anonymity   57
   experimentation as expression of agency   36, 39, 40, 58
   fragmentation of nature in experimentation   37, 51
   laws of nature   37–9
   laws of science   53
   outside of nature   35, 38–9, 48, 51–3
   virtual distance from the world   41
Ladyman, James   73, 178–9, 185–7, 220n12, 223n36-37, 224n39, 230n36, 240n3, 243n6, 244n10,18,20
Laplace, Pierre   21–2, 24, 218n1
Larkin, P.   160
laws of nature
   and agency   22, 27, 29, 34
   anti-realist accounts   220n15
   contingent   220n13
   and continuity   60, 63, 66–8, 70, 81, 112, 241n19
   evolving   220n10
   and habits of nature   30
   and intentionality   22
   and laws of science   30
   origins   5, 12, 22, 33, 41, 48, 63, 68, 79–80, 95, 129–30, 132, 144, 155, 164, 170, 175, 199
   regulators or regularities   24–9, 31, 45, 49
   synthetic product of the mind   188, 244n23
laws of science. *See also:* habits of nature; laboratory; laws of nature
   and agency   22, 33, 36, 50, 57, 64
   agent anonymity   57

discovery of   22, 28–9, 34, 36, 50, 179, 188, 222n23
distinct from habits/laws of
    nature   29–31, 33–4, 39, 41, 45, 48–9, 72, 173, 176
evolutionary   27–8, 33–4, 45
fragmentation of nature   9, 65–6, 69–70, 78, 81, 83, 129, 199, 232n51
hierarchy of   176–80
history of   28–9, 31–2, 55, 173–4, 178, 181
and human interests   180
idealizations   36–41
instrumentalism, scientific   173–4
laws and causes   22, 60, 67, 72, 82, 95, 153, 167
mathematization   47, 178–9, 181, 184–5, 187, 222n22, 223n37, 224n39
measurement   42–5, 223n31
multiplicity of   184
outside of nature   29–30, 35–6, 41, 43–5, 47, 55, 132, 184, 188, 207
place of   188
real patterns   185
restoration of continuity   64–7, 69, 81, 83, 140. See also: fragmentation of nature
scale   45–7, 244n10
and tensed time   234n25
uncontaminated   53, 174, 176, 178–9, 181, 188
underdetermination of   178
unification of   32, 47, 177, 179–80, 182–3
unnatural   25–6, 30, 35–6, 39, 41–2, 44–5, 49–50, 175, 186
Leibniz, G. W.   219n7, 221n20
Lewis, David   228n22, 230n38
Lewis, H. D.   169, 243n2
Libet, Benjamin   15–19, 48, 86, 95, 217n9,12, 218n15-16
Lichtenberg, Georg Christoph   61–2, 119, 226n4

Mach, Ernst   43, 222n28
Mackie, J. L.   227n16
MacNeice, L.   184
Maudlin, Tim   25
Maudslay, Henry   225n52
McClelland, Tom   190–91, 196, 244n1
McDowell, John   245n12
mental
    actions   191, 195–6, 244n1
    causes   129, 134, 241n16
    contents   84, 122, 127, 210, 215n6, 216n10, 236n37. See also: propositional attitudes
    entities/items   6, 84, 98, 127, 129, 204, 238n51
    events   3, 126–7, 144–6, 151–2, 191, 214n3, 225n48, 235n35, 236n35, 237n42, 238n50,52. See also: propositional attitudes
    holism of   115, 117, 122, 126. See also: propositional attitudes
    illusions   7
    representations   205–6, 214n3, 246n13-15
    states   1–2, 7, 116, 119–20, 122, 153, 190, 204–6, 208–10, 213n1, 214n1,3
Merleau-Ponty, Maurice   205, 216n14, 242n11
Metzinger, Thomas   208, 246n14
Millikan, Ruth   214n3
Mill, John Stuart   22, 52–3, 76, 156, 218n4, 224n47, 230n39
morality
    and agency   165. See also: agency
    moral luck   13, 162
    moral responsibility   13, 76, 135, 155, 162, 217n8, 238n58, 241n24
    and propositional attitudes   234n28
Mumford, Stephen   140, 219n7, 221n16, 231n47, 240n9,12
Munchausen, Baron   163

Nagel, Thomas   12, 154, 216n4, 232n52
natural laws. See: laws of nature

necessity, causal. *See:* causation:necessity, causal
neurodeterminism. *See:* brain; determinsim
neuromania 217n7
neuroscience. *See:* brain

objects
    and agent-causation 144
    and causation 136–7, 141, 239n2
    embodied subject 139, 241n18
    and endurantism 138, 146, 241n19
    and fundamental physics 240n3
    nature of 138, 239n2
    and perdurantism 138, 146, 240n6
    and property causation 139–41, 221n16
outside world. *See also:* agency; consciousness; intentionality; perception

Peirce, C. S. 30, 220n10
perception. *See also:* agency; intentionality; perception
    and action 190, 195
    and agency 7
    causal theory of 2–7, 84, 108–9, 215n5, 230n35, 244n3, 245n3
    of causation 61
    facing the world 6, 8, 98. *See also:* intentionality:facing the world
    and intentionality 3–4, 8, 49, 55
    objects exceed experience 96–7, 241n19
    and perspective 6
    subject/object distinction 5–8, 55, 97. *See also:* agency
    temporal distance 99
    virtual distance from the world 5–6, 8, 53, 55–6, 73, 83, 99. *See also:* consciousness
perdurantism 138, 146
Pereboom, Derk 217n8
person. *See:* self

physics, fundamental 47, 177, 181, 221n21, 224n39, 240n3. *See also:* sciences, special
    micro-physics 45, 178–80, 182–3, 185, 228n19,28, 229n28,31, 244n10
Popper, Karl 50, 102, 224n44
possibility. *See also:* action; agency; causation; intentionality; time
    absent in the material world 100–01, 231n41
    and action 105, 153
    and agency 102, 161, 210–11
    anchored to the present 102
    and consciousness 210
    fallible 97
    and intentionality 104
    nature of 211
    and perception 99
    post-tensed time, shared 103
    and probability amplitudes 234n29
    and propositional attitudes 105
    and shared knowledge 98–100, 102
    tensed time, temporal distance 96–7, 99–101, 104, 127, 211, 239n1
Price, Huw 71–2, 79, 228n24-25, 238n56
property causation. *See:* objects
propositional attitudes
    and action 106–7, 115–22, 211
    and agents 142
    and becausation 113
    and the body 137
    and causation 105, 109, 111, 122, 126–7, 134, 143, 150
    as causes and effects 107–15, 127
    denied existence 105
    dispositions 236n41
    distinct from their objects 109
    and "eliminative materialism" 234n28
    and enactivism 204–5, 208
    hierarchically related 121
    holism in actions 122–6
    holism of the mental 115, 117, 122, 126

and intentionality   114, 120–21
and neurodeterminism   117, 126–9
non-material outcomes   124–5
outside of nature   132
and possibility   105, 124
and the representational theory of
    mind   210
and shared knowledge   98
and time   126, 134
unreal   236n39
purpose   18, 90, 92, 95, 148, 156, 168, 190,
    197–8, 200–01, 223n31
and intentionality   54
purpose/telos   87
and agency   162, 168
and attention   193
and causal relations   141
and embodied subjects   146
entertained/envisaged   90
and outcomes   124, 237n46,48
and temporality   89
Putnam, Hilary   28, 175–6, 220n15,
    223n31, 243n1-2

quantum indeterminacy. See:
    indeterminacy:quantum
quantum mechanics   46–7, 73, 174–5,
    178–81, 183, 221n21, 223n31,35,
    228n19, 231n42, 234n29
limited scope of   185
and neural activity   185
quasi-agency. See: agency:quasi-agency
Quine, W. V. O.   50, 55, 137, 184, 221n19,
    224n43, 225n53, 240n4

Readiness Potential   16–17, 19
realism   24, 28–30, 33, 36, 173, 175–6,
    180, 182, 188, 227n12, 242n28. See
    also: anti-realism
and causation   66, 75–6, 133
Laplacian   21–2, 78
and laws of science   243n1
ontic structural   181, 224n39
real patterns   185–7, 220n12, 244n17
structural   181, 224n39

Reid, Thomas   70, 229n33
relativity   223n30
representational theory of mind
    209–10
Rorty, Richard   175, 243n3
Rostowski, Adam   227n12,15, 232n54,
    243n5, 244n13, 246n18
Ryle, Gilbert   238n49

Sartre, Jean-Paul   88, 160, 163–6, 213n1,
    215n6, 216n14, 235n30, 241n22,
    242n6,10-11, 243n13
Schlicht, Tobias   208, 214n3, 246n13-15
Schlosser, Markus   92, 195, 204–7, 211,
    218n16, 230n34, 233n7,11, 245n5,
    246n1,7,12,17
Schwenkler, John   205, 207, 246n2,5,11
sciences, special   31, 47, 177, 179, 243n5.
    See also: physics, fundamental
inferior   183, 223n37
Searle, John   120, 179, 181–2, 238n55,
    244n8,11
self, the   42, 100, 121, 142, 165, 170, 182,
    199–200, 209, 241n20, 242n26
and action   147–9. See also: action
and agency   151, 154, 160, 163. See
    also: agency
and causation   148–9, 151, 154,
    241n23-24. See also: causation
cause makers   150, 230n34,
    241n23-24
embodied subjects   88, 138–9, 141,
    145–8, 152, 240n6
facing the world   151
and intentionality   151. See also:
    intentionality
and the natural world   141
outside of nature   154
self-defining   240n3
self-unifying   146, 240n3
and tensed time / temporal
    depth   145–6, 160, 240n6
Shearer, Harry   93, 233n12
Shoemaker, Sidney   139, 240n8
Smart, J. J.   135, 227n10, 231n45

Smolin, Lee   220n10
Spinoza, Baruch   168, 243n1
Steward, Helen   198–200, 245n2
Strawson, Galen   162, 226n3, 242n5
structures, mathematical   47, 178–9, 181, 185
supervenience. *See:* consciousness:supervenience

Thalos, Mariam   46, 83–4, 179–80, 223n33-34, 230n40, 231n47, 232n49,53, 244n9-10
that-it-is. *See:* what-is / that-it-is / what-is-there
time-gap experience   204–5
Tolstoy, Leo   59, 92, 203
Tomasello, Michael   215n7, 245n7
Toribio, Josefa   206, 246n9

Ubuntu   161

virtual outside   5, 7, 9, 41, 46, 51, 53, 55–7, 73, 88, 96–8, 104–5, 170, 184, 203, 209, 215n6, 235n30

Wegner, David   148–9, 241n21, 242n4
Weinberg, Steve   177, 179, 243n4
what-is / that-it-is / what-is-there   9, 46, 50, 53–4, 56, 83, 96, 101–2, 109, 114, 151, 167, 170, 179, 188, 198, 210
Whittle, Ann   239n2
Wiggins, David   239n2, 242n10
Wilkes, Kathy   214n1
Wittgenstein, Ludwig   82, 103, 200, 232n50, 234n23, 245n8
Wolpert, Lewis   221n17